PEPSI DEMACQUE-CROCKETT was born in London and grew up in Notting Hill. She had a gift for music and would later discover that singing and dancing were her main passions in life. She left home to tour the world as part of Wham! and spent the following decades on stage and in studios doing the thing she loved most: singing. She now lives in St Lucia with her husband James and her gorgeous dog Shabby. She is writing her first novel. @pepsidemacquec

SHIRLIE KEMP grew up in North London surrounded by a large family. After a chance meeting with George and Andrew, she became part of Wham! and later formed Pepsi and Shirlie. Since then, she has discovered her passion for photography and styling and has created shoots for interior design magazines worldwide. She married Martin Kemp from Spandau Ballet and has two beautiful children. She now lives in the lovely English countryside with her husband and her beloved dogs. @shirliekemp

Published by Welbeck
An imprint of Welbeck Non-Fiction Limited,
part of Welbeck Publishing Group.
Based in London and Sydney
www.welbeckpublishing.com

First published by Welbeck in 2021. This edition published in 2022.

A CIP catalogue record for this book is available from the British Library

ISBN
Paperback – 978-1-80279-216-4

Typeset by Roger Walker
Printed and bound by CPI Group (UK) Ltd, Croydon, CR0 4YY

10 9 8 7 6 5 4 3 2 1

MIX
Paper from
responsible sources
FSC® C171272

www.welbeckpublishing.com

All photos courtesy of Pepsi and Shirlie from their personal archive.

PEPSI & SHIRLIE

IT'S ALL IN BLACK AND WHITE

WELBECK

To my first best friend, my first love;
my mother Agatha.

Pepsi

To Martin, Harley Moon and Roman;
I love you.

Shirlie

Introduction

Over the last 40 years, we've lived a thousand lives. We've travelled the world together and watched each other fall in love, achieved our wildest dreams, had our hearts broken, grieved, grown, learned and evolved. We celebrated each other's successes and were there for each other in times of need. We've changed, but part of us has remained the same: we've stayed the best of friends.

Our friendship began one windy day in 1982, in less-than-glamorous surroundings. We met for the very first time outside Finsbury Park tube. We feel it was *like at first sight*. Over a car stereo, a cassette tape and a journey to Bushey, Hertfordshire, we bonded. We had no idea that we were on the first of many journeys together and that soon we'd be travelling all over Europe, Australia, America, China and Japan. Or that no matter where we went, together, we'd find a way to make every exotic destination feel like home.

At the start of the eighties, the world felt very different. We'd both been teenagers during the seventies – a dreary and difficult decade, especially if you were young and in London and you didn't have much money. The era was defined by political and economic turmoil and as young kids, we felt it. It's remembered as a period of power cuts, strikes and bad fashion. We remember it as a time when most families struggled to get food on the table, when everyone was worried about staying in work and when sexism and racism were rife among society. Pepsi's parents, Agatha and Roger, had arrived in the UK in the late fifties from St Lucia, keen to do their duty for the Commonwealth, to work hard for the 'Mother Country' and create financial support for home and family. The British government had promised that they would be made welcome and that Britain needed them to come and work. The 1971 Immigration Act was supposed to preserve the rights of Commonwealth citizens, but it did not protect them from the racist abuse, instead it confronted them with the slogan, 'No Dogs, No Irish, No Blacks' when trying to find somewhere to live. However, it was also a time for young people to be daring and creative. Everything was up for grabs, everything could be destroyed, then reinvented. Punk revolutionised youth culture and gave us a space to express ourselves. We knew we didn't want to live the same lives as our parents and for the first time, we were starting to see that it was possible to do things a different way. We were dreaming of a thrilling future – and our musical heroes were showing us how to rip up the rulebook and do it for ourselves.

So, in 1982, anything was possible for us – a pair of twentysomethings who hadn't been to university, who didn't have any money, who dreamt of singing and dancing, but ultimately lived for fun. Everything felt new and life was a shiny question mark. We had no idea what was lying ahead, but we wanted to say yes.

This is our story from the beginning to the 'till we meet again'. It's all here. We hope it inspires you. No matter what highs, lows and challenges lie ahead, we want to show you how we found the strength to get through it all, how we have embraced so many changes and surprises, and how our friendship has evolved throughout it all.

Lots of love,
Pepsi & Shirlie

1
Pepsi – A little girl with a big dream

Can you dream while you're awake? The therapist and spiritualist Dr Wayne W. Dyer wrote in his bestselling book, *The Power of Awakening*, 'Dreaming while you're awake can make you feel limitless.' By the time I read those words, I was an adult woman who had travelled all over the world. I'd experienced fame and fortune. I knew how it felt when your dreams come true – and also how it felt when life becomes tough and those dreams no longer nourish you. But I was startled. 'Dreaming while awake' described so many moments of my life, especially a strange feeling I struggled to explain to others. 'Déjà vu' might be the closest expression we have.

Something can be wholly new, while feeling completely familiar. When something happens that you couldn't possibly plan for – and yet, it feels as though it was always meant to be. And for as long as I can remember, my recurring dream, sleeping and waking, was the same: I was by a microphone. Strangely, the dream was silent – soft without sound, as though someone had muted a television – but I could feel the vibrations of the music. A vast crowd pulsed and swayed, and I swayed along with them. I knew they were all dancing to the sound of my voice and yet, the silence was peaceful and freeing, as though we had all been submerged underwater. As a very young child, as a teenager and as a grown woman, I would have that dream. And I'd never stop seeking out the feeling that matched it. The giddiness, the elation, the euphoria and the sense that anything and everything was possible.

Aged five, I found the feeling in the playground. I'd persuade a friend to lift me up, hooking her own arms under my armpits, so that together we'd become a human carousel. She'd spin, gathering force and speed, and I would carefully point my feet, in their tiny white plimsolls, in imitation of a ballerina. That sense of being up in the air, maybe about to take off at any moment, was euphoric. I can still remember the specific sensation of being let go, my feet suddenly reaching solid concrete, not knowing whether I was up or down – and finding it thrilling, exciting, addictive. Aged 22, I found it at PAs and stadiums, riding the roar of the crowd, boosted by their energy, dazzled by the chance to entertain them, honoured to share in their joy and delight. Those were the rare and wonderful moments where the way I felt inside seemed to match what was going on outside. I was a dreamer and I grew up in my own little world, and in my own company.

Looking back, I realise that I've always been someone who likes to fantasise and who has a big imagination but at first, I dreamed in secret. No one I knew had ever shared any desire or a dream to go out and do exciting things, or see the world and experience all it had to offer. Life was tough and complicated enough without wanting too much and letting your big, messy ambition get in the way ... that way surely lay disappointment. Most of the time, I didn't get the little things I longed for, never mind the big ones due to many mouths to feed and money being tight. And sharing my dreams would make me vulnerable. What if people laughed at me? I still can't get over my good luck. It was hard for women like me to make those dreams realities, yet I manifested it.

I was born in West London, in 1958, but my story really begins in a different West, thousands of miles away, on an island in the West Indies called St Lucia, in a small fishing village called Canaries. Its history dates back to the seventeenth century, when settlers moved over from the neighbouring French island of Martinique and embarked upon a sugar plantation within the Canaries valley. They brought with them French customs, culture, words and an enslaved population to work the fields. This is my heritage and where patois or Kwéyòl comes from – a language that evolved within the slave population as a mixture of French and African dialects. It is still widely spoken by islanders today. Canaries is a beautiful place. Tucked into the coastline, there's a stunning view everywhere you look. Until 1960, it wasn't even possible to get to the village by road – you had to go by boat. It was calm and quiet, with sunshine, ocean, tropical plants and warm breezes. Why, you might wonder, would anyone ever want to leave?

In the twentieth century, two things happened.

The first hit Canaries particularly hard when the price of sugar dropped and the estate and the sugar plantation upon which the village relied for work closed and was abandoned by the owners. Without another source of employment, it was very hard for people to support their families; fishing and farming were all that was on offer, life was tough. After the Second World War the opportunity arose to help rebuild England from the rubble of the Blitz.

The British government actively encouraged Commonwealth citizens to do their patriotic duty and help out. My parents were among them. In 1956, my father moved to London and my mother followed him in 1957.

We're used to hearing about how hard life was in Britain after the war but there are details missing from the story; those of the Caribbean men and women who served in the British Forces – wanting to help and do their best for their country even though Britain was thousands of miles away. The Commonwealth had a complicated infrastructure and while it was hard for everyone everywhere to get back to normal, it was especially difficult for Islanders, who were quickly discovering that you can't live on sunshine alone.

During their war work, many had developed an affinity for the UK and they yearned to return. They opened their minds and hearts to the people and culture that felt so different, yet so familiar. For tea, biscuits and the BBC, they didn't mind a little cold and rain.

I think my mum, especially, was very keen to help Britain 'get back on its feet'. Like many St Lucian women, she loved the Queen. It wasn't just a case of listening to the speech at Christmas or knowing the words to the national anthem, in her family home in St Lucia, a picture of the Queen took pride of place on the wall. To Mum and her friends, the Queen was a fashion icon and no matter how hot it got on the island, she'd emulate her by copying her outfits as best she could. I've seen pictures of her, dressed like the Queen. I love imagining her on the ocean liner bound for England, one of hundreds of beautiful black women, smartly dressed in pretty dresses with matching hats and white gloves. There would have been *many* brooches too, I'm sure.

Sadly, like so many others, my parents did not find a warm welcome waiting for them when they reached the UK. Racism is still a terrible fact of life, but now, it's not tolerated in the same way. We recognise the breadth of it and we challenge it. There are laws that have been made to protect the rights of all citizens to live, work and exist, even though it's not always easy to ensure that these laws are upheld. But when my parents arrived, racism was something they were simply expected to live with.

It must have been the worst, cruellest shock to them both. They came to London, believing there was work for them to do and that they were needed. But, like so many of their friends and family members, they weren't welcomed. London was a dangerous place for them. There was an increase in racist attacks in the summer of 1958. The Notting Hill race riots would break out, in which young white men – Teddy Boys – violently attacked the homes of black families in West London, causing injury, chaos and devastation.

Teddy Boys were one of the youth subcultures to emerge after the war. They were gangs of young men who dressed in an elaborate Edwardian style – hence the 'Teddy', listened to the rock'n'roll music coming from America and rejected the UK government's call for post-war austerity. Not all Teddy Boys were racist, but there were many young, disaffected men who fell for the fascist message. Of course this was at the time of Enoch Powell's Rivers of Blood speech which my dad found amusing because it was so ridiculous. Many newspapers were also publishing the same racist messages and calling for an end to immigration.

Some years after he had arrived in the UK, Dad was violently attacked by Teddy boys and stabbed. He shrugged it off and simply turned up at the nearest hospital, asking for stitches. I often wonder what it must have been like for him, having to walk the streets in fear. He didn't want to speak about what happened to him. I think he wanted to think of it as a case of being in the wrong place at the wrong time and leave it at that. But I don't think Dad wanted to think about how vulnerable he was, or to consider the reality of the country he'd already given everything up for.

These days, knife crime is sadly all too familiar and on the news constantly, especially in London. It pains me that it is still so prevalent to this day.

Dad always enjoyed a drink but after his attack he started to drink more heavily. As well as being filled with St Lucian friends and family, our neighbourhood was where many Irish people lived. At the time, Irish folk were treated badly too and sadly experienced much of the same prejudice as us. Dad found work as a labourer and his Irish colleagues took him under their wing. They were the ones who got him interested in racing and taught him how to bet on the horses – a passion that remained with him throughout his whole life. They were also the ones who encouraged him to the pub after a hard week's work on the construction site.

As you may have gathered, life was very hard for everyone. Our family was managing on very little money. Dad's work was back-breaking but now he also knew that wherever he went, he might be attacked – and he'd usually be treated appallingly. He didn't have the same freedom of movement that he'd been able to enjoy back home. Now, as an adult, I can understand why alcohol provided a temporary answer. The only men who offered him friendship and support loved drinking. Together, they could drink to forget and drink until they fell over.

During the working week, Dad didn't touch a drop, but he was a Friday binge drinker. As soon as he got his wage packet, the pub would be his first stop. He was usually a happy drunk, singing, dancing and being too generous with his friends – but there was never enough left for his growing family.

'Go on down to the pub, get your father out,' Mum would tell my brothers and me. We *dreaded* Fridays. The moment we dragged my father through the door – no mean feat when you're a little kid – the screaming would start. Mum was frightened, frustrated and furious. And sometimes, Dad would raise his hand to her. It takes a long time to get over a trauma like that. I still remember my brothers and I making ourselves as small and still as we possibly could – and worrying that the anxious thump of my heartbeat would draw attention to me. Years later, I'd find a kindred spirit in Shirlie, who had gone through some of the same difficulties with her own mum and dad.

It took me a long time to realise that this experience had a major impact on me. When I look back, I feel heartbroken for that little girl. She should have been outside, playing and feeling carefree. Not standing in the darkened doorway of a gloomy pub, begging her daddy to come home. I was forced to grow up very quickly. The other hard part of this was always wanting to protect Mum and keep her safe. I worried about Dad, but I worried about worrying too. I never wanted to add more to Mum's plate – not when just putting food on it was a major source of stress for her. She did so much to make our home a happy one, but when it came to sharing my hopes and fears, I didn't want to overwhelm her, or ask for anything she might not be able to give me. Also, in the sixties and seventies, we just didn't share our emotions in the way we do today. I'm so glad this has changed and I think we're all happier and healthier for it, but back then, 'feelings' meant being hungry or sleepy, not sad or scared. I think that's why I bonded so quickly with Shirlie – she was the first person I'd ever met who'd ask, 'How are you feeling?' and really want to know!

Life was difficult for my mum. Dad did not treat her well and she struggled. They were very different. Dad could be charming, but he was completely unreliable, never where he said he'd be, when he said he'd be there. He didn't seem to care about all of the things that held a family together. But Mum cared deeply. When I think of everything she did for us, I think of that Peggy Lee song 'I'm A Woman'. She cooked, she cleaned, she held down a job and she was passionate about making sure that my brothers and I were both well fed and well presented at church on Sunday. But I think she was exhausted. 'Mummy, why don't you come to my school open day?' I'd ask her. I wanted her to be proud of me and how hard I tried for her. 'I don't have the time,' she'd say, honestly. 'Look, as long as you're good, I'm not worried about you. All I ask of my children is to go to school and don't bring a policeman to my door!'

Church brought her a lot of comfort, and I think that she found structure, community and support there. Every Sunday, she would bring me to Mass. Over time, I'd be joined by my little brothers, David, Max and Robbie. Mass was something I had complicated feelings about. On the one hand, it was so long! And so boring! And Mum would get so grumpy, as we fidgeted and whispered and climbed all over the pew. (What *was* it about sitting still that made my ankles itch?!) On the other hand, it was a chance for me to dress up. When I was little, I loved dressing up. No matter how hard up we were, Mum cared passionately about making sure we all had 'best' clothes. I'd have a bright, colourful dress, often covered with pink or blue flowers. Now I know that the fabric was probably polyester, which was very popular at the time, but to me, it felt like gossamer, shimmering and fluttering around me. My hair was tied up with shining red satin ribbon, but my shoes were the very best part of my outfit.

Most of my shoes were bought for substance, not style. My feet grew fast and it wasn't worth spending a lot of money on something I wouldn't be able to wear in a couple of months, so Mum favoured canvas shoes – or jelly sandals. The second-hand stall at the market *always* seemed to have jelly sandals, no matter what time of year it was. Who was donating all of these shoes? Where could they be coming from? Even now, if I see a pair of jelly shoes being sold in a beach kiosk, I'm transported straight back to Portobello Market. There's Mum chatting to a neighbour, loaded down with bags of fruits and vegetables, as I fiddle with a buckle and wonder whether it's actually possible to die of boredom and who the shoes used to belong to. If the stall's stock was anything to go by, West London was populated entirely by giants and dolls. We wore those shoes all year round, too. In fact, it didn't matter if they were a little bit too big, because in winter, you added thick socks. And in the summer, when your feet got a little sweaty, you could rinse your shoes out in the sink and the next day, they'd be ready to wear again!

Once a week, I had freedom from jelly shoes and I could wear my beautiful black patent leather shoes to church. When we could afford them, these were from Clarks, which was, among our community, the very last word in smart footwear. They looked especially good with crisp white ankle socks. Carefully, so my mum wouldn't notice, I'd sit in the pew, pointing and admiring my feet. I felt like a ballerina again. It wasn't as much fun as being whirled around the playground, but Mass was a good place to lose myself in my daydreams and fantasise about that moment when I'd be singing in front of an audience.

In a strange way, church was a great rehearsal for what was to come. When I was seven, I made my first Holy Communion and I loved dressing in white, with a special veil, and feeling the congregation's eyes on me as I sipped the sweet wine – the Blood of Christ – for the very first time. At home, I rarely got to be the centre of attention. Usually, it was something I wanted to avoid. When things were bad with Dad, it was safer to escape, to hug the walls and try to disappear. But when I was in church, I knew everyone was looking at me with joy and approval. I was safe and when everyone stared at me, I knew they were admiring me. But as much as I loved the feeling of having an audience and wearing a special outfit, I was relieved when I could go home, put a T-shirt on and play outside with my brothers.

Years later, I'd remember this feeling when I was with Wham! I loved the thrill of running on stage, dressed in a great outfit, and seeing a stadium crowd roaring with joy. I also loved the relief of running off the stage, knowing that soon I'd be taking off my great outfit, putting on a dressing gown and slippers and curling up with Shirlie for a good gossip!

Mum taught me to celebrate femininity, creativity and ritual. When I was little, I thought that a lot of her habits, tips and tricks were slightly embarrassing or 'just something mums did'. Now, I realise just how amazing she was. With almost no money and even less time, she looked for ways to express herself, colourfully and joyfully. She never complained and she never, ever gave up. She was brilliant at conjuring up something out of nothing.

There was nothing Mum couldn't do with a sewing machine. Even though she grew up admiring the more formal British fashions, I think that arriving in London made her miss the bright colours and bold patterns she used to see in St Lucia. She was always looking for bargains to surprise us with, and even when things were especially difficult with my dad, she'd look out for smart, colourful shirts and leave them for him to find in the wardrobe. Dad loved them. He'd strut proudly, as though he was wearing catwalk couture. 'It could have been made for me!' he'd announce in delight. And sometimes, it (sort of) was, if Mum had altered the colour or changed the buttons.

Jeans were Mum's favourite – no denim item could escape her scissors or her imagination. At this time, bell bottoms were all the rage. Mum loved to make them, cutting along the seam of your jeans and sewing in a panel of bright fabric. In the seventies, there was a bit of a make-do-and-mend hippy ethos and I sometimes wonder whether that was why bell bottoms were so popular. They were an affordable craft project! In years to come, I'd be stunned when I discovered the strange tips and tricks that stylists used in order to create iconic looks for stage shows and photo shoots. Perhaps if her life had turned out a little differently, Mum could have been a stylist or a designer.

That wasn't the only way in which Mum predicted parts of my future. Shirlie, George and Andrew loved the pool and the leisure centre – and later, Shirlie and I would get seriously into spas. But my first experience of public bathing was far from luxurious. Every other Saturday afternoon, I'd make my way to Wedlake Street for a trip to the public bathhouse.

We did have a bath at home, but the gas used to heat the water was so expensive that this worked out a little cheaper. It was a treat to have as much hot water as you needed – and the best days were when it was just Mum and me. This meant we both got a bath to ourselves and I'd luxuriate in the water. I loved being alone and being by myself in the bath felt so peaceful. Everywhere I went, I'd be told off or laughed at for daydreaming. When I was in the bath, I could dream to my heart's content.

However, it wasn't the same story when my little brothers came along with us. They'd share a bath, and I'd go in with my mum, and it was impossible to relax. First, my brothers loved to mess about, laughing, joking and splashing each other. Thanks to the tiles and high ceilings, the sound echoed and every single bather was disturbed. To be honest, they were probably even more disturbed by Mum, shouting 'SHUSH!' and 'Don't do that!' from across the way.

If I was sharing a bath with my mum, it also meant that she'd be scrubbing me. It was a little bit like having my own personal massage therapist. The only difference is that Mum would never ask, 'Is the pressure OK? Is that too hard?' She'd go at me with the soap until she was convinced that even my bones were clean. Still, I have very happy memories of the bathhouse. I loved curling up on the chair, feeling the heat and steam, soft as a blanket, as I waited for the bath to fill up. And I loved the thought of my mum occasionally getting a little bit of time for herself, when my brothers weren't in tow. I don't think I realised how much I was constantly worrying about her until I saw her in the bathhouse, when that worry was released for an hour. I knew my dad wasn't causing her extra worry in that moment and no one was asking her for anything, so I could relax too.

The bathhouse was closed in 1980, although the swimming pool remained open. I can understand why they were phased out. As living conditions and sanitation improved, there was much less of a need for them, which was as things should be. I don't really think we should go back to a time when families had to go out to bathe once a week. However, I do think about how important the bathhouse must have been to my mum, who was constantly working, worrying and doing things for others. Even though modern life is easier, I'm certain there are still many stressed women who need a quiet hour by themselves once a week. Back then, the bathhouse gave those women somewhere to go. Years later, I'd learn that Shirlie's husband Martin used to go to the public bathhouse in North London with his family. It's funny to think that so many people of our generation were in that position, watching their parents scraping together the pennies in order to prepare for their weekly wash.

Parts of my childhood were painful, but I truly believe I was meant to grow up in the exact way I did, with all of the ups and downs that my family presented me with. Both my parents taught me so much. Through Mum, I learned about positivity and perseverance. She showed me that it's possible to find joy during the darkest days and that most of the time, life isn't about major highs – often the greatest achievement is to keep on going, looking for reasons to be cheerful. Mum inspired love in everyone she met, usually by showing them kindness. I think that's the best way to be. Even to this day, members of my extended family often remind me how much love they had for my mother for the many kindnesses she showed them.

My dad taught me some more complicated lessons. He had traumatised us, disappointed us, badly let us down and failed to provide for us. Looking back, I think he just couldn't handle the responsibility of a growing family to look after. He left that to my mother, and deep down, I think he knew he had let us all down. Perhaps he wouldn't have needed to seek solace in alcohol and his life could have been very different if only he'd had the courage to take full responsibility and face his inadequacies.

Long after I left home, my youngest brother Robbie had the courage to confront him. Robbie had grown up cowering and afraid, with the rest of us protecting him when Dad was really ranting and raving, but over time, he grew into a young man – a young man who was taller and broader than his father, from being a hod carrier on a building site. One night, he heard my mum's voice, pleading with Dad to leave her alone.

'You're not to touch her again,' he told Dad, pinning him against the wall.

Miraculously, this altercation was the beginning of my dad changing his ways. Perhaps it was a combination of shock and shame. As his youngest son looked him in the eye, he was forced to confront the fact that this was a stronger man, and a man who would stop at nothing to protect his mother. He knew he had to change. Dad's binges had been getting longer and longer. As he became more dependent on drink, he was no longer waiting for the weekend and so the amount of alcohol his body had to metabolise was making him seriously ill.

After my brother shouted at him not to raise his hands to our mother again, and Dad finished his binge, his body went through delirium tremens (DTs), a full and very physical alcohol withdrawal. The symptoms are serious. It causes extreme shaking, shivering and sweating. Sometimes you feel as though you're freezing to death and sometimes it's as though you're burning up – and the irregular heartbeat might be the scariest part of all. I think Dad thought he was dying – well, I suppose he'd come close.

As Dad sweated out the alcohol, he had a series of terrifying fever dreams that he could barely bring himself to talk about. All he would say was 'God spoke to me' – and he never touched alcohol again.

Dad taught me that who we are is never set in stone. He hurt so many of the people he loved, but he showed me that anyone can change. I learned that disease and addiction are powerful and painful, but it's never too late to alter your course and say sorry. As well as the hurt he had caused his family, the alcohol must have done untold damage to his body but when he passed in 2002, he was sober and relatively at peace.

I think Dad also taught me a form of independence. It's funny that Shirlie and I had such similar upbringings but have such different approaches to love and romance. Shirlie's Dad was so angry and unpredictable that I think it made her want to seek out someone kind, loving and gentle, who would always protect her. My dad's anger and alcoholism made me realise that I couldn't rely on any man. I was never especially bothered about boys. My girlfriends would get very excited about crushes, but my brothers cured me of any silliness or sentimentality – 'They're just *boys*,' I'd sigh. Good for climbing trees with, not falling in love with. But more seriously, I think I saw how much my mum struggled and suffered. She had such an independent spirit and could have done so much with her life, if only she'd had a little bit of luck and a few more opportunities. I never wanted to be trapped. I never, ever wanted to have a husband who always made me worry about where he was, who he was with or what he was doing. I certainly didn't want to rely on my children to bring my partner home from the pub, before going through his pockets in search of any remnants of the week's wages.

I knew that all I wanted – *needed* – was to pursue my waking dream. The on-the-stage feeling. The flying-through-the-air feeling. And it didn't matter if anyone thought I was strange, or silly, or just another dreamer. I knew, in my bones, that there had to be life beyond my little patch of Paddington and I was going to look for it.

I was going to follow the music and dance to my own beat.

2

Shirlie with an 'ie'

M y hand swooped, forming extravagant loops and curls: *Shirley. Shirley. Shirley.* My name was the only thing I could write without too much trouble. School was scary, and no matter how hard I tried to learn, nothing ever seemed to stick.

The sixties were supposed to be an era of peace and love, but that message had yet to reach our school room. Now, I know that so little was understood about children and how to encourage them and support them. Child development wasn't something anyone ever talked about. We certainly didn't know that there was a word that explained why I had so much trouble keeping up with my classmates. I guess because I missed so much school through illness, it was a difficult task to catch up every time. Although I was never diagnosed, I am sure that I may have had some sort of dyspraxia and possibly attention deficit hyperactivity disorder (ADHD). Even with friends around me, I felt so shy and insecure. I really didn't have much confidence growing up and certainly not at school. It slows everything down as you're battling against your own fear of getting it wrong or making a mistake. I spent a lot of my lessons daydreaming, gazing out the window until I heard an inevitable, 'Shirley Holliman! What did I just say? Why aren't you paying attention?'

Every day, I hoped that, against all odds, school might get a little bit better. Every day, I was disappointed. But when we were practising our handwriting, I found a release. My name was the only word that I was confident I could spell. Actually, I was more than confident.

I didn't particularly like the name. But seeing Shirley Bassey share my name made me feel extra special. Sometimes I would spend hours practising my autograph as if I was about to go on stage. I had no idea why that was, and still don't but back then it seemed a lot more important than writing my times table. Shirley Bassey was also my dad's favourite singer, and I liked that we had that in common. Dad was a difficult man – he'd roar and rage, and sometimes he'd make our little house shake with his angry outbursts. But when he was in a good mood, there was no one I felt closer to. Music meant almost everything to my dad and being another Shirley was an honour. I liked Shirley Temple too. I'd seen some of her old films and I loved her dancing. I often secretly thought it would be fun to have a life like hers and that I'd be so much better at singing and dancing in Hollywood than simply surviving in Bushey. Still, if I ever got to Hollywood, or even down the road, to the West End,

I'd need to make myself stand out. Perhaps there were too many Shirleys. Was there a way I could make myself a little bit more eye-catching? Was there a way of becoming more memorable? Here I was, little Shirley Holliman, sometimes 'Snagglepuss', when my dad was in a good mood. I was small for my age, easy to overlook – and when I wore my sisters' hand-me-downs, I'd pretty much disappear.

Shirley … One interesting thing that we had learned in school was that there were different ways to make the sound that came at the end of my name: *Shirley … Shirlee.* I wished we could slow down and study this; I loved playing with words, finding the jokes, tricks and double meanings. I loved *telling* stories, creating things, but there was never any time to play: we had to do everything perfectly, first time, without making any mistakes or we'd be punished.

Shirley … I permitted myself a tiny, secret smile as the rain drummed against the window pane. Maybe one day I'd be leaving a theatre, or in a beautiful big car, one of the American ones my dad adored, signing my name for someone who had seen me sing or dance … *Shirley … Shirlie.*

Shirlie looked just right. At the time, I was too little to put that feeling into words, but it looked happier and brighter. It was just me – there was something extra-feminine about the 'ie'. I was putting my individual spin on my name. Making it truly belong to me.

At home and at school, I often felt lost. Now, I think we'd call the feeling anxiety. Back then, we weren't having conversations about mental health. We'd go to see a doctor if there was something wrong with our bodies, but no one ever spoke out loud about this feeling of uncertainty – I think it was just down to being alive.

Back then, big families were much more common and I was a typical fourth child. I shared a bed with two of my sisters because there wasn't much room in our terraced house. It was noisy and constantly chaotic. It made sense – when you have lots of children, cooped up in a small space, life will get loud and messy. But the only way for me to deal with the drama was to get very, very quiet.

I didn't realise quite how anxious I was until I went to tea at my friend Jocelyn's house. She was my next door neighbour, but living on a council estate back then no one's front door was locked so we would just wander in and out of each other's houses freely. And most days I would wander into Jocelyn's back garden. She had a family who wanted to keep things calm and quiet. Even now, I'm transported straight back there, where we'd play dolls. She had a beautiful little wooden playhouse called Wind Whistle, which looked like a little beach hut painted in pastel colours. It was so orderly and neat. Wind Whistle in our imaginations turned into a cinema and dolls' hospital. Mum never had any time so I would walk myself over to Jocelyn's house to sit on a nice blanket. Her back garden became our playground and our dolls all had starring roles in our make-believe games. I loved mini doll tea sets and I would take mine with me in a basket. Our days were simple: there was no big adventure, in our imaginations Wind Whistle was always a beach hut or a hospital, there were jam tarts and orange squash. My own back garden was a builder's yard, while my friend's was a place to go and feel safe – I just wanted to make the dolls go to tea and talk quietly and politely to each other.

Years later, when I was getting into art and photography and needed a creative space, I built an outdoor office in the garden. 'You need to think of a name for it!' said my husband, Martin. "Oh! I think I should call it "Wind Whistle"' I said, startling myself. I hadn't thought about Jocelyn or her dolls' playhouse for *years!* But Wind Whistle is a word that perfectly evokes creativity and calm for me. A place of refuge and peace, for when life is getting a little bit too much.

I wish five-year-old Shirlie had known about all of the joy in store for her – and that some of the mad adventures lying ahead would be wonderful ones. But back then, afternoons at Jocelyn's house were the high point. School was terrifying and overwhelming, a world of slammed wooden desktops, scratchy blackboards, cruel teachers who didn't care if they made you cry, and written sentences so confusing that they might as well have been in code. Home was better, because it was where my lovely, cuddly mum was. And when my dad was in a good mood, it could be the happiest place on earth. But it was also shabby and dowdy, where the cushion on the sofa was only there to cover a huge hole and our dining room table would often be covered in oily car parts, thanks to Dad's experiments in mechanics. And because I shared a room with my big sister Lorraine and my little sister Nicola, I had nowhere to go for a quiet five minutes by myself – you couldn't even be in the bathroom for two minutes without someone banging on the door.

It was amid all this chaos that I became seriously ill. When I woke in the early hours of the morning, sandwiched between Nicola and Lorraine, I hoped I was just having a bad dream. A *very* bad dream. Our little bedroom was melting. Even though the lights were off, there was a strange brightness, a flickering. The walls were pulsing – no, *melting*. Somehow, the sides of the room were sliding down into puddles, hitting the threadbare carpet. Frightened, I screwed my eyes up tight, but that didn't seem to help.

It couldn't be a dream, because I was hotter than I'd ever felt in my life. I had to get up, I had to get out! The trouble with sharing a bed, and being in the middle, is that the covers are weighed down at either end. It was as if I was stuck in a straitjacket, but I wriggled out and my temperature was only going up dramatically to the point where I was aching and stumbling, trying to get to my parents.

I had to get to Mum and Dad.

Everything was distorted, I was unable to see and I felt so fuzzy and hazy. I was so out of it and I really didn't know what was going to happen. It was such a whirl.

It was hard to get across the landing as the floor kept swirling and spinning. The next thing I remember is leaving the house on a stretcher, wrapped in a thick red blanket. Everything seemed upside down as they held me and took me to the hospital. By then, the pain was unendurable. Unable to hold back anymore, I screamed and sobbed, 'I want my mum!'

'Don't worry love, she'll be here soon,' said a kindly paramedic. 'But we need to make you well again.'

In the ambulance, the paramedic did his best to keep me conscious. 'Well done, you're being so brave,' he told me. But I didn't feel remotely brave. I just wanted to be at home. I wanted to shut my eyes tight and discover this had all been a dream after all. The worst was to come. As soon as I arrived at the hospital, I was taken to a big clinical room with bright lights. I was laid down on a red leathery couch, although it may have been a plastic bed that was really hard, surrounded by nurses and doctors. They grabbed my arms and legs and pinned me down to give me a lumbar puncture. This is sometimes called a 'spinal tap' and I often wondered if it's because the pain is turned all the way up to 11! A long, thin needle was pushed into my lower back to collect my cerebrospinal fluid. I could hear my mum crying as she watched this horrific scene in front of her. I was screaming so hard and thinking, *how can my mum let them do this to me?*

Mum, Mum …

They must have thought it was better she wasn't there so they told her to leave. Before she left, she put her coat near me and that was the only thing I could squeeze for comfort – I think she understood how grave the situation was and she had to let the doctors and nurses do their best. I had meningitis and getting this painful treatment on arrival almost certainly saved my life. Usually, an anaesthetic is given before the procedure but in my case, there simply wasn't time.

Fortunately, meningitis was and still is very rare. (When I was ill, some of the vital vaccines in use today had yet to be developed.) It's usually caused by something airborne, but it's very difficult to 'catch' it, or work out where it came from – or why some people are more susceptible than others. I'd been sharing a bed with my sisters, but they were absolutely fine.

I've often wondered whether the stress and anxiety that I was experiencing at school made me especially vulnerable to the illness. It probably didn't help that I was always very small for my age. When I was born, even the smallest baby clothes were too big for me. Lorraine's old babygros wouldn't fit – Mum had to dress me in clothes from Lorraine's dollies instead! Later in life, I'd become fascinated with the work of the bestselling writer and motivational speaker Louise Hay and the link between the brain and the body and how different thoughts and emotions can sometimes make us ill. Of course, I didn't know any of that at the time and although I sometimes felt a little homesick in hospital, I soon learned to love it.

Once the infection had been treated with antibiotics, I felt tired and weak, but I started to get better almost straight away. In hospital, everything was clean, organised and ordered, and no one was allowed to make too much noise. I had everything I craved. At school, I was being constantly told off for things I didn't even know I'd done. In the hospital, the doctors and nurses told me I was a good girl if I managed to eat most of my dinner, or sleep through the night. But best of all, in hospital, my parents were loving and tender. Usually, at home, my dad would shout at my mum and it would make her cry. But when they visited me in hospital, they knew that it wasn't the right place to argue. I think they made a real effort to try and get on with each other to make sure that I recovered. Now that I'm a mum, I know what they would have gone through and how the worry would have made them worry about each other. After all, I nearly died and when I think about going through that experience with Harley Moon or Roman, I feel quite sick so I'm sure that almost losing me made them appreciate each other so much more. In hospital, my world felt so much safer. Everyone was kinder, gentler. I was still shaken up after my traumatic ordeal, but I have many happy memories of that time too.

Even after I left the hospital, I was treated a little differently by my family. Home was still loud, messy and intense, but when I came back from hospital everyone made an extra-special effort to keep quiet so that I could recover better. I could feel that they were being quieter, gentler, and the chaotic atmosphere had disappeared. Being little made everyone much more protective. To my dad, I suddenly seemed even smaller and more vulnerable, and he was desperate to protect me and wrap me up. I could see how this whole experience had scared him into thinking that he might lose me.

One Saturday, Dad took me to the Wimpy in Watford, where I loved sitting at the bar on the red leather stools.

It made me feel so grown-up, sat next to my big dad like we were in an American diner just like the ones you see in films. I remember my dad ordering this amazing strawberry milkshake. That was my first milkshake and it started off my lifelong love for them. Taking my last slurp, still trying to get the remains of the milkshake out, Dad said, 'Come on, let's go down the road and get you a Snagglepuss coat.' I didn't quite know what this coat was, but I was loving the attention. We then went to this shop which I hadn't ever been to before. Certainly upmarket from C&A, it was very old-fashioned with big wooden floorboards and well-spoken sales assistants who seemed to know my dad. At least, I felt like they knew who my dad was, so when I saw the leather jackets hanging up, I wondered if that's where he got his coats from. As a child, I loved fur coats but I didn't quite equate that they were from the animals I also loved. Of course, wearing a fur coat now would be the last thing that I would ever do.

My dad said, 'I'd like to get her a coat, that cream and white speckled fur coat.' When I put it on, I saw the biggest smile on his face and was delighted because once I was wearing it, I truly became his Snagglepuss. Then the sales assistant placed a big furry hat on my head with these big pom poms to tie it as my dad continued smiling – 'Oh, she has to have a fur muff to complete the look!' My dad totally agreed. Wearing all of those items together, I truly felt like my namesake 'Little Miss Snagglepuss', all soft, warm and cosy like the Hanna-Barbera character from the cartoons.

But of course, Dad could make life very difficult for everyone too. Sometimes it was as though he was operating under his own weather system. When he was in a good mood, it felt as though the sun had come out, but suddenly huge grey clouds would loom on the horizon and no one would understand why. He marched to his own beat. I knew what made him happy – music, especially old rock'n'roll and jive tunes – and huge old American cars. But no one could work out what was making him angry. And he was angry often.

Just as I didn't really have a word for my own anxiety, I didn't have a word for Dad's moods either. Now, I realise he was probably struggling with depression. If he'd had the help he needed, his life, and ours too, might have been completely different. But I think it was a very hard time for both of my parents. Anger was the only emotion that men were allowed to express and although my dad seemed especially furious, my mum was under plenty of pressure to simply put up with it, just because of the times we were living in. I can't stress enough how different the world felt then. It was very, very hard to end a marriage, no matter how painful things felt, or how unhappy you made each other. You were expected to put up and shut up, and keep up appearances. Mum always had people in the house having tea and talking. She was the agony aunt of our neighbourhood. One of her biggest strengths was having so many friends and family members that she could listen to, help and in turn confide in. Maybe I learned through her how important friends are when times get too tough.

This is also why I'm so proud of my son Roman for doing so much work around mental health in 2021. I never want to go back to those dark days when people didn't share their feelings. I've seen, first-hand, the problems it causes. Now, I realise that there were probably plenty of families like mine, screaming and shouting behind closed doors, but then, I felt as though there were no families as volatile as mine. I felt isolated and sometimes desperately lonely.

I knew I had to look outside my family for the closeness I was craving. I needed gentle, quiet, reliable, unconditional love – and I had an idea.

'Dad, you know you've been asking me about what would make me feel better, after hospital?' I said one day before I left the hospital. 'Well, I've been thinking …'

'What is it, Snagglepuss?' asked Dad, possibly about to run out the door and find me another furry coat.

'The thing that would make me happier than anything in the world, the thing that would make me feel better forever, is a pony.'

Now, saying, 'Daddy, I want a pony' is one thing if you live in the countryside, in a big house with plenty of space and there is plenty of money. Saying it when you live in a council house in Bushey is a bit like saying, 'Daddy, I want a spaceship.'

But my dad, for all his faults, was a determined man. I think it helped that I wasn't a spoiled kid. Even though he'd showered me with presents, I'd never asked him for anything before – certainly not outside Christmas and birthdays. I went on and on about how much I wanted this pony.

He sighed, but he was smiling.

'If you want a pony, you're going to have to buy it yourself,' he told me – which seems ridiculous in retrospect.

I didn't have a job, but our dad was always very generous with our pocket money – he would give us £5 a week. He told me I could get a paper round and that's exactly what I did. I got an early morning paper round but then I think he was worried about letting me go out early in all weathers so he did the paper round with me!

In no time at all I had saved up £65 and was ready to buy my pony. Because my dad worked as a builder and labourer, he knew quite a few travellers, who of course had plenty of horses for sale. He drove me to the caravan site where my palm was sweaty with my money, ready to let go and ride off on my horse. One of the guys my dad knew took us to a field with lots of horses, most of them tied up on heavy chains. They were mostly skewbald and piebald – but I didn't want one of those, I wanted a white pony. And just when I thought that I spotted a little white pony in the distance, pointed to it and said, 'What's that one?', my dad immediately said, 'It's too small.' But it was the prettiest thing I'd ever seen so I didn't care how big it was. And with the blink of an eye, one of the boys jumped on his back and rode it over to me – and that was the one I bought.

But there was only one problem and that was I didn't have anywhere to keep my pony. It couldn't stay in our garden and we didn't exactly have a spare field. They said I could keep him there until I found him a home. The funny thing was, one of the boys would ride the horse bareback with just a piece of rope around his head that he'd made and he would ride it to me, through our council estate every other day, so that I could see him. Eventually we found a field for him but I realise now that it wasn't quite the right way to go about buying a horse.

I was born loving animals, but now for the first time, I had something that was just for me. I could lose whole days in that field, not noticing if I was getting cold or hungry. I didn't even need to ride my pony, I just wanted to stroke and cuddle him and be with him. At home, Mum was so busy with all of us – she'd have to go and make dinner, or one of my brothers and sisters might need her, or my dad would come in and shout at her. For me it was just nice to have something to love and take care of, it gave me a great sense of responsibility.

I think that time really helped me creatively, too. For once, I had the headspace to think, grow and dream. At school, I struggled to express myself and if I wrote anything, I'd just be told off for my spelling. No one seemed to care about content or meaning. But in the field, just talking with my pony, I was free to express myself in songs and stories – I didn't have to make sense.

After a few years, disaster struck: 'Snagglepuss, I'm so sorry, we just can't afford to feed him anymore,' my dad explained. It wasn't a complete shock. I'd heard the tense conversations between my parents that quickly turned into arguments. Dad's work was always a bit erratic. During the sixties, it seemed as though there was plenty of work for everyone, but as the seventies dawned, life was becoming harder for everyone. Occasionally you'd hear scary words on TV or on the radio, like 'unemployment' or 'recession'. I didn't really understand what a recession was, but I knew it made grown-ups angry and scared. Most of the arguments and stresses at home seemed to be connected with money and not having enough of it. I knew that if my dad couldn't find a way to keep my beloved pony, it wasn't possible.

We had to sell him in the end, but I was pleased he went to a good home. Luckily my life was to have plenty more horses in it to love and to care for. I loved to daydream about my dear pony having all sorts of romantic adventures, meeting friends and going up and down the country, but by that point, I was completely pony mad. It made life a little easier at school. Even though I'd always rather be with animals than people, now I had a passion and a hobby, as well as a way of making friends.

When I was 12, and moving up to senior school, I met another pony fanatic – a girl called Tracey. At the time, there was a real craze for horse riding. There was a hugely popular children's TV series, *Follyfoot*, based on a series of books that captured the level of obsession and created new converts. For lots of girls – and their parents! – horse riding was a smart, aspirational activity and perhaps a way of showing off a bit, partly because it was so expensive to keep a horse. I was never interested in riding, I just wanted to be in a field, stroking my horse and talking to it.

Tracey and I were worlds apart. Her family were wealthy and they lived in a beautiful house on the nicer side of Bushey, but our shared passion united us. (To this day, I think that's the best thing about loving animals. It doesn't matter who you are or where you're from, animals can bring all sorts of people together.) Also, Tracey was a rider – an extremely talented one. I think that set the tone for many of my major relationships that were to come, later in life. I wasn't interested in competing with Tracey, or comparing myself with her, I only wanted to support her and applaud. It brought me so much joy to see her success. In years to come, I'd recognise this exact same feeling when George played me a song that he'd written, when Martin got the part of Steve Owen in *EastEnders*, when I saw Pepsi acting on stage for the first time. Nothing makes me happier or prouder than seeing the people I love excelling.

With Tracey by my side at school, I could survive. Lessons were hell, but I had horses. I was also discovering punk. It seemed crazy, really. I'd grown up tiny and timid. As Snagglepuss, I couldn't say boo to a goose. I always felt lost and lonely, unable to make myself heard. How could punk possibly be for a girl like me?

Well, punk was perfect! First, the music moved me. I'd grown up dancing with my dad, loving jive, soul and those beautiful artists with big voices. But I'd had to share those songs. My dad's huge, gleaming radiogram was his pride and joy, but he decided when we listened to music and what we listened to. He'd be furious if I put one of his records on without his permission. Punk wasn't meant for parents, it was all mine! I loved the screech of The Sex Pistols, discordant and wild. If that sound could be music, then anything was possible.

The other thing I adored about punk was that it was all about image. Now, when I think about my love of art, photography and flowers, and my obsession with all things elegant and feminine, I can't quite believe that punk was where it started. But the brilliant thing for shy girls was that your punk clothes could do all of your talking for you. Just as my furry rabbit coat had made me look cuddly, cosy and defenceless, my punk outfits created my attitude. Bin bags were brilliant and you could get quite creative with them. Sometimes I'd rip up edges into streamers, but other times I'd pin, drape and make an outfit that looked quite sleek.

My lovely mum was not a natural punk, but she was my biggest ally. To be honest, if she'd hated it, I think I would have found it hard to keep it up, as I never wanted to hurt her. But I wonder whether she got a vicarious thrill from my wild looks. I think she loved it. As a Teddy girl, she completely understood the link between fashion and music so it never bothered her that her daughter came down one day with chopped-up green hair, dressed in bondage clothes! She was very expressive and in some ways very different to women of her generation.

Once, as we were walking home from the shops, we were chased by teenage boys who were making fun of the way I looked. Well, I *had* covered my hair with a whole Crazy Dyes box of bright green colour!

'Yuck, she's got snot in her hair! Snot hair! Snot hair!' yelled the boys.

I rolled my eyes. It was hardly an original insult. Still, no one likes being shouted at in the street. But Mum stuck up for me. 'At least she's being creative! You're boring!' she yelled back. Now *that* was punk! Many years and two grown-up(ish) children later, I realise how smart Mum was. I think she knew it was a phase and she was happy to let me be an obnoxious teen girl for a while. To be honest, if she'd told me off, there's a possibility that I might still have green hair! She loved my kettle handbag too – I suppose technically, it was more The Wombles than The Slits, and it wasn't very practical on a night out.

Punk gave me a purpose and even though Mum supported me, I could still be naughty. One night, I dragged 13-year-old Nicola out to see X-Ray Spex in London, dressing her up as a punk. 'If anyone asks, you're 18!' I said, mussing up her hair and trying to gel it into spikes.

But at school, I think the teachers thought I wasn't destined for much. I'd tried and tried, constantly struggling, only to get told off. It was the disappointment of trying so hard and when my work would come back covered in red marks and crosses it made me lose confidence in what I was doing. I knew I had something wrong – that my brain is faster than my hands and eyes. In those days, teachers didn't seem to realise that there are different ways of learning and there might be a different path for me. When I was very little, it was hard enough, but when I was a teenager, things didn't get any better. School still didn't make any sense and therefore the teachers gave up on me as much as I gave up on school. As my school years progressed, I would sit at the back and hope that they wouldn't notice me. I'd hide behind a copy of *Melody Maker* or *NME* to screen myself off from the rest of the classroom. School wasn't a place for me to develop and grow. I counted down the days until I could escape.

The moment came sooner than I expected.

My friend Tracey had an announcement: 'Shirlie, I've got some news. My family is moving to Sussex,' she said one morning, as we waited outside our form room. 'They've found a great place in the country with loads of land, there will be plenty of room for my horses. It means I can really concentrate on my riding career and make a go of it. At the moment, I don't have enough time to practise. I need to be doing it full-time.'

My heart sank. Of course, it made perfect sense. Tracey was so talented. Unlike me, she was on an exciting path, she had a future. But she was the only person who could make school bearable.

'Oh … Oh no! What will I do without you?' I said. I didn't want to show her how upset I was, but I felt devastated.

'Well, I think you should come with us. I've talked to my mum and dad, they love you, and they think you'd be the perfect person to help out. I need a groom, someone who really knows horses. I can't think of anyone better. We're going to have the best time! Will you do it?'

Of course I'd do it! That day, nothing could touch me. None of the teachers could upset me, no matter how much they shouted. 'Shirlie Holliman, stop staring out of that window, we're supposed to be doing long division!' yelled the maths teacher. I smiled, dreamily.

I wouldn't need long division in Sussex – horses don't care about tests and exams!

Still, perhaps I should have broken the news a little more gently to my mum. 'I'm moving to Sussex!' I cried, as soon as I got through the front door. Mum was kind and gentle as always. 'That sounds wonderful,' she said. Only now do I realise how brave she was to let me go and how much room she gave me to follow my own path at the tender age of 16.

At first, I was happier than I'd ever been. I didn't realise what a big change in my life moving to Sussex would be, because it was the real countryside. There was no public transport, instead one bus that came every four hours if you were lucky. Even then I didn't know where the bus would actually take you. Sussex was definitely the rural idyll I'd imagined it to be. I went from being the girl who went to punk clubs in London to staying in seven nights a week in a country mansion. The work was hard, but I never complained because I was going straight to the stable where I was working with the horses I loved. Being a groom is physically very demanding and it was the perfect occupation for an anxious person, but working side by side with Tracey brought out the best of me: I'm good in partnerships and Tracey and I had that strong friendship.

Watching Tracey was thrilling, too. She had always been a wonderful rider, but out here, without any other distractions, she was really able to excel. It was intense and it took me a little while to realise I was feeling isolated.

Tracey's older sister lived in London and was really into the London club scene and fashion so Tracey and I would eagerly await her arrival to see what she was wearing and what music she was listening to. She always had a *Vogue* magazine under her arm. The thing about the late seventies and eighties, especially if you were young, was that there was this anticipation about what was coming next with music and fashion. It just represented the time and gave you your identity. We never saw it as a trend but something to be excited about, something to belong to and look forward to. Tracey's sister used to bring that to us, a glimpse into the latest haircuts, while Tracey and I were smelling of horse poo and straw, wearing our joggers and rubber riding boots. She looked like Alexis Carrington Colby from *Dynasty* while we were these two tomboys on a farm.

One day, some friends of Tracey's parents came to visit as they lived in London too. They had a newspaper cutting, with a rave review of a London gig. 'Our friend's son's in this band, they're going places!' they said. 'They're really good. Next time you girls are in London, you ought to go and see them.'

The band was called Gentry and I couldn't take my eyes off one of the boys. I asked if I could keep the picture as I thought they looked really cool and casual. I suddenly became excited and wondered if this was the next big thing I had been waiting for. Maybe my life was calling me back to London to enjoy some of this scene that was coming out of it. Tracey and I arranged to go to their next gig, a few weeks later – we got the train from Sussex to Holborn, but when we arrived at the venue, we saw a sign on the door saying sorry the gig had been cancelled at the last minute. You never know why these things happen but I guess I was never supposed to see Gentry live on stage.

Luckily for us, Tracey's sister would always forget her *Vogue* magazine when she left, which Tracey and I would read and tear pages out. Fashion was becoming our next obsession. The thing is we were both very slim. Tracey was tall and athletic and I was small and petite, but even so we couldn't help but notice that all of the models were very, very thin. And we started to become preoccupied with getting thinner ourselves – we realised we couldn't be thin enough.

I've always had a small frame and a quick metabolism. When I was younger, I loved fast food and fizzy drinks, but these were real treats and back then, it was almost impossible to get hold of McDonald's in the Sussex countryside! Tracey wanted to keep her weight down in order to be a faster rider. We sustained ourselves on Kellogg's Country Store cereals and nothing else. A bowl for breakfast, another bowl for lunch and one for dinner while working out, sweeping yards and riding horses. Again, in those days there was no body positive movement and women did all sorts of dangerous things to be unnaturally thin. I don't think I was ever in serious trouble, but when I was feeling sad and lonely, not eating properly meant I was extra unhappy and unhealthy.

I started to feel desperately homesick and insecure. As well as missing the fun of London, I wanted my mum. And although seeing Tracey's progress was exciting, I was becoming scared. It was becoming increasingly clear that she was getting better and better, while I was getting stuck. I was working for my keep, but I wasn't earning any money. I had no qualifications and no real future. I wasn't overly ambitious and didn't know what I was missing out on, but strangely I felt that I was missing something – I just couldn't put my finger on it. 'What will I do?' I wondered out loud when no one else was around. It was a constant niggle that I found harder to ignore. Then one day, something happened that was about to break my heart and make the decision for me.

My dad had bought an Alsatian puppy, Henry, for me to take and move to Sussex with. I guess that was his way of protecting me and he knew the best way was to give me a dog to look over me. I was standing in the field one day when out of the blue Henry shot off and ran out into the road. As I stood there powerless, I watched him get hit by a car right in front of me. I was frozen. It was the biggest shock and I was completely devastated – Sussex never felt the same again.

At that moment, I knew there was no future for me in Sussex. I didn't really want to go back home but there was nowhere else for me to go and staying put was no longer an option. But was there anything waiting for me in Bushey? I doubted it at the time yet it turned out a fate much bigger than I could have imagined lay in store for me ...

3

Pepsi – Finding my own beat

come from a culture where rhythm is *everything*. Anyone who spent any time in West London in the sixties and seventies will remember the music of the streets, the beat and the melody that punctuated every turn you took, the sweet sounds drifting out of every shop doorway and car window. Island sounds, drifting and lapping, like waves against the shore.

Music was in my blood and in my bones. I wish I could tell you that there was a moment when I decided I *had* to sing and making music was a conscious choice. The truth is it never occurred to me that I couldn't. I sang at church, with my family. I sang to the radio. And every Thursday night, when we all gathered together to watch *Top of the Pops*, I saw that making music mattered.

Top of the Pops was a great leveller. I didn't know anyone who didn't watch it. Every single person at school was tuning in because you had to know who was number one! My cousins, my brothers and sisters, even my parents, who thought that a lot of the youth culture we loved was nonsense, they always made sure that they were around to see what was going on. It was where we learned about new music, new dances and just as importantly, it was one of the very few places where we could see other black people on screen. (Of course, in those days, most houses only had one tiny TV and there was no such thing as Sky or Netflix. We didn't even have Channel 4 in those days! If the telly was on, you *had* to watch *Top of the Pops*.)

Even though my world was filled with black faces, when we turned the telly on, we rarely saw ourselves reflected. Occasionally there might be a story about racism or immigration on the news. At the start of the seventies, ITV began to show a sitcom called *Love Thy Neighbour*, about a black family in Twickenham who move next door to a racist white family. It starred Jack Smethurst, Rudolph Walker, Nina Baden-Semper and Kate Williams.

Love Thy Neighbour was criticised heavily. I think it was supposed to reflect the times we were living in. All over the UK, communities were becoming more integrated, but racist attitudes prevailed and everyone found it hard to adjust. However, in some ways, the sitcom exacerbated a real problem. At my school, there were so many other black kids that the show didn't have a huge impact, but I've talked to people who were some of the only black students at their schools and they used to dread Friday mornings after the programme had aired. The white students would copy the racism they had seen on TV. However, my family adored *Love Thy Neighbour*! I still remember my brothers jostling for space on the tiny two-seater settee, hugging my knees and squeezing up to make room, and the magical, choral sound of my parents laughing together, rich and harmonious. Why? When it was on, it was one of the only times we could all come together and watch people who looked a little bit like us.

So, *Top of the Pops* meant so much to us because it was another opportunity for connection. We didn't see black performers every week, but there was always the exciting chance that someone who looked like me might be there, singing and dancing to one of the songs I'd hear around the neighbourhood. Maybe that's where the first creative seeds were sown. My earliest role models were people like Shirley Bassey, the Jamaican singer Millie Small with her song 'My Boy Lollipop' and American artists like Gladys Knight and Aretha Franklin – strong and powerful women who were able to make beautiful music. Our family home was small, and slightly shabby. It was cosy and my mum worked hard to keep it spotless, but once a week, *TOTP* opened a window onto a gleaming, glittering, distant world. The screen twinkled like a priceless jewel in the corner of the lounge, shining brightly and contrasting sharply with our typical 1970s brown carpet.

Still, if I'm honest, it took me a little while to work out whether I was a doer or a dreamer. At times, I could be quite practical and good at getting things done, like when I was 17 and wrote to the council to tell them my birthday was coming and it was time for me to get my own flat.

I longed for independence. Still, when the school careers advisor sat down with me and asked me to make a plan, I felt a little lost.

'Have you thought about nursing? Or working in a shop?' She frowned at me over her smeared spectacles. I felt a heavy sigh brewing and held my breath – I didn't want to fog up her glasses! Her office felt like a cupboard, a narrow room with one tiny window. It was not a room to talk about your hopes and dreams – my options seemed even more limited than the floor space.

'Maybe something where I could travel?' I suggested, suddenly inspired by the inch of blue sky I could see through the window. I knew I longed to see the world. I'd been to St Lucia, my parents' home country once, with my mum, and it had been a magical and exotic experience. I'd do anything to be around more warmth and sunshine.

'Well, there are two jobs here, one in an antique shop and one in a travel agent. Maybe you should try the travel agent,' she said, shutting her notebook.

End of discussion. My fate was sealed – or so I thought.

It was a confusing time. Months before, I'd hoped that I might try to apply for art school. In the art room, I'd found myself. I'd loved working with paints and bright colours. In maths or history, the minutes would pass like hours and I'd find myself daydreaming, doodling, praying for the end and hoping I wouldn't get shouted at for staring out the window. But when I was in the art room, time went by in a flash. If I was working on something after school, it could get dark outside and I wouldn't notice. My teachers thought

I was talented. 'Helen, if you work hard at this you could go to art college. I'm really impressed with your work!' she said to me. It was one of the few times I felt that a teacher showed me any encouragement about my future prospects. So I began to wonder whether it was something I could explore. Then, my portfolio was stolen.

At first, I was worried that I'd mislaid it, or been careless. Had I left it on the bus? But deep down, I knew I'd always been incredibly careful with it. It was precious. To this day, I don't know who took it, but I know that someone was jealous. Now, I realise it was typical teen behaviour and there is part of me that regrets not trying a little bit harder to track down the thief and my work. But back then, I just didn't want to make a fuss. Things were hard at home, especially between my parents. I didn't want to give Mum anything else to worry about, so I pretended to myself that I didn't care and I wasn't really bothered. My portfolio was gone and my art school dreams went with it. But I could do something else – I was going to be a travel agent!

These days, I think that if you work as a travel agent, you really do get an opportunity to travel, so you can speak with some authority on a destination. But in the seventies, as a school leaver, my glamorous new job did not come with any adventurous perks. Oh, I travelled all right, all the way to Queensway. To really change things up, sometimes I walked and sometimes I got the bus. It was the time when package holidays were taking off and many people in the UK were going abroad for the very first time. The role of the travel agent was to give them some guidance and support before they got off the plane. However, the travel agency was based at the Rank Xerox office and my responsibility was to compile and type out the itinerary for the travelling sales reps. There was no intention of creating a fun-packed holiday in the sun for them. The objective was to get them close enough to the exhibition hall where they were selling photocopy machines for the company, so no Lanzarote on the beach for them. After almost a year, I just had to give in my notice because the job was so dull and boring with no chance of an adventure holiday in sight. I had no idea what I was going to do next, but I felt totally free when I walked out that building with my P45 in my hand. Already, in my head, I was imagining my plans for the evening and how I was going to celebrate my decision by dancing the night away.

Of course, that's not how my mother saw it. 'What's wrong with you?' she cried, hands in the air, as if asking God Himself why her daughter couldn't just get a proper job. 'What are you going to do with yourself now? You need to work! We *all* need to work!'

'Mummy, I don't know,' I told her. 'I just want to sing. You know I love to sing and dance!'

'Yes, but that's not a proper job, is it?' she said, shaking her head.

Of course, I had to find some paying work from somewhere, but I realised I needed to change my priorities. Work was there to support fun, adventure and opportunity. I did everything that came my way, as long as I could sing and dance as much as I liked. For a while, I even served Meals on Wheels, meeting people from all walks of life, with so many different stories to tell. That was when I knew I needed to start creating stories of my own.

It all started to happen just after I got my name. I think it's all thanks to Crackers. In the mid-seventies, Crackers was a hugely popular funk and soul club, just off Wardour Street in Soho. The best thing about Crackers was their daytime sessions. On a Friday lunchtime and Sunday night, a DJ would play a set and we'd all come down from school to dance. It was a different world. It was full of kids, but there was nothing creepy or sleazy about it. Every single daytime clubber was there to hear the music. We *loved* it. And that's where I found my tribe. London's coolest, most creative people were hooked on these amazing tunes and we discovered each other. There were no plans or expectations, just a brilliant vibe. We'd all come together and dance. At the time, I didn't even drink alcohol. When people went to the bar to get a round in, I just wanted something sugary to keep my energy levels up.

'Hey, girl, what will you have?'

'Just a Pepsi, thanks!'

'Come on, don't you want a beer? A rum and coke or something?'

'No, no, a Pepsi for me!'

You can guess what happened next.

A name can change everything. At school, on my birth certificate and to the wider world, I was 'Helen'. 'Helen' felt official, proper, necessary and for a long time, not really me. At the time, lots of families like mine, who had moved to the UK from other countries, were taking care to give their children recognisably English-sounding names. Now, I've come to understand my name, but then, being called 'Helen' felt like a tacit acknowledgement that my family didn't belong everywhere and we needed to assume other identities in order to stay safe and fit in. Many years later when I moved to St Lucia, I learned that the island has the nickname 'The Helen of the West', its beauty said to rival the mythological Helen of Troy, the most beautiful woman in the world. Only then did I realise why my mother had called me Helen and that she had done so in honour of our home island.

My family called me by my middle name, 'Lawrie'. Again, I've come to love it and for a long time, I didn't really think about it. I grew up in a part of London where I was surrounded by family, not just parents, brothers and sisters but aunties, uncles and cousins too. Now, I realise I was very lucky. At the time, it felt like another identity that was being pushed upon me. As Lawrie, I couldn't just be – everywhere I went, everyone would see my father's daughter, my brother's sister. We all knew each other's business and no matter where I went or what I did, chances are, someone would spot me. It wasn't even that I wanted to get into trouble! I'd come home and my mum might say something like, 'Oh, Auntie Alice just saw you in the shop!' As Lawrie, I had no privacy whatsoever.

But being Pepsi felt really, really special. It was a joke, a nickname, and all it meant was that I loved dancing and fizzy drinks. Still, it was the first time I felt that I had something that belonged to me, a word for the woman I was becoming. As Pepsi, I felt independent, creating an identity that didn't necessarily have anything to do with my home, my family or where I came from.

I knew something had changed one afternoon, arriving home from Crackers after an afternoon of dancing, glowing with energy, my muscles tingling. As I walked up our road, I heard a voice behind me: 'Hey, Pepsi, where you been?'

Instinctively, I started to turn around to reply. Halfway through, my hips locked, catching up with my brain. Hold on, that was Mum's voice. How did she know to call me Pepsi? What was going on?

'Why are you calling me that? Where did you hear that?'

She smiled. 'It's your name! I hear everyone saying it, your brothers, where's Pepsi?, there goes Pepsi. Don't think I don't know what you get up to!'

I could hear the warmth in her voice.

As I've said, my mum's life was not an easy one and we both worried about each other. I wanted to enjoy as much fun and freedom as possible while making sure that I didn't cause her any extra anxiety. She worked hard at keeping food on the table with an odd job here or there, ironing or cooking. She desperately tried to make do on very little money and she had to deal with my dad, his drinking and his other bad behaviour. But in that moment, I knew, deep down, she was like me. Life made Mum into a worrier. On the surface, she was a stressed, harassed woman, simply trying to get by. At her core, she was a giddy, giggly girl, a carefree person who loved music, dancing and fun. As Pepsi, I could be my true self and honour that part of my mum.

One of the people I met when I was dancing with the Crackers crew was a lovely young woman named Yasmin Evans. You might remember her as Yazz! She was extraordinary – she had a huge smile, piercing eyes and an incredible body. Tall, slim and graceful, she was filled with a vivacious energy.

My proper introduction to Yazz was when Chris, the bassist in the first band I was in – Pastiche, invited her to a rehearsal. Later on, she became a second vocalist in the band and we started to spend a lot more time together. Yazz and I gravitated towards each other. We seemed to throw ourselves into the music in exactly the same way. She was dazzling – confident, ambitious, but never egotistical, just quietly sure. Later, I found out that she'd been a successful teen athlete and it made so much sense to me. She was filled with a quiet drive, focus and determination. However, she also had a tremendous appetite for fun.

We spent so much time together and were always seen on the dance floors together at parties and in the clubs. Then someone on the scene seeing us as a duo asked us to put a fashion show together.

Yazz had begun to start working as a model and moving in that world, but I wasn't sure how I was going to fit as I had zero experience in that area. We decided to call it 'The Black and White Show' as we wanted a full-colour spectrum of models. Amazingly, we did the event, which was held at the Grosvenor House Hotel in Hyde Park, and it was a great success. Some of the models had experience walking down the catwalk, some were dancers. Each girl and boy was stunning and just knew how to show off the outfits designed by fashion students we had selected. We made no money to speak of, but it was a fabulous evening. It was my introduction to the can-do, creative spirit of the eighties. A mix of the glossy and the homemade, a wild, gorgeous mix of people and ideas, it felt like an extension of the club scene. Everyone had come from completely different backgrounds and families and areas of London, but we were united by our love of music and our desire to express ourselves freely. Yazz had a fantastic can-do attitude and it inspired me and gave me confidence. She was my first best friend – the first woman who told me that she wanted to know what I was thinking and feeling, the first one to see and celebrate my potential.

After the fashion show, I was all ears when Yazz had ideas. One day, she announced loftily, 'Let's go to the South of France! St Tropez!'

My brain was asking 'How? With what money?' Other than my trip to St Lucia with my mother, I'd never been abroad before. Certainly not on my own. Our annual family holiday was usually a day in Margate.

'I've worked it all out,' said Yazz airily. 'We can get a coach and go camping!'

A coach, a ferry ride and the most basic accommodation. I knew that these trips have a very strict itinerary, with timed, scheduled stops, and we wouldn't get many opportunities to go off exploring. But Yazz had other ideas.

'There's a stop in Paris, we're going to go straight to the Champs-Élysées.'

And we did. While the rest of the group disembarked and waited to be told what to do, we scarpered. It was a glorious blur, a whistlestop tour of the City of Lights. We didn't make it up the Eiffel Tower, but we saw glittering shop windows, gorgeous clothes, eccentric people – with Yazz by my side, I felt the world opening up to me.

But the most fun was to come. We only just managed to get back on the coach, soundtracked by the grumbles of the poor passengers who had been waiting for us. Gazing out of the window, I daydreamed as we drove past green fields and farmyards. The French countryside was beautiful, but to this city girl, it was getting a bit dull after an hour or two. I couldn't wait for us to reach the bright lights of St Tropez!

We arrived at our campsite. 'Yasmin, where are we?' I groaned. 'This is the middle of nowhere!'

Those bright lights of St Tropez must have been a good 10 miles away.

However, Yazz was not fazed. 'Don't worry, I have a plan! Let's, ah, go for a walk.'

The walk turned out to be a hike across many muddy fields. It was hot, sweaty and my feet were aching, but I was thrilled to be outside, with my best friend, having a French adventure.

'We're nearly there!' said Yazz, cheerfully. 'Not long now.'

We loved dancing so much that our excitement gave us extra energy.

After a couple of sweaty hours, we could see the sea! A constellation of lights glinted on the horizon and we beamed at each other. As we got nearer and approached the famous bay, we could make out figures. Gorgeous girls, elegant women dripping with diamonds, dapper men in three-piece suits, everyone tanned, wealthy, stylish and sophisticated. And there we were: two young girls from West London in scruffy jeans and decidedly damp T-shirts.

For a second, I thought about turning back to our tents but Yazz took my hand. 'We made it, let's go!' she cried and we ran the rest of the way.

She had a nightclub in mind. We could feel the beat pulsing through the tiny, darkened doorway. However, there was a problem – the queue. I didn't mind waiting, but I was worried about the long line of ultra-glamorous people in front of us. Everyone looked like a model, or was carrying a handbag that probably cost more than a car. What chance did we have? But when we got to the front, Yazz beamed a cheery (and *fairly* English-sounding) 'Bonjour!' To my surprise, the surly bouncer beamed back and we were in.

We didn't stop at the bar and we didn't even take a minute to check out the beautiful people around us – we were on the dance floor as fast as our legs could carry us. Joy surged up inside me. I couldn't believe we'd made it all the way to St Tropez! In another reality, I was following the rules, fed up, watching the clock on the travel agent's wall, wondering whether I'd ever be able to escape the office, or my family, or a future like my mother's. But here I was, with my best friend, who was brave enough to break all the rules, and having the time of my life. Still, Yazz wanted to go one step further.

There was a swimming pool at the centre of the dance floor. It was tiny – really, more of a swimming *pond*. People were standing beside it, posing, sipping their drinks, keen to look as cool as possible. But Yazz wasn't interested in posing – and she jumped straight in the water!

It's a cliché to say that we danced the night away, but we did. We weren't interested in meeting men, or celebrity spotting. We stayed until the club shut at 7 a.m. and the sun was already high in the sky. I don't know how we found the energy for the long walk home, but we managed, exhausted but euphoric.

We recovered with a day of sunbathing; we found a local beach, an idyllic stretch of soft sand, quiet and comfortable. We could just about hear the soothing murmur of waves lapping against the shoreline. However, there was one problem.

'Yazz, everyone here is topless!' I whispered, crossing my arms over my chest protectively.

'Yeah, I know!' She laughed, whipping off her T-shirt and presenting her body to the sun.

I'd felt horribly self-conscious about my breasts ever since an awful incident that happened when I was 12. I was walking home from school, wearing a vest under my uniform. I'd been trying to ignore my breasts, but it was getting more difficult. Already, my body was making it harder for me to run around and play like my brothers and I was doing my best to hide it with baggy clothes and lots of layers. But that day, as I walked past a building site, I didn't manage to conceal what was happening to me.

'Oi, love! Give us a jiggle!' called the workmen.

Shame pulsed in the pit of my stomach and I felt it burning my face. I was so embarrassed. Looking back, I'm angry. I can't believe that grown men would sexually harass a very young girl. I was in my school uniform, for goodness' sake! At the time, I thought it was all my fault. My shoulders hunched, I lowered my head and did my best to shrink into the background. I was not one of nature's wallflowers. Instinctively, I was not shy or retiring, but those workmen made me feel so self-conscious and ashamed of myself.

Slowly but surely, as I discovered clubbing and dancing, I'd been shaking off that shame. Any kind of rhythmic movement is a wonderful way to calm an anxious mind. Being in your body does wonderful things for your brain. For most of us, the desire to move is something we're born with. We're all designed to feel happy and relaxed in our own skin. Self-consciousness is something we're unfortunate enough to learn through painful and negative experiences.

On the beach with Yazz, my mind travelled back to my childhood. I was that young girl, my arms crossed over my chest, head down, determined not to cry. I was a little older, awkward and squirming as my mum helped me into one of her old bras, adjusting the straps, trying to make it fit – 'It's not perfect, but it will have to do.' I was fanning myself on a summer's day, too hot, sweating under baggy layers. And then, I was on the floor at Crackers, euphoric and joyous, free from everything but the beat.

I looked at Yazz – tall and lean, elegant, with the body of a model. I was shorter, more curvaceous and top-heavy. But it was her self-confidence that I saw, blooming and lighting up her skin. That was what I wanted. I took off my T-shirt and felt that gorgeous Mediterranean sun against my skin. The heat made me feel softer and smoother, the warmth was melting every memory that had ever made me feel bad about my body. It helped that we were surrounded by bare skin. Everyone, of all shapes and sizes, was bare-chested on that beach. No one was staring at anyone else, no one was making a big deal out of it. Because everyone was relaxed and happy, they looked beautiful. That meant I was beautiful too. I stretched out on the sand, closed my eyes and let my dancing body rest.

After we got back from France, life continued as normal. Yazz was doing more modelling work and taking part in fashion shows all over Europe. I was doing any odd jobs that came my way. I was really happy. I had my little council flat, my life was filled with music and I was beginning to make my own way in the world. Still, Pastiche rarely performed. We rehearsed endlessly and ad-libbed and jammed together. I wanted to sound like my heroine, Chaka Khan, but making music seemed to come more naturally than promoting or pushing ourselves into the limelight. But I had made a name for myself in the area as a singer. This led to me getting calls to contribute my vocals to sessions and gave me the opportunity to hone my vocal skills.

Still, I kept thinking about my recurring dream. I *knew* I was meant to be on a stage, in the lights, performing for an audience. It didn't feel as simple as ambition, or a longing. I could feel it. I'd known that sense of excitement, euphoria and freedom so clearly it was like a premonition. Then, one day, I got a phone call.

I'd just got in from a Meals on Wheels shift and I was feeling a little tired and a little sweaty. I was just about to start to peel off my grubby clothes when the phone rang. Sighing to myself, I thought, *I bet that's Mum, she knows when I get in. If I get changed before I ring her back, she'll be all "Lawrie, I know you were home, you answer the phone when I ring!" She'll definitely call me Lawrie, that will mean I'm in trouble*. Grumpily, I picked up.

'Hi, is that Pepsi?'

I didn't recognise the voice – warm, well-spoken, slightly posh. Not old-fashioned, BBC posh, just very clear and confident, with the slightest hint of Soho in the mix.

'Um, yeah, hello?'

I did *not* sound clear, or confident. Just very, very confused.

'Great! I'm calling from Simon Napier-Bell's office, we look after some of the most exciting up-and-coming bands and we're looking for someone new for a band. Are you free to come in for an audition next Tuesday?'

'Ah … yes! Of course.'

'Great, we'll see you then. We're going to send a bike with a tape for you to learn – just let us know where to send it.'

The voice took my address, gave me an address for the studio, then hung up.

Thank goodness I had next Tuesday off! I sat down and thought for a minute. The mysterious voice hadn't given me any clues about how they knew who I was, or how they got my number. This was so exciting! Was this the beginning? My destiny?

Probably not. My dad didn't teach me much, but through him I learnt never to get my hopes up. Even though I was young, I'd been promised all kinds of things but none of them had ever materialised. They got lost or got drunk away. Maybe this was a session singer job? I'd be able to make the music I loved and I'd get a few quid in my pocket. I'd go in, do my best and that would be that. Girls like me had no business thinking of destiny. I pushed the audition out of my mind for the evening and never considered it may have been a hoax.

When the day came, I was so worried about tempting fate that I didn't even dress up – I arrived at the studio in jeans and a T-shirt. The studio was a small, brick building, not far from where I lived. I knew enough people who were starting work in the music industry to know this was typical. It wasn't going to be glossy or glamorous – studios were small, scruffy spaces where people went to work. To be honest, I was relieved. I think that if I had walked into something that was all chrome and glass, it would have made me nervous.

'Hi there, I'm here for the audition,' I said to a young guy, dressed as I was in jeans and a T-shirt.

'Great, come through, it's just here,' he said.

I'd been practising with the tape, doing my Chaka Khan-style ad libs, and I was keen to get going. So keen that I forgot to take off my jacket! In fact, I stood there, headphones on, singing my heart out and moving to the beat, with the strap of my handbag still on my shoulders. The song was a fairly generic backing track and I still didn't know who I might be working with. As the final bars faded out, I smiled to myself: I'd been lost in the music, but deep down, I knew I'd nailed it.

The young guy was pleased. 'OK, that was fantastic, you did great! Come out of the vocal booth and let's have a chat.'

Simon Napier-Bell, Wham!'s manager, was in the studio and had been watching me and listening to my vocal. He had an upbeat energy and smiled as he spoke.

'So, how do you feel about going on tour?' he asked.

Wow! That sounded exciting – although I wasn't sure what it meant. I could be going to Bangkok, I could be going to Birmingham. How long would I be away for?

'Er, yeah, that sounds really good! Who would I be touring with?'

'It's Wham! Dee's left and we need someone who can replace her.'

'Wham!?' I bit my tongue before I could say 'those white boys who rap?'

'We'll set up a meeting with them, a rehearsal, see how

you get on. Then we've got a show coming up on Sunday. If that goes well, you're on! We'll be in touch!'

'Great, thanks! I guess I'll see you later.'

A little dazed, I stood up and looked for my handbag – oh, yeah, I had auditioned with it.

I had absolutely no idea that my life had changed in that moment. Back then, I couldn't think beyond the next week. I was going to get paid for music, maybe even a show! Wow! I didn't share this opportunity with anyone, I kept it to myself just in case it didn't work out. But the hope in my heart had been ignited but I had to keep it under wraps. No point in disappointing anyone else but me.

It was arranged that I'd get a lift with the other girl, Shirlie Holliman. She was going to pick me up at Finsbury Park and drive me out to the rehearsal. I'd seen Shirlie on *Top of the Pops* and I was nervous. She was incredibly cool – this gorgeous, petite punk pixie with white-blonde hair and a dress to match. When I'd seen her on screen, I'd been really drawn to her energy. She wasn't full-on, she never seemed to try too hard. Instead, she had a slouchy, sophisticated deadpan vibe and it was magnetic. Everyone loved watching the boys, George Michael and Andrew Ridgeley, and they were the stars of the show. Still, there was something about Shirlie that caught my attention and kept it there.

Again, I'd not bothered to dress up. I knew it was a rehearsal and I needed to move, so it was my beloved comfortable Levi's and another T-shirt. Also, I think there was a bit of me that knew, as the new girl, that it might be weird for me to be too Wham! or to turn up as anyone but myself. I couldn't compete with Shirlie, all I could do was be me. I walked up the crowded steps, overwhelmed by sounds and smells. Anyone could be here, that was the magic of London. Some of these people were homeless, some were going to posh offices, to shops, theatres and school. Was anyone here like me? Perhaps another girl was going down the steps and getting on the tube to go to *her* very first rehearsal.

As soon as I was outside on the pavement, I saw her. The blonde pixie, from the telly, *in her own car*. A very groovy little white Ford Capri with a black vinyl roof. She looked up and smiled. I got in and shut the door.

'I'm Shirlie! You must be Pepsi!'

Nervously, I fingered the plastic case in my handbag. I'd brought a demo tape with me, wanting to show her that I was professional, I had a decent voice, *I could do it!* But did I dare give it to her?

The plastic was getting slightly sweaty under my fingertips. 'Um, I brought a tape ...' I pulled it out and Shirlie slid it straight into her stereo. My own voice blared out from the speakers. This was normal, right? I looked out of the window and tried to rearrange my face.

I'm cool! I'm relaxed, I do this all the time!

Shirlie grinned at me and any awkwardness and tension dissolved immediately.

'Oh my God, your voice is incredible! You sound just like Shirley Bassey!' she told me.

'Thank you so much. Shirley Bassey is my favourite!'

And we were away ...

When I got into the car, I wasn't sure how I was going to keep the conversation going but after that, we couldn't stop. We were going at it, to use an expression of my mother's, nineteen to the dozen. Now, at the time, music was quite tribal. I loved funk, soul, R'n'B – and I assumed that if you were in Wham!, you must be a diehard pop fan. But Shirlie listened to absolutely everything. She told me about growing up with her dad's records, learning to jive, loving everything and everyone from Little Richard to Peggy Lee. Every time one of us mentioned a musician we loved, the other would wave her arms and say, 'Oh my goodness, *me too!*'

By the time we got to Bushey, we were best friends.

I'd wondered whether we'd be rehearsing in another studio like the one I'd auditioned in, but we appeared to be pulling up into a smart suburb, in front of a house unlike any I'd ever been in before. It was detached, neatly painted, big and bright, with lovely picture windows. Everything gleamed. 'Come in!' said Shirlie, beckoning me. I felt a little nervous. It seemed so cosy, and so homely. For the first time, I felt myself falter. I had come to do a job, planning on doing my professional best, working hard and going home, but I was walking into people's lives.

A smiling, dark-haired woman burst forth, radiating warmth: 'Welcome, welcome! Cup of tea?' It was George's mum, Lesley! I wasn't just joining the band, I was meeting the family. It felt like a date. Just in case it couldn't be any clearer, I noticed an enormous photo on the wall, the essence of the colour-saturated eighties – George and Andrew, beaming, with Shirlie in the centre, all three faces smiling at me. This was the group Wham!-And this wasn't a professionally shot photo of Wham! at work, this was three best friends, having the time of their lives. They lived their chemistry. Wham! was simply an extension of their friendship and here I was, joining in.

I think the three of them sensed it. As soon as I was in the room, everyone went out of their way to welcome me and put me at ease.

'We're so, so glad you're here! Thank you so much for coming,' said George. He was so smiley, but I think he was as shy of me as I was shy of him.

Andrew was immediately high-energy and gregarious: 'Pepsi, brilliant you're here! We're so pleased you're joining us!' He went over to shake my hand and then pulled me into a quick hug. He was charming. One of the poshest people I'd ever met, but so wonderfully at ease. I relaxed.

Once we got started, we *really* got started. George's initial shyness disappeared and it became clear that he loved working as much as I did. We were all in the zone, working out choreography for 'Young Guns (Go For It!)' and 'Club Tropicana'. I kept looking at Shirlie and noticing George looking over at her too. We all wanted to reassure each other and keep the chemistry and connection going.

I focused on getting the moves right, but the glorious thing was that George didn't want me to follow anything rigid. We were all supposed to look loose and free – 'On stage, we're creating something that everyone who watches us feels that they can be part of,' he explained. So I let myself go, just as I had been doing on dance floors all over London.

Everyone was happy – and everyone wanted to make sure that I was happy too. 'Was that all OK, Pepsi?' said George. 'Are you enjoying it? Will you come and dance with us on Sunday?'

'Definitely!' I said, smiling.

On Sunday afternoons, before the Top 40 was announced, Capital Radio hosted and broadcast a dance party. Groups of fans would come along and watch their chart favourites on stage and the whole thing was broadcast live. It was very important to me that my family knew what I was doing. However, my mother wasn't entirely sure what was going on, so I enlisted the help of my brothers.

'Look, I'm going to be dancing on the radio on Sunday afternoon and I really need Mummy to be listening,' I told them.

'Dancing on the radio? What are you talking about?'

'It's on Capital, before the Top 40 – I'm going to be the dancer in a band. You know Wham!?'

They knew Wham! but it wasn't a hoopla moment, they just took it in their stride, no big reaction. They were happy for me because they could see I was happy.

'Yeah, yeah, we'll definitely make sure Mum doesn't miss it.'

The record company sent a huge car to pick me up, which caused a bit of a stir. As I was driven through London, I stretched out, trying to relax. Was I nervous? I didn't have anything major to remember. Andrew had said, 'Just smile, try to have a good time!' *I could do that!* When we got to the venue, the nerves kicked in. The crowds were starting to gather outside the building. Hundreds of screaming girls, maybe thousands of them. *I could do this.* A familiar sense flooded my body. Of course I was nervous, but there was something else to this. I knew this feeling: it was my dream, my destiny. I knew how to do this, I'd been literally dreaming of it for as long as I could remember.

When I saw Shirlie, she greeted me like a long-lost friend – 'Pepsi! Brilliant! You're here, I'm so pleased!' We changed into our outfits – very short, flippy Fila tennis skirts and matching tops. I tugged at my skirt, a little self-consciously. Thank goodness I was wearing a decent pair of knickers!

I will never forget hearing the first beats of 'Young Guns' as the lights went up. The roar of the crowd wasn't just an expression, they actually roared! I'd never seen so many people in one space. It was the middle of the afternoon, but it could have been midnight in Studio 54. They were screaming, laughing, crying and every single one of them was dancing. It was a pure, concentrated wave of joy. My instincts took over. I started to move to the music and I did not stop. *This* was my dream manifested!

At first, I let myself get lost in the rhythms of the sound and the stage but when I remembered, I tried to pay attention to George, Andrew and Shirlie. Not because I was forgetting what I was supposed to be doing, but because watching them gave me the confidence to naturally bring out my own performance alongside Shirlie. It was the beginning of my pop education. In his sitting room, George had been ultra-focused, kind, a little quiet, while Andrew was more vocal and encouraging in a really fun way. On stage, George was transformed, the epitome of a superstar. His presence and energy were dazzling. Andrew's charisma and jovial energy was enhanced on stage and really drove the girls wild. The chemistry between George and Andrew was obviously central to the whole Wham! experience and the crowd responded to their camaraderie with wild screaming. These were not just 'white boys who rap', Wham! had something really special going on.

We were only performing for two songs and when we ran off the stage I felt energised and electrified. I didn't know quite what had happened, but it felt so addictive that I was tempted to run straight back on again and do my own encore. But the atmosphere backstage was just as exciting. I was surrounded by light – Shirlie, George and Andrew were all lit up, beaming at me.

'Pepsi! Did you love it? Did you? Did you have fun?' asked Shirlie.

'You were so, so good!' added Andrew. 'Did you enjoy it? Isn't it amazing?'

George echoed them. I was touched and shocked. I'd assumed that they would probably come back with feedback and say something like 'oh, you started a bit too soon' or 'you were supposed to be on the right during the intro'. Their joy and generosity were heartwarming. They had been doing the thing they loved most in the world and they wanted to share it with me. They wanted me to love it too.

'It was the best, ever!' I said, meaning it with all my heart.

From that moment, there was no doubt: I was with the band.

4

Shirlie – 'The cool punky girl'

There's no doubt that being part of Wham! defined my life. Not as a performer, musician or even as a creative person, but as a friend. The songs were so special and my time in the band brought me so many opportunities to travel the world. But friendship was at the core of everything we did. Between them, George, Andrew and Pepsi taught me everything I know about love, loyalty and having fun.

Maybe the most important thing I learned from the boys happened first. Don't judge someone on their appearance – in fact, don't judge. When it comes to friendship, we can be quick to rush to conclusions. It pays to be patient.

OK, I'll be honest. George and Andrew were in the year below me at school, and I barely noticed them. When you're a teenage girl, you wouldn't dream of hanging out with the junior boys. Plus, I was a punk. My life was all about scheming to go and see Siouxsie Sioux and the Sex

Pistols, getting into as many gigs as I could, bleaching my hair, dyeing it green, dressing up in bin liners when I went to gigs. Once, I even turned an old kettle into a handbag.

One lunchtime, we were waiting to go back into our form room, which was also the music room, which was set on a stage with big curtains. Behind the stage there were large concertina doors leading to a classroom. How funny that my clearest memory of George from school was me being on stage and him walking in and out of the music room with his violin case. I certainly wasn't into classical music and if you'd have told me years later that I would be sharing yet another stage with that boy with a violin case, I would never have believed you.

I wasn't the sort of girl who liked to make fun of anyone, but it was as though he was from another planet. I also remember Andrew, mainly because he was very neat-looking. He wore his blazer and his school uniform perfectly and he had a big grin on his face as he would walk past. I thought he was very cute and sweet. Even though we went to the same school, Bushey Meads, and we all lived within a couple of miles of each other, our lives were completely different. When I left school at 16, I assumed I'd never see them again mainly because we weren't friends and didn't have anything in common.

It took a series of mistakes and misadventures to make me reconnect with the boys again.

When I came back to Bushey after two years in Sussex, I felt lost, frightened and timid. I had no idea where I was going, or what I was doing.

One evening, my brother took me to the local pub, The Three Crowns. 'Come on, Shirlie, you need to get out of the house! It will do you the world of good,' he said, trying to make me move. He was expecting me to protest, but I simply nodded, numbly: 'OK.' Usually, I wouldn't be seen dead in the pub. It was an old-fashioned place full of miserable old men. In fact, before I'd left for Sussex, I'm not sure I'd ever set foot inside a pub. Sometimes I'd walk past and hear waves of grumbling, unhappy chat pouring out of the doorway. I always thought pubs were for dads who wanted to get away from the family. If you wanted to go to fun places, you went to gigs, you went dancing, you went to London. You didn't want to go and listen to lots of grumpy old people complaining into their ales.

Still, while I'd been away, something had shifted. There were no grumpy old geezers muttering. Instead, it was buzzy, full of young vibrant people having a good time. There was still a photo of a girl in a bikini being used to sell packets of peanuts and that damp smell of beer, and cigarette smoke was still lingering around – I never liked the smell of pubs. But there was a change in the mood. The old men were standing at the bar alongside bright young things – kids my age in well-cut, brightly coloured clothes. I could hear genuine, happy laughter, there were smiles in their voices. At the time, I was worrying that nothing would ever make me smile again. Even though I wasn't yet 20, I felt careworn and exhausted. I couldn't think of a single thing to feel optimistic about yet even I could tell that while I'd been away, something had changed. The eighties were beginning to get going – and after a decade of hardship, they were going to be better than anything that had come before.

Still, as I sipped my orange juice, I struggled to summon up the spirit of the eighties in my own soul. I was scared, rubbish at small talk, and convinced I had nothing in common with the other revellers, who were all blowing off steam after work, having left a glamorous office somewhere. I was a barely educated, unemployable someone who was better at communicating with horses than people. 'Just five more minutes,' I told myself, then I could claim to my brother that I had tried my hardest and I could give up and go home.

'Shirlie?'

I didn't immediately place the voice, but it was friendly, clear and familiar. Quite posh. But I didn't know anyone posh – certainly not anyone I'd expect to bump into in the pub.

'Shirlie, is that you? It's Andrew! From school!' he said with a big smile on his face.

Squinting to look, I thought, *Is that the young boy with a perfectly cut blazer, the kid in the year below me with a nice smile?* It had been years but I knew he was still around, because I'd seen him walking along the road when I drove back to Bushey from Sussex. In fact, I'd very nearly swerved. Had he just stepped out of a salon? Surely there was no barber in Bushey who could give a young man a trendy haircut like that? At the time he had on a fisherman's stripey T-shirt and those pale blue peg trousers were pretty special too – he was wearing the same outfit tonight.

'It's so good to see you! Will you come and sit with me, catch up?'

I looked around and I was no longer fed up, in fact I was quite excited – I suddenly met this person and we instantly clicked. That's when the jukebox played 'Start!' by The Jam. 'I love this song!' we said, simultaneously. We started talking about music and didn't stop until the landlord called last orders. I told Andrew everything, from dancing to jive music with my dad when I was a little girl, to my teen love of punk. He blushed a little. 'You know, before we knew who you were at school, when we didn't know your name, we used to call you the "cool punky girl,"' he admitted. Now it was my turn to blush! Sure, I'd been a punk, but I'd had no idea anyone thought I was cool! Quite honestly, I had no idea that anyone, anywhere, had noticed me at all.

As I felt the warmth spreading to my cheeks, I looked at Andrew again and for the first time, I felt like someone had plugged me back in and revived my sense of fun and passion, especially about music. He smiled the whole time that he was talking to me and it was impossible not to smile back. The little boy from school had grown into a cool, confident young man – but he still wanted to impress me. Being caught in the full beam of Andrew's smile was special. I felt huge excitement that I connected with someone – I wasn't feeling like the loser who had to go back to Bushey.

Andrew asked me everything about where I'd been living and what had happened to me after school. He was so funny, no one had made me laugh like that for years. I think it's what you call charisma and he had plenty of it. We talked about life for ages – well, I didn't think we could have been chatting for more than half an hour, but suddenly the landlord was calling time.

'Will you come and see my band soon?' asked Andrew. 'We're called The Executive. The lead singer is Yog, from school. You remember my friend Yog? You must have seen us together?'

As I'd not paid much attention to anyone in the year below at Bushey Meads, Andrew's friend didn't come to me straight away, but I was curious. 'I'd love to come along!' I said.

Just then I heard my brother shout, 'Shirlie, come on, time to go!' We hastily made a plan for me to watch their rehearsal in the next couple of days. After all, being around bands was my favourite thing – this boy seemed perfect.

I introduced my brother to Andrew as we walked to the car but he wasn't as impressed with him as I was.

'Is this *your* car?' he said, admiringly.

I looked at my car, a knackered B reg Austin Mini Estate. It was my first car and I felt quite proud of it. After all, I was the only one here with a car and so I had a queue of people wanting a lift home. It was the one bit of independence I could still cling to. So, when Andrew suggested a few days later that I pick him up on the way to the rehearsals, I was keen. I didn't even mind when he asked me to pick up this Yog guy, who I still couldn't place. I was curious: who was he? Would I recognise him?

It only took me 10 minutes to drive to Andrew's house. He was already outside when I arrived.

'Yog lives out in Radlett,' he said as he climbed into the front seat of my Austin mini. 'Do you know the way?'

I did. It wasn't that far from Bushey, if you look on a map. If you get lucky with the lights you're there in 15 minutes. But as we drove there, Andrew and I just chatted and chatted. In what felt like no time we were outside Yog's house.

Even though it was just around the corner, it had a completely different feel. There were trees, flowers and a sense of symmetry and space. As we pulled into the street, he said, 'Here we are, this is it,' and pointed to a really pretty cream house with a semi-circular drive in front of it. I pulled up and parked the car on the road.

As we waited on the doorstep, I wasn't sure who to expect. Would this Yog remember me like Andrew had? I doubted it because I couldn't recall who he was. The door opened and I held my breath.

'Andrew! Shirlie! Come! Come on in!' I'd thought Andrew was the happiest, smiliest person I'd ever met, until I met Yog. He was quite tall, with tight curly hair, but what I noticed most about him was his energy. He looked confident and so open. I could see why they were such good friends, they really mirrored each other in charisma and friendliness. As Yog closed the door, he and Andrew both shot upstairs, leaving me behind. I had no idea where to go as I stood there in the hallway feeling awkward because in my house you wouldn't be able to run upstairs with a boy under any circumstances. Then I suddenly heard Andrew shouting, 'Come on, Shirlie, come upstairs!'

I'd thought Andrew had changed beyond all recognition, but Yog's glow was something else. Now I remembered who he was, he was that boy holding the violin case outside the music room. Yog had developed a kind of aura. He had a truly magnetic presence, it was impossible to look away. Although I couldn't formulate the thought into words at that point, it would have been easy to imagine him in a stadium, surrounded by tens of thousands of screaming fans. It seemed weirder to see him standing in a hall foyer, on a thick white carpet, examining a pile of post on an occasional table.

As I stepped into his bedroom, Yog said, 'Shirlie! Andrew told me you were coming along, I'm so glad to see you.'

'It's great to see you too, Yog. By the way, why do they call you Yog?' I asked, genuinely interested.

In a funny Greek accent Andrew shouted, 'It's short for Yorgos.'

But I was none the wiser.

'It's short for George in Greek,' Yog added.

That satisfied my curiosity.

His room was small, with a single bed and a white carpet and I remember thinking how neat and tidy it was with his record collection on the shelves opposite the bed. I walked over and looked at his album collection. I remember seeing everything from Elton John and Queen to ABC and The

Human League. Just as with Andrew, I instantly had a rapport with Yog. When I asked what their music was like in The Executive, George put on a cassette for us to listen to. I was instantly impressed, especially with the voice.

In that moment, I think the first seed of Wham! was planted. It's hard to explain, but being with George and Andrew simply felt right and made sense. We didn't have to explain ourselves to each other, there was no awkward small talk or catching up.

Yog suddenly said, 'Hey guys, we've got to go! We've only got the rehearsal studio for a couple of hours and we have to get to Watford, let's go.'

The Executive also featured Andrew's younger brother, Paul, and a childhood friend of George's called David. They weren't bad, but they were a ska band and more like The Specials, which is a band they all loved. It made me realise how important chemistry between bandmembers was and unfortunately, it didn't look like it was really working – I think they all got frustrated with each other and maybe George decided the band wasn't for him at that time. I never saw The Executive perform other than at that one time in the rehearsal room.

Still, George's talent was undeniable, as was his chemistry with Andrew. When he sang, I simply couldn't take my eyes away from him. He transformed the space – his voice and his attitude belonged in a spot-lit stadium. It was hard to watch him and remember that he was surrounded by old boxes and brooms! I'd never heard a voice like that before, someone who had such softness and sang in these otherworldly tones.

He had such a feeling in his voice, it gave me goosebumps. A star was born and to this day, I don't think there is anyone with a voice like his – that's what made him so special.

'You were really good,' I whispered, staring at my boots.

'Thank you,' said George, smiling. 'Any chance of a lift? Fancy The Three Crowns?'

It's really difficult to describe George's relationship with his gift. He knew how extraordinarily talented he was, but in a strange way, that knowledge made him modest. He wanted to be the best that he could possibly be, but he longed to achieve excellence on his own terms. I knew he was pleased that I loved his voice, but he didn't sing because he craved approval and adulation. It was a gift that was given to him and he knew that. His gift gave him the ambition to keep him moving forward, knowing that was his destiny: a life in music.

On the way to the pub, I soon realised that George's humour matched Andrew's. Both of them were witty and sharp and hilarious. I'd met George a matter of hours ago and I felt like I'd known him all my life. I'd never met two boys that bounced off each other as well as they did. Together, we'd crack jokes and put on silly voices. 'Don't make me laugh!' I'd beg, knowing that if I didn't stop giggling, tears would come to my eyes and I'd struggle to see the road.

When we were at the pub, I didn't drink so I was able to drive the boys home afterwards. I dropped George off at his beautiful house and as he closed the door to my car, he said, 'See you soon.' I remember turning to Andrew after he had gone and saying, 'Aw, I really liked him, he's really nice!'

There was a tacit understanding that the three of us were completely bonded from that point. We didn't know it, but that was the beginning of Wham!

After that, I went to a few more rehearsals for The Executive, but the band was gradually running out of steam. Some of the other boys were trying to get proper jobs and George was writing the most incredible songs, on his own. In those days we had cassettes and ever since I knew him, George loved to play me his songs in my car. Half the time I think he only wanted a lift so he could play me his songs. I guess it was the nearest thing to imagining how it would sound on the radio. There were some ballads that he played and they were so sad and the lyrics so intricate – I became fascinated by the extraordinary ability that he had. Some of them were never released – he was like that, he would throw away songs that most bands would die to have on their album. They were brilliant, but not really suitable for a ska band. Later, instead of going to rehearsals, the three of us would go out. Now that we had my little car, the world was our oyster! Well, London anyway.

George was getting part-time jobs by now. For a while he was DJing in a dinner and dance restaurant called Bel Air and I went with him a couple of times. He was earning good money playing songs for after-dinner guests and he was also an usherette at the Watford cinema. Soon, the three of us were inseparable to the point when George was working,

Andrew and I would go and watch a movie while he was walking up and down the aisle, showing people to their seats with a torch and taking their tickets. It was brilliant – we either had half-price tickets or he got us in for free.

I also had a job in a restaurant called Ponderosa, so the boys would come in whenever I was working so they could take the mickey, but I knew it was because really, they wanted to be with me while I was on my shift. Our other friend David Austin was also a lifeguard who got us into the swimming pool for frcc. All of our entertainment was taken care of and very often the three of us would go to the local leisure centre, swim in the pool and then go dancing in a local club – quite often, I'd turn up with wet hair. Life felt very spontaneous. My car could transport us anywhere we wanted to go and I loved driving us there.

But things were changing in the eighties and the spirit of Wham! evolved on our dance floors. It was the era of the yuppie – the young, upwardly mobile professional – but we were so the opposite. Our life was simple, with no deadlines or meetings – we were living our passion, not our profession.

George and Andrew were into great bands that they introduced me to. Andrew would play Aztec Camera and Scritti Politi, which I'd never heard of. They rebelled against the establishment by laughing at it. And there was plenty to laugh about. Now I was no longer lost – I felt I'd met my soulmates and it was exciting to spend my days feeling free with them. There was a feeling that anything was possible.

This suited me perfectly. I'd come back from Sussex, terrified about what my future held – or *didn't* hold. I'd been lying awake fretting, ashamed of my lack of qualifications and my inability to plan. I'd felt so lost and George and Andrew had found me and said, 'So what? It doesn't matter!' The boys reminded me that I was young and that having my whole life ahead of me was a good thing. They taught me to live in the moment.

'Wham Rap! (Enjoy What You Do?)' was born out of being in that moment. The first time I heard George rap, it was all about McDonald's. We were sat in the car eating our McDonald's. The boys loved root beer and George would start singing – 'Root beer, apple pie, give me an order, those French fries …' and then we'd all just start singing about McDonald's with everyone adding a line and laughing. So, from that silly song, George was thinking about rap – it was almost like his fun thing. 'Wham Rap!' was such a tongue-in-cheek song – it really made you smile. I don't know if people took it seriously, but that was us: you were on the dole but you had soul.

We found a nightclub in North London that was playing the music we loved and every Thursday we would be there without fail. I would head to Miss Selfridge to get something to wear as the New Romantic scene was hotting up and to get noticed, you had to look the part. I'd pick up things like ra-ra skirts and tucker boots. We started to take it more seriously, practising dancing in George's bedroom. We would practise because when later we would go out, we wanted to hit the dance floor. Now we took it more seriously but we lived for those nights – that's how it started for us.

There must have been a point where George started to

think that there was a future in music for him and Andrew and me dancing. Such a shame I never had that conversation with him to ask, 'When did the penny finally drop?' It was during those early trips to clubs that I realised George had two sides that were almost fighting to get out – the confident part and the shy part. While Andrew was a full-on extrovert, George sometimes felt very self-conscious. I think that deep down in his core, he knew he was on a mission. His purpose on this earth was to make music, that was what he was focused on and he felt sure of his gift. He was never, ever arrogant, but then he didn't feel any need to prove himself as a singer or a songwriter – he was very secure.

On the dance floor, we had the most incredible chemistry. George came alive and would swing me around with such confidence. When I thought he would let go of my hand, he would grab me and spin me around. Always, he had a big smile on his face when he would dance and he would look me in the eye. We had such strong eye contact that everything else would disappear and we could be back in his bedroom for all we cared. It was a gift that we were able to give to each other. On our own, we could be shy, quiet, awkward kids, the sort of people you might not look twice at. Together, we became a magnetic, unstoppable force.

Looking back, I wonder whether that's where Andrew's confidence came from too. I think Andrew is one of those rare people who didn't grow up feeling shy or awkward. That's where his charisma comes from, he's always been very gregarious and open.

By experimenting with rap, completely by accident,

George and Andrew were able to start to discover their sound. The seventies had been a difficult, deprived time for almost all working families and by 1981, a deep recession hit as the UK government tried to control inflation. A movement started to protest the shockingly high unemployment figures – three million people in the UK were out of work and the first People's March for Jobs happened in 1981. It was really difficult for women to find work, especially girls like me, who had a miserable time at school and struggled to get their exams. Only 15 per cent of students stayed in higher education or went on to university.

My friend Tracey was lucky – even though like me she didn't excel at school, she was sponsored to showjump. Every other girl I knew was working in a shop, or working in a hairdresser's, or would soon be a stay-at-home mum with children of her own. Of course, there's nothing wrong with taking any of those routes if that's what makes you happy. Some didn't have options or freedom but I found my freedom with George and Andrew.

Now, my own children, Harley and Roman, pursue their professional passions because they have grown up knowing that if you have a talent that makes you happy, then you have a right to embrace it – and that your friends and family will get behind you and help you on your way. But back then, 'Enjoy what you do' was a *radical* message. Dreaming was discouraged. Even though the boys were clearly talented, their families initially didn't believe that they could make a living in the music industry. Everyone was so, so anxious about unemployment and simply getting by. So even though 'Wham Rap!' was a tongue-in-cheek, slightly naughty nod and a wink to the situation we found ourselves in, it was a revolutionary anthem. It told young people that being on the dole didn't mean a loss of dignity – in fact, it said that there was dignity and decency in enjoying yourself and that living through a politically problematic period didn't mean that you stopped being entitled to having a happy life.

The song started to evolve, slowly, and it was exciting to see that George and Andrew were capturing our mood. Ironically, the more ambitious the boys became, the less I worried about the future – I was so excited about watching them finding their musical path and seeing how happy it was making them.

I knew it was only a matter of time before the boys were offered a record deal. They were both desperate to get signed, I think partly because they really wanted to validate their decision to pursue music. As we drove around in my car, we'd talk about our hopes, dreams and frustrations. 'I just want a record deal!' George would say, sighing. Even though we were having fun together, he and Andrew were working so hard on what Wham! would become. I had no doubt they would get signed, and soon, but it was their journey. I loved the dancing, being with them and hearing what they were working on, but I felt that the music was their project. I loved singing, and even wrote my own songs in secret, but when your best friend is *that* talented, you don't necessarily want to push yourself into the limelight. George and Andrew were busy recording on the 8-track. George also played the bass and the keyboards and would lay down all the melodies as well as sing – they were literally creating music in his bedroom.

I still remember George's eyes shining when he shared the news that they had been offered a record deal – 'It's happening!' he cried. Turns out The Three Crowns was a magical place for us because one night, the boys met Mark Dean, who owned Innervision records. The boys must have been impressed by this and sent him their tape. When I arrived at George's house, the two boys couldn't wait to tell me. I thought I was going to explode with pride, I was overjoyed for them both.

A little while later, George had a handful of white-sleeved vinyls of 'Wham Rap!' I had booked a holiday to Ibiza with an old school friend and George said, 'Take these with you and tell all the DJs in the nightclubs to play them.' *I'm not taking those in my suitcase*, I thought, thinking he was mad, but he managed to persuade me to go running around all the nightclubs. What's hard is that when working, most DJs have their headphones on and they're not looking out to the dance floor, so all I remember was that I stood frantically in front of their booths waving this white label record and shouting at the top of my voice so they could hear me, 'This is my friend's song, please play it!' I remember I had success in one place and when it came on, I jumped on to the dance floor, so happy that my friend's song was being played live. The best thing about it was that I was so pleased I got rid of all those white labels and I didn't have to take them home with me. It gave me more room in the suitcase to bring back my new suede Ursula Andress boots that I bought in town. Also, I couldn't wait to get back to show off my Ibiza tan.

So, the boys were excited to see me and I picked Andrew up to go to George's house, as was our routine, not knowing that they had actually been asked to do a PA in a club. But I wasn't expecting George's next words: 'Will you come and dance with us?'

If George was asking, I was dancing, but I was confused: 'Of course I'll come, but, er, what's a PA?' I was so naïve and I think that was part of Wham!'s charm! I certainly had no ambitions when it came to a pop career, but it did make me wonder how the boys were going to do it. After all, Andrew played guitar while George sang, but would it just be a duet? It seemed quite awkward for it to be just the two of them, so it made sense to bring me and another girl on stage with them. After all, when George and I danced together, everyone stopped and stared, clearing a space on the dance floor to watch us. Why not make the performance official?

That first PA – public appearance – was in Haringey in a club called Bolts and it was to be a showcase for Wham! In my head, it wasn't a big deal. I thought that we would do what we do when we go out dancing in clubs together and now we would do it on a stage in front of people. I always thought that once you were signed to a record company, your songs would get played on the radio – I didn't realise you had to actually do club performances.

As the date drew nearer, Andrew started plotting and planning. One night, when we were at our local pub, he made a suggestion: 'Listen, I've been thinking about this PA,' he said, as we waited at the bar. 'It would be good if we had another girl, I think. More professional. We could do a bit more of a routine.'

I nodded. Practically speaking, I knew Andrew was right – I couldn't think of any other groups that had just one backing dancer. There had to be two girls. The trouble was that I knew this would mean major change. For me, our friendship had always been the most important, precious force. I was excited about what the boys were creating and I'd do everything I could to support them, but I was also trying not to think about how their success might change our dynamic. I wanted them to have everything they wanted and for the world to know how talented they were, but I was scared this might mean that eventually, we wouldn't be able to spend Saturday mornings messing about at the leisure centre. And if another girl came into the group, the dynamics would shift – we'd have to be together and professional, we couldn't act daft or make inside jokes.

Still, rather than search the country for a glossy, glamorous trained dancer, Andrew decided to keep things local. He managed to find another dancer inside The Three Crowns! Amanda was someone we'd known for a while – she was a local girl, a pub regular, and just like me, she would rush to the dance floor the moment anything

Above: Pepsi's dad Roger.
Left: Pepsi's mum Agatha.
Right: Agatha & baby Pepsi.
Bottom: Pepsi as a baby.

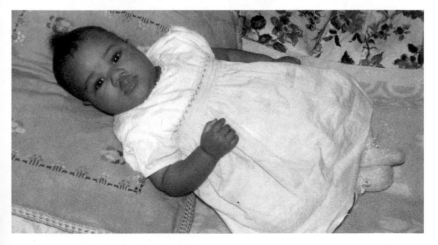

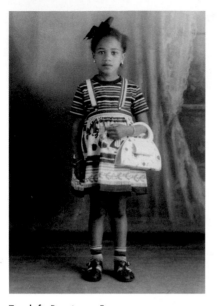

Top left: Pepsi age 5.

Top right: Pepsi school photo.

Below left: Pepsi, Agatha and brother David.

Bottom right : Pepsi, Agatha and Roger at her first Holy Communion.

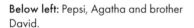

Top Left: Pepsi in the middle with her brothers, David and Max.

Top right: Pepsi's youngest brother Robbie and mum Agatha. 'He would eventually stand up to our father Roger.'

Above: Pepsi at primary school.

Above: Shirlie with a monkey, aged 4.

Below: Shirlie, her mum Maggie and sister Nicola.

Top right: Shirlie age 5.

Bottom left : Early David Cassidy fan.

Top: Jocelyn's back garden. Shirlie with Jocelyn playing with dolls and her two sisters.

Above: Shirlie and Bobby the pony.

Top: Shirlie, Brighton.

Above: George and Shirlie on Brighton Beach.

Top: Shirlie and Andrew in Japan.

Above: George, Maggie and Deon Estus.

Pepsi and Shirlie in 'Club Tropicana' dresses.

with a beat came on.

I think we were nervous about asking her. We didn't want to make too big a deal out of it – especially because we weren't getting paid! But it was important to me that she took it seriously, especially because I was so excited for George and Andrew and I wanted her to be impressed by the boys. Happily, Amanda was really keen: 'Of course, that sounds brilliant! I'd love to do the PA,' she beamed.

George was delighted: 'Great, we'd better have some rehearsals at my place!' he decided. It was a bit of a squash, but we all squeezed into my little car and took to the white carpet. He was very focused and it really rubbed off on the rest of us. We knew we needed to come up with a routine, but we didn't want it to *look* like a routine. Even though we were trying to give ourselves a bit of choreography and structure, we wanted to appear spontaneous and fun. That idea remained at the core of Wham! even when we were playing stadiums. George used to say, 'I want everyone in the audience to be able to imagine themselves on stage with us.'

Together, we were all good at feeding off each other's energy, and responding to the music. Amanda and I both wore white – I'd found a little skirt and top from Miss Selfridge in Watford – we wanted to look coordinated, but not matching.

The big day dawned. 'Are you nervous?' Amanda whispered to me as we loaded bags into the car boot. I had to think about it – 'I don't think so. Maybe a little bit for the boys.'

It was so strange. For years, I'd wondered whether I might

be the shyest, most self-conscious person in the world. Now, here I was, about to perform with my friends and as happy and relaxed about it as I was when I danced with my dad in the front room on a Sunday morning! Still, in years to come, I'd go to see Harley and Roman in school plays and recognise a familiar feeling. It was a kind of stage fright by proxy. I didn't feel remotely nervous about my performance and I can't stress this enough, I knew that anything George did on stage would be brilliant – he was a perfectionist and I knew this performance had to be spot on.

Still, moments before the music started, I looked out at the clubbers and thought, *Oh, they're going to hate us*. After all, when I went out to a nightclub, I went to dance. I'd feel pretty grumpy about being made to clear the dance floor to watch some kids doing their thing – we were interrupting their big Saturday night!

Just before we began, I noticed that there weren't any other women in the club. We had an all-male audience, young and beautifully dressed in perfectly pressed shirts and bright, tight white jeans and vests. It didn't dawn on me that this was a gay nightclub. I felt relaxed and comfortable, and it took me a moment to work out why. I'd always felt a little uneasy about male attention. I never felt sexy and I certainly didn't go out of my way to look it. I wanted to be cool, funny and sometimes silly – and these were all words that described the way I felt when I was hanging out with George and Andrew. Subconsciously, a remote part of my brain registered that Amanda and I weren't going to be ogled or judged. These men looked sophisticated, but also friendly and interested –

they wanted to watch and see what we had to offer.

As soon as the 'Wham Rap!' double-clap beat kicked in, my instincts took over. I was aware that this was a performance and I kept remembering to check in with Amanda, Andrew and George most of all. This was new for all of us. We had big smiles on our faces and we were pulling out our best moves. Everyone was staring at us and we were having so much fun moving to the music. By the time I heard the opening bars of 'Young Guns (Go For It!)', I felt exhilarated. I didn't just dance like no one was watching, I danced like the peasant girl Karen in *The Red Shoes*, letting my feet control me totally. *I might never get to do this again,* I thought. *I've got to make this count!*

The music stopped and to my utter shock, I could hear clapping, cheering and even whooping and screaming! The audience all had smiles on their faces as they waved their hands in the air. I looked around me: George looked elated, but slightly stunned. Amanda was grinning and Andrew was jumping up and down, hugging us all. If you'd told me that in a few years, we'd be playing to tens of thousands of people at a time, in Australia and Japan, I wouldn't have believed you. But while it's a pleasure and a privilege to play international shows, I've never had a performance high *quite* like that first time, playing to a couple of hundred people in Haringey.

It took me a few moments to remember what I'd *really* been looking forward to all day. We weren't getting paid for our performance, but we'd been promised a meal afterwards. Free burgers and chips, and as much Coca-Cola as we could drink! This was the most glamorous thing that had ever happened to me by far. I knew my brothers and sisters would be bright green with envy. I felt like a film star!

By the time Norman, the club's owner, came over to chat, I was stuck into my second pint of Coke. 'That was fantastic, we all *loved* you! Please come back and do it again,' he said, grinning. 'Any time,' I said, slurping, before realising that this was amazing news for George and Andrew – not just an excuse for me to get more free drinks!

5

Shirlie – New girl called Pepsi

Sadly, Amanda soon left us – 'It's great fun,' she explained. 'It's just really hard to fit it in with work. After a day on my feet at the salon, it's hard to come and do a performance at the club! And I can't leave my trade, especially because we're not getting paid for these PAs.'

'I don't blame you,' I sympathised.

I was doing various odd jobs in shops and cafés and still living at home. In many ways, I was lucky. Because the unemployment situation was so bad, everyone's parents were anxious and constantly on at them to get a job, but Mum always said, 'Love, I don't mind what you do, as long as you can give me 10 pounds a week for the housekeeping.' Because I had no qualifications, there weren't many jobs I could try to get, if I wanted them – my CV was a strange one, after all.

Still, I was torn. The record company kept talking about the future, which seemed to become bigger, better, shinier and more exciting. Now, I realise we should have been a bit more cynical. I think some executives were looking at the boys with nothing but pound signs in their eyes. It's a dangerous combination – they were enormously talented, gorgeous, passionate and vulnerable. But I couldn't help but be swept up in their vision and their enthusiasm. And it became clear that once he got past his surface shyness and insecurity, George was very intuitive and sure. He wasn't just an exceptionally gifted singer and songwriter, he understood, long before the rest of the world caught up, about the power of being a band with a brand.

And I worried. Day by day, I cheered along with the boys and every single success. They inspired so much love in me. I don't think there's anything more exciting than watching your favourite people realising their hopes and dreams but very occasionally, when I couldn't sleep, a sad, scary feeling threatened to overwhelm me. They were obsessed with what might happen in the future and I was completely content to live in the present. I didn't really want to be a pop star, but what would happen if these dreams came true?

By now, Andrew was my boyfriend and George was my best friend but the three of us were inseparable. We complemented each other and nothing ever felt awkward. Still the idea of having lots of girls screaming at them worried me – our relationships could be affected if they became famous. But then, if they became megastars, they wouldn't need me anymore surely? What would become of our late-night drives and heart-to-hearts? I'd been trying to teach George the basics of driving. He wouldn't need me to be his driving instructor anymore. Would I now be replaced by a limousine? Even worse, would they have any time for me at all?

Just before the very first PA, George and Andrew had gone to the studio to record some of the songs for the album that would become *Fantastic*. Now, at the time, the music had never really been any of my business. It sounds odd, but as I've said earlier, I didn't expect them to involve me. Music had been their project before we became friends and they wrote songs together. I was always really excited to hear what they were working on and delighted that the world would soon hear George's gorgeous voice but I suppose I knew I could never compete. I loved music so much, but George really did have the voice of an angel. I know I was able to bring something extra, something that he needed to the club performances, but he didn't need me to help him carry a tune.

Still, I got so caught up in the excitement of performing the first PA that it took a while for me to realise there was something odd about the experience. I'd assumed we'd be singing to a backing track, but we were miming to the music that the boys had recorded in the studio – 'It's much easier this way,' explained George. 'We don't need to worry about being mic'd up, we can throw ourselves into the dancing and really put on a show!'

He's got a point, I thought. Our dances were very high-energy, and no one wanted to hear us singing while we tried to get our breath back!

Then, two things happened. After Amanda left, Innervision – the record company – found another girl for the group. We knew Wham! was going places when we stopped having to recruit our own dancers from The Three Crowns! Now, I'd been a bit scared of things changing when Amanda joined us, but that had worked out OK. Of course, it's always a little strange when another person joins a very close-knit gang, however, Dee C. Lee's arrival really changed things in a way I couldn't imagine. A truly lovely, down-to-earth, kind-hearted woman, she was also really beautiful.

'She's been in a band called Central Line, they've had hits in America,' Andrew explained.

And when I met her, I realised that Dee was also a real grafter. That suited George perfectly, as he was working so hard too. She was sweet, she was fun and she never complained about work, but it really was work now. And Dee had a life outside the group. She danced with us all day long, but this was a professional gig for her and she had another life.

Still, Dee looked great, she was ambitious and she was a *fantastic* singer – she had a really delicate, beautiful voice. The trouble was that she had no way of using it in Wham! I hadn't thought much about my own singing until the record company had some exciting news: 'Great news! *Saturday Superstore* want you on this week!' A scout had seen one of our PAs and suggested Wham! as a booking.

Saturday Superstore was a big deal. It was the hot new weekend show – and even though it was aimed mainly at kids, it was watched by pretty much everyone in the country. It was young, it was fun and it was one of the few places to see bands perform. In those days, when there were only three channels, if you were on TV absolutely *everyone* would see you. This could be a huge break for Wham!

'Do you want to be on telly with us?' asked George. 'It's only miming again, just like the PAs.'

Was I keen? I'd already bought the dress! I didn't care if I was miming, because everyone was miming on TV. But something was bothering me. 'George,' I asked, hesitantly, 'what about the girl you have on the track singing, won't she be annoyed that she won't be on TV instead?'

George shook his head – 'No, she's a session singer. She sang on this record. You're the one we want performing with us!'

At the time, I accepted it all without questioning it too much. The TV company had all kinds of weird rules, so I didn't feel that bad that I was miming even though it wasn't my voice. Still, part of me felt crushed. I knew I could sing that part anyway, and it was a shame that it wasn't my voice on the record.

Years later, I was watching a documentary about eighties pop, and I had a real shock. A woman I'd never seen was onscreen, talking about how upset she was with me! And it was to do with the fact that I was miming to her vocals at that time. How ironic that we were both upset about our roles in 'Young Guns'. I managed to contact her and apologise for my part in that and I feel like we have now made our peace with it. What's even stranger is the way that we choreographed the song: 'Shirl, listen to the lyrics,' explained George. 'I need you to play the angry girlfriend. Act as though you're really pissed off with me. Think *fury*.'

At the time, I thought fury – then caught George's eye and creased up. The idea of being angry with him was too much, it made me laugh. Looking back, I think I did a decent job, but the real singer was probably out there somewhere, looking pissed off.

I'm sure that if I'd really thought of myself as a singer at the time or made it my business to get more involved in the music, I would have been given a chance to sing more. But you have to remember that although I loved singing, at the time it wasn't necessarily a big part of my dreams and ambitions. All I wanted was to spend as much time with my best friends as possible. It was as if we'd all been paddling in the same stream and suddenly I found myself caught in the current of a fast-flowing river! I was happy to go with the flow, in every sense.

Poor Dee never really spoke about it, but I could tell she was becoming increasingly frustrated. She did dream of a career in music and I think that in some ways, being part of Wham! must have been really tough for her. As time went by, even Andrew was doing less and less in the way of songwriting. He was very talented musically, but it was blindingly obvious that George was a superstar and it made sense for him to be doing as much as possible. Dee had a gorgeous voice and no way of showing it off to its full advantage.

At the time, the London music scene was pretty cosy and cliquey. Everyone knew each other and we all had friends in common, we'd bump into each other at various London bars. So, although Wham! and The Jam were very different groups, Dee had become friends with Paul Weller, who loved her voice and had an exciting project that he wanted her to be a part of.

When she broke the news, it wasn't especially dramatic – but there was one surprise. 'I've been chatting to Paul about his new band – he'd like us both to come and sing for him!' she said. 'What do you think?'

I laughed. 'No, Dee, don't be daft! He doesn't want me, he's just after you!' I told her. I knew Paul wanted Dee in the band and not just for her voice. I'd never met him but I just knew what was going on. For me, leaving George and Andrew was *unthinkable* – but if I did, I knew I might be playing musical and romantic gooseberry. Now, I'm not sure that I would necessarily have changed the course of pop history by joining The Style Council, but it's funny to think about what might have been.

Yet again we had to say goodbye to another talented person. We understood Dee – especially George. 'This is a great opportunity for her, she needs to go and do what she loves,' he mused. He knew how much music meant to him and really empathised with Dee's opportunity. But before Dee left us, we all got to go out to Ibiza and make the 'Club Tropicana' video.

Promotional videos were fairly new and they were about to become a new art form. By the mid-eighties, record companies had worked out that a brilliant video could help a band break America and they were worth investing in. However, when we made the video for 'Young Guns', the budgets were so tiny that we wondered whether the producers were expecting change from a 20-pound note. All I remembered from the 'Young Guns' shoot was spending all day on my feet in a hot stuffy club, where they used a dodgy smoke machine that pumped loads of smoke into a small area. We were all choking, I genuinely thought they wanted to kill us.

How clever of them to come up with a song that just had to be filmed on location! The song 'Club Tropicana' was so fun, the video needed to be special too. The boys had never been to Ibiza. I had but my last time was spent flogging white label vinyls. So I was looking forward to going back. Ibiza was such an unusual holiday destination – hippy, sexy and young and pretty wild – so when George announced, 'We're all going to Ibiza!' I couldn't believe my good luck. Sure, we were going there to work, but as far as I was concerned, it was a holiday with my best mates, where I could show them what it was all about.

George loved the sunshine and heat just as much as I did – 'Shirl, I've had a thought. Let's go out a couple of days early, just me and you, so we can catch up and get nice and tanned before we shoot the video.' Although we would have topped up ourselves with a lot of Sudden Tan. 'Brilliant, I'm in!' I beamed. Before the record deal was signed, George and

I had spent a lot of one-on-one time together and I missed it badly. I loved being with the others, but I couldn't wait for the two of us to have a proper catch-up.

Most pop fans know that 'Club Tropicana' was filmed at Pikes hotel in Ibiza. Founder Tony Pike was a legend, I've never met anyone like him. He liked to think that he was part of the inspiration for 'Club Tropicana', which could almost be about the hotel. Pikes brought 'Club Tropicana' to life, it was perfect. George's lyrics were about Club 18–30 holidays, but admittedly, it's hard to tell where one idea stops and the other one starts. As George led me by the hand around this quaint, sexy, boutique-style hotel, he pointed to the pool and my jaw dropped. As we walked around it, I noticed a man with a leopard skin G-string and a large Stetson and skin that looked like tan leather. When he introduced himself as the owner, Tony Pike, he certainly had everything on show – I didn't quite know where to look!

The hotel regulars included Grace Jones, Tony Curtis and Freddie Mercury, whose 41st birthday party is still commemorated with a charity event every September. (Famously, Freddie ordered a cake in the shape of the Sagrada Família, the beautiful Barcelona cathedral, and had it flown to the island in his private jet. The cake did not survive the journey and so, at the very last minute, Tony had to find a baker who could make a birthday cake for 500 people, with hours before the party was due to start – he did it!)

There was nothing Tony loved more than seeing a woman in a bikini. I realised quickly how much he loved women. He was like a cartoon character, you could see his eyes popping out of his head as he chatted up literally every female that walked past him. I would purposefully try to avoid Tony as I hid behind palm trees trying to get to the pool without him stopping me.

Anyway, staying in any hotel was exciting for me as I was always thrilled about getting clean towels and crisp sheets, and taking back the tiny soaps and shampoos for my mum. George told me to come and see his room, which he was very excited about. The rooms were beautifuly decorated and each had its individual charm. George's room was much bigger than mine and his whole ceiling had mirrors. 'That's strange, why would you want mirrors on the ceiling?' I said to him as he burst out laughing and said, 'Why do you think, Shirlie?' Then the penny dropped. Jumping on his bed, I said, 'I want this room' and that was that – I ended up staying in George's room until the others got here. It was so beautifully decorated; it had these moody, soft boho-style lamps and the whole vibe was relaxed and sexy. That was the great thing about Ibiza, it was one of the most unique places I'd ever visited.

The day after we arrived, we headed for the pool. We chatted with Tony. He was vying for a part in the video, suggesting where he could come in. Generally, we spent the day relaxing and having a good time topping up our tans. By the second day, I was feeling completely relaxed but something was bothering George – he suddenly seemed very awkward. He propped himself up on his lounger, leaning on one elbow. Usually he seemed so confident and sure of himself. What was going on? His chest, glistening with sun oil, rose and fell as he took a deep breath.

'Shirl, I've got something I need to tell you …' He paused before adding, 'I'm gay.'

I looked at him and thought about what he had just said. For some reason I wasn't surprised. It's not that I ever thought about him being gay or straight but I think I was surprised how uncomfortable he felt saying it.

'That's OK,' I said, nodding. 'What about Andrew?' he asked. 'Andrew's not going to be bothered,' I answered.

It made me sad that he had to worry about what those closest to him might think about who he was, or that it could change their relationship with him. I knew I had to make him feel OK about it and not make a big deal out of it, so I turned to him and said, 'Is there any of that oil left? I need to do my back.'

Was that all he was worried about? I could see that just telling me had eased his anxiety. His shoulders had relaxed, his breathing returned to normal. I *hated* thinking that he'd been worried, or the thought that coming out to me had caused him any fear or doubt. But it's hard to explain. I'd never, ever thought about George's sexuality – he was just my friend and I loved him.

Now, with hindsight, I appreciate that it was a very different, difficult time. It's not all that long ago, but attitudes towards sexuality and identity have changed beyond belief. I'm so glad that now, my children are growing up in a world where they are told that everyone is deserving of respect and should have the space to express themselves and their sexuality is no one's business but theirs, but also, they should be able to shout it from the rooftops if they want. However, at the start of the eighties, the earliest reports of AIDs and HIV were appearing in newspapers. There was very little knowledge and a huge amount of misinformation. Of course, we'd been aware of gay celebrities, or people in the public eye, but even that was very limited. A couple of television presenters and comedians were publicly quite camp, but the idea of anyone with any kind of profile speaking about being gay was almost unheard of. Conversations about sexuality were confusing at best, cruel and judgemental at worst. It would be almost impossible to come out if you were a footballer or a politician, or anyone who hoped to be taken seriously.

The media could be vitriolic. Elton John and Freddie Mercury were hounded over their private lives. First, it was hard to see how their sexuality was anyone's business and second, I think it's important to realise that the climate is not the same as the one we're lucky enough to live in today. Now, there's a lot of pressure on everyone to be a role model and to speak out for rights and equality. In the seventies and eighties, any mainstream artist who did so would simply struggle to survive.

So, when George came out to me, the most significant part wasn't to do with who he was, but the fact that he trusted me enough to share something intimate and personal. And I treated it as something personal – it wasn't anyone else's business. George was still the same beloved friend he had always been. Perhaps, with the benefit of hindsight, I was a little anxious for him, knowing that he was set for stardom and understanding that would come with a terrifying amount of scrutiny. But mostly, I was unfazed because I knew his talent was so huge that I couldn't see anything that could stop him.

Still, perhaps because George and I had found a chance to relax together – or perhaps just because of the location and the lyrics – the 'Club Tropicana' video shoot gave me some of my happiest memories. I certainly don't remember paying for any drinks, there was plenty of sunshine and I got the best tan of my life! The four of us really bonded, it was like a mini vacation. Watching the video now feels a little like looking at a holiday album. Maybe it felt like a celebration of the end of the beginning. In a short space of time, George and Andrew had achieved so much. Not that long ago, getting signed to a record label felt like a dream that was beyond reach – now, the hits were starting to come! Of course, one of life's ironies is that the more success you have, the harder it is to relax and enjoy it. More people are involved and there's more pressure to make your best even better. When we made 'Club Tropicana', I think our hopes outweighed our expectations.

When we came back to the UK, the pressure was starting to mount. Our diaries were filling up with concerts and PAs. We needed someone to replace Dee – and fast. There was no question of recruiting from the pubs in Bushey and Dee was going to be a very hard act to follow. We needed a girl who was gorgeous and glamorous, but down-to-earth, with a real sense of fun. Someone who knew how to move, but who could get the 'girl in the club' vibe, rather than expecting dazzling, choreographed routines.

'It will be really fun to work with a new dancer, I can't wait to see who you find!' I said to the boys, smiling.

When Dee joined us, Wham! were not that well-known. Now, the stakes were higher. This would be the third girl that would join Wham! and I was hoping she wasn't a trained dancer because that wasn't our style, or what if we ended up with a crazed Wham! fan, who ruined our chemistry and made everything weird by being obsessed with George and Andrew?

I found myself parked outside Finsbury Park station, watching the streetlights gleaming in the drizzle, waiting to meet the new girl. Watching the streams of people emerging from the steps, I began to feel very excited. All I knew was that this girl was a 'huge talent' and that her name was Pepsi. Maybe it's because I was such a huge fan of fizzy drinks, but that made her sound a little friendlier, less intimidating. A Pepsi would have to be bubbly and fun, surely? You can't be called Pepsi and go around being boring and serious.

I'd been waiting for less than five minutes when I saw a beautiful woman emerge from the exit. A tall, striking black girl with excellent posture but in a perfectly normal outfit, jeans and a jumper, a smart but comfortingly scuffed leather bag slung across her torso.

She seems sure-footed, I found myself thinking – I had a feeling I was going to like her.

This confident girl approached my car, leaned over to look at me and knocked politely on the window: 'Shirlie?' It was a little bit like a blind date! We were expecting each other, but we weren't *quite* sure who we were expecting. Perhaps we should have worn carnations in our buttonholes. 'Hi, I'm Pepsi!'

'Of course, um, get in.' It's only now that I realise how strange it must have been for her too – sitting in the passenger seat, beside a girl she'd never met, who was going to drive her. 'How are you doing?'

'Good, thanks, you?'

Oh, no, were we in for an hour of small talk? This was going to be a long journey! I hoped the traffic would clear up a bit. Luckily, Pepsi had an ice-breaker: 'I just recorded this, is it OK if we play it?' I nodded, she handed me a cassette and then the most gorgeous, powerful, rich voice filled my little car. I was stunned. 'Oh my God!' I turned to her, overwhelmed. 'You sound *just* like Shirley Bassey!'

Pepsi beamed, shocked and delighted. 'What? Shirley Bassey is my favourite singer.'

'Mine too!'

The ice wasn't just broken, it had all melted away. It might have been grey outside, but in my car, the sun had come out from behind the clouds. We started talking about the music we loved and found we simply couldn't stop. It reminded me of my reunion with Andrew in The Three Crowns. In what felt like five minutes, we'd arrived at George's house.

I was pleased that Pepsi and I had already connected with each other before we met the boys. She seemed so nice and normal, and without any airs or graces, I found myself being curiously protective. We weren't rehearsing in a cool studio, or a special venue, we were on the white carpets in the front room. And I knew George and Andrew would be really generous and welcoming, but what if Pepsi didn't get on with them? What if they didn't really get on with her?

I needn't have worried. Andrew bounded up, introduced himself and hugged her hello. 'It's really great to meet you,' said Pepsi, acting over-confident. I could tell George was immediately impressed with her focus and dedication. 'Really great job!' he said, as she nailed 'Young Guns' pretty much instantly. She'd come here to work and learn. But my clearest memory is of George and Andrew, watching me, watching Pepsi. At one point, Andrew indiscreetly nudged me in the ribs: 'You like her? You're getting on OK?'

'Shhhh!' I replied.

I really, really did like her. And then, I felt myself relax too. Of course, George and Andrew wanted to work with someone who was really talented and right for Wham! – and that was Pepsi down to a tee. But what really made her right was our chemistry. The boys wanted to make sure that we worked well together and that I was completely happy and comfortable with her. Bringing in someone new was an important decision and they trusted me to make it. I felt so much better and could throw myself into the rehearsal.

After four hours, at least 20 rotations of 'Young Guns' and I don't know how many cups of tea from George's mum, Lesley, we felt ready.

'So, Pepsi, will you perform with us on Sunday?' asked George. 'We'd love to do the show with you!'

She nodded. 'Yes, please!'

The big day came. Would Pepsi show? She was in a different car from us, coming from West London. Even though it was a long time since that first PA in Bolts, and I'd lost count of the number of performances we'd done, something felt a little different. I had a Christmas morning tingle. I was nervous, I was excited, and I felt as though we were on the brink of something very special. Pepsi was quiet when she arrived and we dressed up in our matching tops and flippy skirts. It made sense – and I really liked that she was trying to stay calm and keep her head together.

Before too long, we were backstage, listening out for the announcer to say, 'And now, the group you've all been waiting for … it's Wham!' We danced out towards the roar of the crowd. No matter how many times I heard the 'Young Guns' intro, I'd always get a shiver when the first beats dropped.

I glanced over at Pepsi. There is nothing that can prepare you for performing in front of thousands of people. Really, the numbers lose all meaning. You have no idea of how many people are in front of you, it's just a wall of joy. I knew these girls were screaming for George and Andrew, but they were screaming, they were having the time of their lives and we were part of that. And Pepsi was in her element. Her moves, her body, her posture was pure 'cool girl at the club', but in her eyes, I saw something else: she looked as though she had come home.

I felt exactly the same way. I'd never get used to that magical feeling or take it for granted. I'd spent so much of my life feeling scared, or self-conscious, worrying that I was in the wrong place. Being surrounded by happy faces, beside my best friends, I knew I was just where I was supposed to be.

We were barely offstage when the three of us ran to Pepsi, desperate to share the magical feeling, to be part of her first time.

'Did you love it?' cried Andrew.

'You were brilliant!' said George.

'Isn't it amazing? Isn't it great? You're great!' I added, breathlessly.

Pepsi nodded, beaming. It was as if light was pouring out of her eyes – we were in a dark, gloomy corridor, but she made it glow. We didn't have to ask her anything else. From that moment on, she was with the band.

6

Pepsi – The icing on the cake

From the moment I stepped offstage after that first Capital concert in 1983, life started to move fast. I felt as though I had been strapped to a rocket – every time I blinked, I was in the middle of a new adventure.

I couldn't believe I was going on tour! We'd be travelling all over the UK and rehearsals were starting in earnest. We weren't in George's mum's front room anymore, but a busy rehearsal studio in North London. We had a band, sound technicians, representatives from the record companies, a tour manager with a clipboard. The rehearsal studio became a tiny city, busy and bustling. I adored it. I've always been happiest when I'm working – well, not counting the travel agency! But for the first time in my life, I was doing what I loved, all day long, and getting paid for it. Every single morning, I woke up buzzing. (Partly because I'd never slept so well. When you're dancing all day long, you tire yourself out and I was out like a light every night!)

Admittedly, a couple of things weren't quite as I imagined. I didn't always love the outfits we performed in. Early on, George and Andrew decided the Wham! brand was quite outdoorsy, fun and sporty, and that was reflected in the look. It was meant to be preppy, upmarket and bright, but also relatable and achievable, something that fans could easily recreate for themselves if they wanted to. So that meant sportswear.

I knew that Shirlie and the boys were quite sporty and they all loved swimming, but as a black woman with Afro hair, I had to avoid the leisure centre – chlorine would dry my hair right out. I once told George this story and he howled with laughter at this unfortunate incident when my cousins and I tried to sneak into a hotel in Piccadilly to catch a glimpse of The Jackson 5. We *adored* them and we thought we had a brilliant idea. The rest of the screaming fans were filling the lobby, so we decided to try to come up through the underground car park and attempt to meet our heroes that way. Unfortunately, as we crept up the stairs, we were met by a security guard, who turned a fire hose on us! It did the trick – we ran away, but we didn't manage to avoid the water. At the time, I wore my hair in an Afro and it looked like I had a crater on the left side of my head! So, I avoided water, where I could. I wasn't going to get in the sea in Margate and I certainly wasn't going to brave the pool in Watford! (Until quite recently, Shirlie thought I just didn't like swimming. No, it's just what a girl's gotta do for her Afro!)

Someone, somewhere, had managed to secure a deal with Fila, and Wham! got sent plenty of free clothes, as long as we all wore them on stage. This was great for a cost-conscious record company, being careful of budgets – and brilliant for a sports brand, who were guaranteed plenty of exposure whenever we wore them on stage, in magazines and on TV. But not for me. Even though my friend Yazz had helped me to feel much more body confident, I still felt very self-conscious, especially when it came to my chest. Our outfits weren't designed to be super sexy or revealing, but they were stretchy and figure-hugging. Shirlie was so slim and petite that she looked cute in everything she wore. Looking back at the photos now, I wish I'd been able to see what I really looked like – I had absolutely nothing to be ashamed of, but at the time, I'd have danced in a baggy jumper if I could. 'Peps, I'm *so jealous*, your body is fabulous, your cleavage is amazing! Show yourself off!' Shirlie would say.

I'd simply stare back at her, baffled. But I could make peace with it. Once I started performing, I was able to lose myself in the work, the music, the fun and joy of what we were doing. I didn't care what I was wearing and I stopped feeling self-conscious. I loved dancing with Shirlie, but it felt as though something was missing.

I was longing to sing. Singing was what I loved most in the world, it was so important to me. After the first couple of rehearsals, I thought that perhaps they were easing me in. 'They want to make sure that I feel completely comfortable and ready, and then they're going to talk about music', I told myself. Still, another few days passed. No singing. I was starting to worry.

'Shirlie,' I whispered one lunchtime, after a gruelling morning when we were refuelling. Our bodies were temples, we were professional dancers – I was drinking a can of Pepsi, she was eating a Mars Bar. 'I've been thinking and I'm a bit worried – when am I going to learn our bits of the songs? When will we be doing, you know, the *proper* singing?'

Shirlie looked a little nervous. Usually, she was always straightforward and easy to talk to. I could ask her *anything*. It really helped me to settle into the rhythm of my new life, to be honest. When I'd seen her on *Top of the Pops* before I'd known her, she seemed so cool that I'd worried she might be stuck-up. But the real Shirlie was fun, funny and frank, open-hearted and quick to reassure me at every turn – it wasn't like her to avoid a question.

She dropped her gaze and looked at her Mars Bar: 'Um, ah, I'm not sure, Peps. I'll ask Andrew.'

Later that day, Andrew came over to talk to me. He put a friendly arm around my shoulder: 'Pepsi, I was just chatting to Shirlie about your singing. Now, we know you're a fantastic singer, but we love having you here, doing what you're doing. Do you want to be singing in the back, with the band, or,' he paused, meaningfully, 'up at the front with us?'

Andrew put it perfectly. He was giving me a choice – I *could* sing, if I really, really wanted to. And of course, we'd be singing along the whole time we were on stage. But in order to get that buzz that I craved, the joy and euphoria I'd experienced during the Capital concert, the feeling I'd dreamed about, had premonitions about – I'd be staying where I was.

It didn't take me any time at all to make my mind up.

'With you, of course,' I told him.

Still, that was the moment when I really understood what my role was. Wham! was one of the first pop groups to focus on image and to make it part of the music. George was so savvy, grasping the spirit of the eighties and understanding that everything he did had to look as good as it sounded. He needed plenty of window dressing – and that was Shirlie and me.

'We're the icing on the cake!' I used to joke.

'The cherries on the icing!' added Shirlie.

'The jam in your dodger?' I tried, giggling.

We were eating a *lot* of sugar back then, we needed plenty of fuel. Oh, for my twentysomething metabolism!

The tour was set to be intense. Our first date was in October 1983, so rehearsals began early in the autumn. Shirlie and I have always felt that our time in Wham! was like a university education and our autumn rehearsals had a real 'start of term' feel. Growing up in London, I used to mark the seasons by seeing how the shop windows changed and noticing different coloured leaves on the ground. When you stopped seeing ice lolly wrappers on the ground and started seeing odd bits of fireworks, you knew the cooler weather was on its way! Still, whenever I was up with Shirlie and the boys in leafy Radlett, I really noticed the leaves shifting from green to gold. Usually, I hated that 'back to school' feeling, but this year, I loved noticing the crispness in the air.

New Year, new job, new me!

Still, at first, I was very careful not to mix business and pleasure.

'Come out! I want to go out! We'll go into town,' Shirlie would beg.

'Sorry, I've got plans tonight. Another time,' I'd say, crossing my fingers behind my back.

It wasn't that I didn't want to hang out with her, but we were still getting to know each other and we had a tour to get through. I knew Shirlie loved all kinds of music, but at the time, I felt pop was work and soul music was my way of relaxing and letting loose. Every day, at rehearsals, I wanted to prove myself and impress George and Andrew with my energy, determination and drive. I knew it would be hard to fully relax on a night out with them. I had to wait to get to know them a little better – and I knew that would definitely happen on tour.

The Club Fantastic Tour was Wham!'s very first tour, organised to promote the boys' first album. In time, Wham! would be able to fill international stadiums but the point of this trip was to build up the group's fanbase. Wherever there were screaming teenage girls, we would be there too! The venues weren't vast, we'd be playing in medium-sized theatres up and down the UK, starting with the Capitol Theatre in Aberdeen. But every single building gave me a thrill. I wonder whether that's where my love affair with the stage started – years later, when I started acting, I immediately felt at home whenever I was in a theatre. Going on tour was expensive. Hiring venues, paying for security, lighting, catering and travel all costs money. As Wham!'s profile was still building, we couldn't guarantee that we'd make money selling tickets. The management would be lucky to break even. Still, the boys' manager, Simon, had a plan: the tour would be sponsored by Fila, and that would cover all of our expenses. The bad news was more short, flippy skirts and tight tops for me – why couldn't we be sponsored by an anorak company?!

Years later, the Capital DJ Gary Crowley, who played the warm-up set on the tour, would describe it as 'the nearest I'll ever get to being in The Beatles' *A Hard Day's Night*'. Admittedly, it was *gruelling*. Initially we flew up to Aberdeen with George and Andrew, but sometimes we'd be driving across the country, starting out early in the morning – 'You girls should get some sleep, we're in for a long trip,' said the driver.

Shirlie and I beamed. 'We can't, we're too excited!' I said.

For a little while, we watched the world roll past the window, transfixed. Sure, I'd been to St Lucia with my mum when I was a teenager, but West London had pretty much been my universe. I'd never thought about going to Birmingham, or Coventry, or Leeds. What would it be like to live there? What did those people get up to? Would they be coming to see us?

We went on some long journeys, but we were so young and inexperienced that tiny things thrilled us. We couldn't *believe* we could go to a McDonald's at a service station!

'Careful, you don't want to get travel sick,' warned George as I tucked into my French fries. Not likely – as if anything could put me off my chips!

After being on the road for a while, we were starting to flag, but the adrenaline lifted my spirits as soon as we parked at the theatre. A few girls were already hanging around outside. I couldn't believe it – all those years ago, I'd been that keen girl trying to catch a glimpse of my favourite band and now teenagers were waiting for us.

Theatres are full of contrasts. The front of house is so glamorous – all red velvet, plush seating, thick curtains and sparkling lights. Then, when you get backstage, there's a strange mix of the fabulous and the shabby. Glittering costumes, big bits of scenery, programmes and posters featuring iconic celebrities and performances past. But there's also peeling paintwork, flickering striplights and occasionally the odd draft or damp patch on the ceiling. I loved it all. Most of all, I adored the *busyness*. We were surrounded by people walking quickly, concentrating, muttering, looking as though they had somewhere very important to be. Everyone was on a mission – and we were in the centre of it all!

From the start, Shirlie and I had a really strong dynamic. Shirlie has always been super intuitive, a little bit psychic, a little bit spooky – and that's when I really started to see it in action. I wondered if she might be a little bit nervous. After all, we were playing to a packed house and I knew that although she didn't get stage fright, she was always a little bit worried about George enjoying the show and meeting his own high standards. But she seemed really calm and centred. Backstage, in our matching Fila outfits, we waited as the crowd danced to Gary Crowley.

'It's nice having a DJ,' she mused. 'It's a bit like we're hosting a party!'

She'd captured the feeling perfectly. We were dancing in the wings, having a great time – and then we were on!

Just as we'd rehearsed tens, perhaps hundreds of times, we watched George and Andrew run on, George in his yellow outfit and Andrew in his red, before dancing on stage for 'Club Tropicana'. How can I describe that feeling? It wasn't nervousness exactly, but anticipation. I was *so* excited to be up there, dancing, energised by my chemistry with Shirlie, George and Andrew. I can understand why people get stage fright, but for me, performing felt more like a cure for anxiety. I was forced to live in the moment. When I was up there, nothing I'd done and nothing I had to do seemed remotely important, I simply had to respond to the feeling the crowd was giving me – my only job was to put on a show.

Also, the lovely thing about a concert like that is knowing the audience have definitely come to see you. They have decided to have a good time before they hear the music. They haven't come to judge, they're on your side. Over the years, I'd find myself performing in a range of venues, to all sorts of audiences. Sometimes, when the show is huge, the crowd is overwhelming. And sometimes, when you're at smaller gigs and PAs, you can tell the audience doesn't really care whether you're there or not. But those theatres were just the right size. There was plenty of intimacy with the audience and Wham! was at a point in the group's trajectory where the fans were truly fanatical. They felt that they were among the first to discover the boys and they had a huge sense of pride and excitement. It was a total love fest.

I felt so far from home, figuratively and literally. Here, I wasn't Lawrie, worrying about my dad's drinking, wondering how to help Mum, hiding in my little flat and living for the weekends when I could go dancing and forget my troubles. Here, I could simply express myself, I had room to breathe. It was magical!

Because this tour was to promote the album, the set list matched it almost exactly, but there were a few surprises. We had to mix up the energy in order to keep things interesting and every so often, the boys would break out into a ballad, so that everyone could get their breath back. It was the perfect opportunity for George and Andrew to showcase their energy *and* their sense of humour.

In keeping with the sporty theme, the song 'Come On!' was choreographed to include an on-stage game of badminton. Admittedly, I was *shocked* when I first saw George dropping the shuttlecock down the waistband of his trousers – 'Shirlie, what is he *doing*? Has he forgotten where he is?' I whispered, panicked. Shirlie's eyes were wide too – I can't believe how innocent we were! 'I'm not sure *what* he's doing!' she whispered back. Then, we watched as George pulled the shuttlecock out and expertly batted it into the middle of a screaming crowd. It was like seeing a tornado in action, watching the whirlpool of girls, desperate to get to that shuttlecock. He always had a plan – he was a genius showman.

But amidst all of the stunts and fun, there were serious, sensitive moments. Even though it didn't feature on the *Fantastic* album, this is the tour where George first started to perform 'Careless Whisper'. It was a truly amazing moment. After the interval, the audience would start to come back. Excited, distracted, they were still settling down and George would blow them away with this utterly gorgeous song. George was an incredible singer, and he really knew how to build the emotion in a song, but he had a quality that went way beyond that. Watching him moved me deeply – it was like something between falling in love and falling off the top of a 40-storey building!

Now, when we go to watch live music, we really want to hear our favourite artists singing the songs we already know and love. I admit that I'm the same. Even though I know what it's like to be on stage, trying to get the audience excited, I'm always happy to hear a hit. So, 'Careless Whisper' was a big risk. It seems crazy to imagine a time when no one had heard it, but back then, it was brand new. And it's a mix of styles, too. It could be pop, it could be RnB, it feels like a ballad, but it's uptempo too. If you'd bought the singles of 'Young Guns' and 'Club Tropicana', it's not necessarily what you'd expect to hear next. But every time, George brought the house down. 'Careless Whisper' was a sexy, sophisticated eighties anthem and it blew the crowd away. Watching from the wings for the very first time, I got goosebumps. It had been dazzling in rehearsals, but this was something else.

Admittedly, the first few nights that we got to watch George, and watch everyone's reactions, we felt as though we were witnessing something incredibly special. By the tenth time, we knew that soon we'd be back on stage, running around for 'Bad Boys', and that this was a brilliant opportunity for Shirlie and I to stop for a quick Mars Bar.

'Can you believe it?' she'd laugh. 'Those girls down there would pay *millions* to swap places with us.'

'I know,' I replied. 'And here we are, relaxing and having a chocolate bar – all in a day's work.'

The audiences were wonderful, but they could be overwhelming too. Sometimes, we'd dance right up to the edge of the stage and smile at the girls screaming and waving. If we made eye contact with any of them, they'd scream out messages for George and Andrew. 'Tell them we love them!' they'd yell or pass cards and banners. We were like a pop postal service. It was complicated – the fans reminded us of just how lucky we were. And it was important to be reminded. Wham! fans were always friendly.

There were times onstage in the midst of a performance when I got such clarity of what Shirlie and my role was within Wham! Maybe you've had that feeling when in a moment of pure exhilaration and time stands still. Now I live in the Caribbean and have experienced what it's like to go through a hurricane, I can say it felt like that moment when the eye of the storm passes directly over the top of you. All of a sudden the tremendous noise and powerful buffeting of the energy ceases, the sun breaks through the dark clouds and all is at peace. That was how it sometimes felt in the whirlwind of a Wham! performance. The totally unique thing for Shirlie and I was that we were right there with the boys up front and experiencing the full force of the crowd's love and adoration, excitement and exuberance yet we were not the direct focus of the attention – we got to experience it from a unique point of view over their shoulders and dancing at their sides. We were not 'twenty feet from stardom', we were less than six feet away and right in the middle of the storm. Our role was to support the boys, to make them look good and act as a reminder that Wham! started on the club dance floor.

Another thing that helped was the feeling of friends, family and community. Even though I'd done my best to show up as a professional, I was starting to find that I couldn't keep things completely separate. It wasn't what anyone wanted. George's sister Melanie was our make-up artist, Deon Estus, the bass player, and his band Dream Merchant were old friends of George's and George even arranged for his cousin Andros to come out to the first shows as a 21st birthday present. We couldn't have been any more close-knit. When you're on tour, you have to be. And you quickly bond over the smallest, silliest things.

We were thrilled whenever anyone asked us to sign their programme – but just as thrilled when we got the chance to luxuriate in a hot bath! When I look back now on that time in those early days of the tour, I feel so fortunate to have shared many special moments of downtime with Shirlie and George, oftentimes just the three of us, lounging around in our hotel room munching on snacks ordered from room service, sharing our individual thoughts on aspects of the show and laughing at the absurdity of it all.

We were tired, we were overwhelmed and we couldn't always have told you what day of the week it was – but in spite of everything, we couldn't miss the fact that the Wham! fanbase appeared to be getting bigger and bigger. There were more and more fans waiting at the theatre and arriving earlier and earlier. Every night, the screams seemed to be getting a little bit louder. It's difficult to look back and make sense of that time, because everything seemed to be happening with such a terrifying amount of speed. It was like cycling down a hill without brakes, unable to control how fast you're going, just hoping to stay on and not crash. Completely exhilarating – but also alarming and scary. It's so hard to take stock and appreciate every single exciting, amazing moment because everything is happening all at once.

Towards the end of my time with Wham!, I found myself drawn to Buddhism and I often wonder whether it was my way of coping with those intense highs. It's a real challenge for anyone's ego. As I said, Shirlie and I knew that in the eyes of the fans and the media, we were the luckiest women alive. Anyone would have given anything to trade places with us for an evening. I was also able to perform and do the work I loved, which was an enormous privilege and a real thrill, but deep down, I knew that one day, I wanted something more substantial than being the cherry on someone else's cake – I yearned to really sing and express my soul.

Watching George do it so beautifully was mesmerising and inspiring, but it wasn't always easy. Being able to observe him and Andrew working the crowd was an opportunity to learn from some of the world's greatest showbiz teachers, but it sometimes made me long for an audience who had really come to see me. But Buddhism taught me about the link between attachment and suffering. I was very lucky to have Buddhist mentors in the Wham! family – Connie the band's PR and Hugh the guitarist were partners and long-practising Buddhists and they provided me with a wonderful foundation in the practice, invited me to meetings in their home and gave me literature and study materials that helped me deepen my understanding of my own inherent Buddhahood.

Performing for a living forces you to confront your ego. We all have an ego and it's no bad thing, but we don't want to be controlled by it. I wasn't worried about George and Andrew, but I was sometimes concerned about the people around them – and around Shirlie and me. The boys' charisma and talent attracted all sorts of people. Plenty were fun, sweet and wonderful company, but a few definitely had ego issues and simply wanted to be seen with a famous person to enhance their own self-esteem. I felt my growing understanding of life from a Buddhist perspective sometimes gave me an almost X-ray vision into people's deep insecurities and hidden agendas.

If Shirlie and I had been different people, I think we would have really struggled with fame and being so close to George and Andrew. But being down-to-earth was our superpower and I think we centred each other and brought it out in each other too. That was the tour when we really started to bond over the importance of home comforts.

'There's a big party tonight, there will be all sorts of celebrities, champagne, do you fancy it?' one of the boys might say when we got to a show in a big city.

Shirlie and I would exchange a look. 'Honestly, after this, I think I'll just want to put my pyjamas on,' she explained.

'Yeah, slice of toast, maybe. Cup of tea,' I'd say.

I didn't even really drink tea, but I was learning how to make it just how Shirlie liked it! I was also learning that Shirlie was a brilliant listener. She was the first person I'd ever met who really asked me about myself. When she said, 'How are you?' she didn't expect me to say 'fine', she really wanted me to tell her. She was so curious and so compassionate. Instinctively, she seemed to know how to make me feel comfortable and how to make me feel included.

When I was on stage, my feet rarely touched the ground – but Shirlie helped me to remain down-to-earth because she wanted to know about my life before Wham! She asked me about music and performing, but also about my family and my roots. Before too long, I felt as though I'd always known her, partly because she was so keen to learn everything about me. And I loved what I was learning about her. On stage, she was the coolest girl in the world. After a performance, wrapped in her giant dressing gown, she was the cuddliest and the kindest. When I started my musical career, I don't think I'd been expecting sex, drugs and rock'n'roll. Still, what I got was pop songs, hugs and mugs of tea – and I'd never been happier.

7

Shirlie – The One

n what truly felt like the blink of an eye, I went from being a teenage dropout from Bushey Meads to a young woman who seemed to have it all. When it came to Wham! and my career, I tended to take each day as it came, without having any expectations. I was happy to be with my friends and delighted to watch as things got bigger and better for us. Work was fun! Sometimes scary, sometimes exhausting and sometimes I got a bit fed up of sleeping at odd hours of the day and washing my knickers in hotel sinks, but I was happy to see where life led me.

But the biggest thing in my life was Martin. I was in love, and when I was with him, I couldn't have been happier. Martin wasn't just utterly gorgeous – he was the kindest, sweetest, gentlest man I'd ever met. I loved making him laugh. As long as we were together, everything was right in my world. I didn't care that he was in Spandau Ballet, I'd have fallen for him whatever job he was doing.

In fact, I often wished he wasn't in Spandau at all.

Don't get me wrong, there were big advantages. We understood each other. Being part of a group, touring, promoting, performing and being pursued by the press makes for a strange old life. I think it would have been difficult if one of us had done a full-time, nine-to-five job. But the times when the two of us could both be in the same country at the same time were becoming increasingly limited. It was a sign of success. The better Spandau did, and the better Wham! did, the less we saw of each other. Every night, on tour, I'd watch thousands of girls screaming for George and Andrew, and the irony would overwhelm me. Often I would think, 'All of these girls, yelling their heads off for the boys. They would do absolutely anything to be up here, where I am. They would give their right arm, possibly literally, to swap places for me. And in my heart, I'm screaming for a boy who's on stage on the other side of the world.'

I met Martin as a Spandau fan. I grew up loving all kinds of music. Buying a copy of *Smash Hits* was a ritual, it came out every two weeks and every time we would rush out to buy a copy. I think we all would have lived *inside Smash Hits*, if we could! We loved it all – the outfits, the lyrics and the gossip. Cool, but friendly and fun, it conjured up an amazing feeling, a real sense of being part of the pop world. Of course I wanted to know what Haircut 100 ate for breakfast and what Adam Ant did to cheer himself up when he was having a bad day!

We were working our way through *Smash Hits* to find the coolest looks and the hottest boys one day when a gorgeous picture caught my eye. It was a couple of the lads from

Spandau Ballet. I'd seen them on *Top of the Pops* and liked them a lot, but it was a photo of the two Kemp brothers, songwriter Gary and the bassist Martin. I wasn't the sort of girl who went around swooning over pop stars – but I swooned over Martin. 'Oh, he's gorgeous!' I told George. 'And he looks really, really kind. You can tell that he must be a lovely person.'

George fell about laughing. 'Shirlie, he's just really good-looking! You can't tell that he's *kind* from that photo.'

'He has a beautiful smile!' I protested.

'Of course he's smiling, he's having his picture taken!'

Still, even though George loved taking the mickey out of me and my crush, he had a project. As things with Wham! gathered speed, and the group got bigger, he decided that Martin and I had to meet. After all, Spandau Ballet were often being spotted at smart bars and industry parties. It was only a matter of time before we bumped into each other.

To be honest, there were a couple of times when I flunked it. We were still in that strange, special, magical time when it looked as though Wham! was on the brink of blowing up – but we still spent our Saturdays messing about. We were pop stars in training, but we were also basically overgrown teenagers. George and Andrew had a record deal, which had been their biggest dream for years – yet it was the dream that came true in order to unlock all the others. It wasn't crazy for us to think that one day soon, we might be in *Smash Hits* ourselves. So sometimes, we'd go to a party straight from swimming – I'd have jeans, a jumper and damp hair that smelled slightly of chlorine – and we'd hear that Spandau were out. They were always surrounded by the most glamorously dressed women, but they were glamorous too. They seemed to typify the eighties, with their big hair and fabulous jackets.

'I think I just saw Martin go over there!' George would hiss out of the side of his mouth. And I'd shake my head, 'No, no, it's not time yet.'

It sounds crazy, and I know that millions of young girls feel this way about the pop stars they fancy, but deep down, I *knew* Martin was The One. I think that's why I didn't want to chase him. Weirdly, I didn't feel insecure. I didn't go out of my way to get his attention. When I saw that picture, something clicked inside me. It inspired a deep, almost profound longing – but Martin didn't feel out of reach. Maybe I'd meet him in six months, maybe it would take six years, but I trusted fate and I knew we'd be brought together when the time was right.

Back then, I didn't know about manifesting – the idea that positive thinking has a real power to it, and that if you want something badly enough, and believe it enough, you can make it come true. Perhaps understandably, it's something that many people are highly sceptical about. All over the world, people are in pain and in danger. You can't tell them to fix things by simply believing things are going to get better and that good times are right around the corner. Still, for me, there has always been something instinctive about it. I've never forced it, or 'manifested' money or fame, but there are certain parts of my life where I've felt the future in my bones and then felt it coming true.

Although I was quietly convinced that one day I would meet Martin, I didn't plan for it to happen after the premiere of a play called *Yackety Yack* in 1982, when I had messy hair and no make-up on. Almost as bad – Martin, along with the other members of the band were wearing quite a lot of make-up. My initial impression was that he was a bit of a peacock. He wore a beautifully cut, silk turquoise jacket and his hair was flowing golden locks in a bouffant style that looked like it needed a whole can of Elnett to keep it together. He still looked *gorgeous*, but he also looked like a pop star. I was overwhelmed by his glamour and I didn't think I could live up to it.

What I didn't know at the time was that Martin had a crush on *me*, too! It honestly never occurred to me that anyone might fancy me because they had seen me in Wham! After our very first appearance on *Saturday Superstore*, I knew that most of the fans were teenage girls who liked George and Andrew – that was who we appealed to. When I thought about the women men found sexy and attractive, I had a very specific idea in my head. I assumed they liked curvaceous, confident women, with boobs and a bum. I was short and skinny, with a straight up and down ironing board figure. I always felt that I relied more on my personality than my looks. I loved messing about, making jokes and putting on silly voices, and I think I started doing this instinctively.

Little did I know at the time Martin had actually spotted me on *Top of the Pops* – and years later he confessed to me that he'd been asking, casually, about 'that blonde girl from Wham!' It's still weird for me today to think about that. We hadn't yet made the charts so we weren't even supposed to be on the show the night that he saw me. We were a last-minute stand-in – we'd been asked because the producer liked what he saw after spotting us on *Saturday Superstore*. Later, Martin told me that he knew it sounded crazy, but it felt like love at first sight and after that night's show, 'Every time I closed my eyes, I saw your face. OK, and your legs!'

This is what makes me think that there might be a little bit of magic in the power of manifesting. It could just be luck, it might simply have been a series of coincidences, but there's a part of me that wonders whether I started to bring us both together from the moment I saw Martin's picture in that magazine.

Still, I didn't know any of that when we were at the theatre. When I saw Martin with the Spandau crowd, I assumed he was a sophisticated charmer who was chatting up different girls every night – or that there were so many girls throwing themselves at him that I didn't stand a chance. I thought he was playing it cool, I didn't know that he was feeling shy. And when he said, 'I'd love to see you again! Will you call me?' and gave me a paper napkin, with his phone number written on it, I didn't know what to do.

In fact, I was dumbstruck. George, however, was thrilled – 'Oh my God, you're going to go out with Martin Kemp! You're gonna be a Spandau girl!' He kept it up all the way home. I felt as though that piece of paper was hot to the touch – it was burning a hole in my pocket figuratively *and* literally, scorching my skin through the fabric of my top.

'Can you imagine how many girls are ringing Martin up? I can't call him! What would I say? And he's on tour all the time and we've got Wham! to worry about, and concentrate on,' I protested.

For the next three weeks, however, George was on my case: 'Have you called Martin yet?' 'When are you going to ring Martin?' 'Call Martin!' That piece of paper thrilled and terrified me. It became dog-eared, ragged. I couldn't stop touching it, staring at it, turning it over, but the idea of calling the number seemed scarier than anything else.

Finally, one night at George's, my dear friend took matters out of my hands, in every sense. Weeks of teasing came to a head when he took the piece of paper away and ran into his sister Melanie's room (she had a phone).

'It's ringing,' he said, putting the receiver into my hand.

Oh, no!

'Shirlie! I'm so glad to hear from you, I didn't think you'd ring!' When I heard Martin's voice, weeks of anxiety and uncertainty were washed away. He didn't sound like a grand, glamorous pop star, speaking to the tenth girl who'd phoned that night. His voice gave me the same feeling I'd experienced when I saw his picture in *Smash Hits*.

At first, Martin suggested taking me out for dinner, but we soon settled on meeting up at Camden Palace. These days, it's known as KOKO and it's right by Mornington Crescent, at the top of Camden High Street. In 1982, it was where everyone who was anyone wanted to be on a Tuesday night. Back then, George, Andrew and I were spending more and more time in London, going to events, PAs and parties, but I was still a girl from Bushey and one who was a little out of her comfort zone. This wasn't going to the pub for a lemonade, this was a big deal: Martin was a pop star and Camden Palace was his natural habitat. Even though I was in one of the biggest bands of the eighties I never felt like a popstar but Martin epitomised everything a popstar should be. I was worried about feeling out of my depth, but it wouldn't feel too intense – there would be lots of people around.

As soon as we'd arranged to meet up, I realised my mistake. I couldn't go on my own! What if Martin was there with his Spandau entourage and I was left standing about like a Billy No Mates?

'George,' I said, 'you have to come with me to Camden Palace!'

Together, we stood on the steps a week later. George seemed to revel in his role as chaperone/gooseberry: 'Are you nervous?' he asked, as we shivered in the cool autumn air. 'What do you think?' I said, staring back at him. But we didn't have to wait for long before Martin arrived. This time, he didn't look like a glam rock superstar– he had normal hair, cut much shorter, no make-up and he was wearing a nice, simple suit. I actually thought he was even better-looking.

'Shall we go in?' he asked casually. Although Martin came alone, he always knew that he would see people that he knew inside. They would all hang out in the same place so he was never alone or in a place where he didn't know anyone.

George might have been slightly annoyed with me by the end of the evening. It was obvious that Martin and I couldn't resist each other. There was a *lot* of kissing– we'd sneak off into a corner and start smooching, and then we'd look up, and there he'd be. Years later, he'd tease us both – 'I will never, ever forget it, one of the longest nights of my life! And I couldn't go anywhere, Shirlie – you were my ride home!' Although he would tease me about that night often, I knew that he had loved playing Cupid.

That was just the start of how George would look after Martin and I. George would make countless seriously generous gestures. But it wasn't just the meals, hampers or holidays, he was so very giving of his love, his time and his *self*. Even so, I think the best thing that he ever did for me was that call to Martin.

Still, the gift of love was a complicated present. What started with that one phone call from Melanie's bedroom became countless snatched phone conversations – three minutes here, five minutes there, Australia to Japan, Los Angeles to London. In those days, you couldn't be constantly connected to each other. I often think of how different it would be for us now – we'd be talking all day long on WhatsApp, only needing the hotel Wi-Fi code. In those days, international phone calls were cripplingly expensive too. Martin sometimes jokes that any money Spandau made got spent straight away on phone bills!

Time zones were tricky, too. I got used to waking up in the early hours of the morning and putting a receiver to my ear, just so I could hear Martin's voice before he went on

Top: Pepsi's first try out with Wham! Captial Radio Best Disco in Town 1983.

Middle: George and Pepsi as a fairy performing 'Last Christmas' on tour.

Bottom: Rehearsal for 'Club Tropicana.'

Left: Backstage on Wham! tour, Shirlie in 'Club Tropicana' dress.

Right: Andrew downtime in Australia.

Bottom: George loved dogs.

Top: Pepsi downtime at the beach in Australia.

Above: Band members with Shirlie enjoying the beach in Australia.

Top: Downtime on tour in Australia with the Wham! band.

Bottom left: Shirlie and George on a boat ride, Australia.

Bottom right: George, Australia.

Top left: Andrew at Rehearsals on tour with Wham!

Top right: Andrew on the Wham! tour bus.

Bottom left: Wham! band on the tour bus.

Bottom right: George on the tour bus.

Top left: Shirlie and Pepsi on the tour bus.

Middle left and above: George, Shirlie Pepsi and Andrew celebrating Pepsi's Birthday, Japan.

Bottom left: Andrew, Maggie and George backstage.

Bottom right: George and Pepsi joking about backstage.

Rehearsing for a Japanese advert.

Top right: China, food for the band backstage.

Left: Shirlie backstage getting ready for the final show.

Middle right: Shirlie, Andrew and Pepsi, China.

Bottom: George and Andrew with the Japanese press.

stage, somewhere on the other side of the world. And poor Pepsi soon became used to my moods – 'Martin's going to call, he'll ring in an hour, or half an hour, and what if he forgets, or what if we have to go and soundcheck and I miss him? Oh, I can't bear it!' For the precious few minutes we had together, I'd light up – and then burst into tears: 'It's so hard,' I'd sob. 'I hate being without him!'

Pepsi was wonderful. She was sweet and sympathetic, but she didn't let me wallow. 'OK, come on, we've got to cheer up. Let's get room service.'

Together, we balanced each other out. I was lovestruck, dreamy and in love. Looking back, I think I must have driven her crazy. I was a young woman who had been given the opportunity of a lifetime and all I could think about was when I was next going to talk to my boyfriend. But Pepsi was pragmatic, ultra-focused and happy to concentrate on her own plans. She was happy to let me talk about Martin and I think she gave me a lot of room to act like an overgrown teenager. She's a couple of years older than me and that's when it started to show. I certainly wasn't boy-crazy – I was only crazy about one particular boy – but I think Pepsi was much more interested in her work with Wham! than chasing after men. To be honest, we didn't really have the chance to date, or to pursue relationships. Missing Martin seemed to take up most of my time and it wasn't as if we were going to big parties where we could meet anyone.

After a show, we liked to get cosy. We all guarded George's voice as though it were the Crown Jewels. If we were coming to the end of a tour, we'd be desperate to go out dancing, but most of the time we'd be tucked up in bed, in our dressing gowns, with cups of tea long before midnight.

As time went by, a new obsession reared its head – I didn't just want to be with Martin, I longed for a baby with him. Princess Diana was pregnant with her first child and constantly in all the papers, photographed in her maternity clothes. My tight, white dresses and tiny Fila outfits seemed to contrast dramatically with the look I longed for. I wanted to wear a sailor dress, accessorised with a bump. Again, Pepsi was always supportive, listening to my longing and teasing me when it all got to be a little bit too much.

I think this was the point when I started to be aware that the dynamics of Wham! were shifting. As the group became more and more successful, there was a sense of things becoming separate between Pepsi and me, and George and Andrew. George's immense talent as a singer, songwriter and performer was becoming globally recognised.

At the time when the boys signed to Innervision, I think they thought that the moment the ink started to dry on the contract marked one of the best days of their lives. In theory, having a record company behind you means that promotion and marketing are taken care of – people are making sure that you're getting heard and all you have to do is concentrate on making music and performing.

George and Andrew had been writing, singing and creating music together since they were little kids at school. Even though I loved music and wrote songs in secret, I wasn't contracted as part of Wham! I wasn't officially signed to the record label. I was paid a wage by their management, but I had no say in any conversations about the future of the band. Suddenly I had the realisation that the boys were going to go on and have a massive career and I wasn't sure of my place in it – I didn't think the format could go on forever. George and Andrew took to stardom like ducks to water but knowing that I had no contract or security left me feeling quite unsure sometimes.

I didn't want the boys to know how challenging I found it, but Pepsi was to become my saviour when we toured. Things really changed when Wham! made it big in America. It was so notably different – all the boys would be taken out to dinner by music executives and other important people, they couldn't wine and dine them enough, while Pepsi and I stayed in the hotel, having room service most nights. The dynamics were definitely shifting. On the Whamamerica! Tour we played to 50,000 people. The audience was full of screaming girls and as I skipped along the stage and caught their eye, I knew I had their dream job. I bet any one of them would have swapped lives with me in a heartbeat – I guess it was still a good gig to have.

8

Pepsi – From Dorset to Hollywood!

My years with Wham! seemed to cover the longest, shortest time. Looking back, I feel as though I spent most of my twenties laughing, dancing or wrapped in a giant Fila dressing gown, being bundled into a car and speeding off to a hotel. But one minute, we were playing little theatres in Dorset and the next, we were in Hollywood!

Wham!'s second album, *Make It Big*, released in November 1984, had done exactly what it said on the tin. It was the first album on Epic and for George, it was a way to break out and give the world a glimpse of the solo star that he'd become. It's common for record labels to make most of the big decisions when it comes to breaking new bands – and most acts, when they're new to the music world, aren't experienced enough to make major commercial decisions, but George and Andrew had a real gift for understanding and planning every part of the process. Moving labels gave them the opportunity to really take control, producing as well as writing and singing. The album wasn't just adored by teenage fans, critics raved about it too.

It would be a cliché to compare the experience to a roller coaster – and not even an accurate one. Roller coasters go down and around, but Wham! just seemed to soar further and further up. The higher Wham! went, the more aware I was of the way that the people around us were changing. So many people were drawn to the boys, especially George, and they saw Shirlie and I as a way to get to him. It could be frightening, particularly as we realised that if these people were moths, it was fame, not talent, that was attracting them. Still, I think that together, we kept each other down to earth. Wherever we went, we brought a little bit of North London with us. We could be in the most opulent, luxurious dressing room in the world, filled with fresh flowers and fruit, and there would be Shirlie, reminding me exactly where I had come from by exclaiming delightedly, 'Oh, good! They've left us some biscuits!'

Despite knowing George was gay, he wasn't out publicly. Meanwhile the AIDS crisis was at its peak and the media were starting to hound public figures about their sexuality and it was something George understandably chose to be extremely private about. Also, teenage girls adored him for a reason – they would be heartbroken if they had to stop dreaming about an encounter with their idol. Plenty would get to the front of a concert and be so overwhelmed by their proximity to George and Andrew, they would fall into a faint. Quite a few of them would quickly learn that if the paramedics had to put you onto a stretcher, there was a decent chance that they might take you backstage. Shirlie and I would nudge each other, giggling, whenever we spotted a girl who seemed to come round quite quickly, sitting up on their stretcher and waving to all their mates as they were brought into the inner sanctum. Good on them, it was very resourceful! It reminded me of my younger days, sneaking into the hotel car park, desperate to get a glimpse of The Jackson 5.

It wasn't just teenage girls, either. All kinds of famous faces fancied their chances with George and would come along to Wham! shows in the hope of getting backstage. One of the most memorable celebrity visitors we had arrived just before our Whamamerica! show in Miami. It was a blisteringly hot, sticky Florida night. We were playing to a sell-out crowd and despite fans and air conditioning, Shirlie and I were having trouble keeping cool. We were in our dressing room, sitting in front of the mirrors, doing our make-up and trying to stay chilled in every sense.

'It's so hot!' said Shirlie, fanning her face.

'You're lucky, you never sweat,' I sighed. 'I feel like if I put much more make-up on, it's just going to slide straight off again.'

Shirlie's unique ability never to sweat was a source of constant fascination to me. George, Andrew and I would fall offstage at the end of a show, dripping. She'd be bone dry.

As I sighed, and wondered whether there were any more fans in the building, there was a knock on the door: 'Come in!' I called. 'We're dressed!'

It was one of the security guards from the venue – a giant, friendly bear of a man, accompanied by a petite woman with a stunning face. Stunning – and very familiar.

'Ladies, good evening!' said the friendly bear. 'Miss Minnelli needs to sit somewhere quiet and out of the way before the show begins. Could she wait in here with you?'

Thanks to the mirrors, Shirlie and I were able to play it cool – or as cool as we could be in the heat – while meeting each other's gaze and silently screaming. *Liza!* Liza Minnelli was an icon for any performer – we'd loved her in *Arthur* and she was unforgettable as Sally Bowles in *Cabaret*. She'd worked with the legendary choreographer Bob Fosse. She was a proper, old school movie star, come to hang out with a pair of British girls, who were eating chocolate and practising our American accents – there may have been a pair of tights drying on the side of the sink.

'Of course, come on in!' I said, hoping I didn't sound as nervous as I felt, and wondering what on earth you're supposed to say to the great Liza Minnelli before a show. Should I offer her a bite of my Hershey bar? Would Shirlie tell her a joke? We glanced around, working out where she should sit, but there was no need: she was a ball of pure energy.

'HEY GIRLS!' she said, radiating charisma. 'Have you WARMED UP YET?'

She leapt around the tiny space, behaving as if she was wearing leg warmers and a leotard, not a little black dress. Looking expectantly at Shirlie and me, she executed a few high kicks, stretching her leg right above her head! The next

20 seconds seemed to take two hours to pass. We'd never warmed up in our lives before! And right now, all we wanted was to cool down!

Shirlie shuffled in her chair, just as I started to think about getting up. It seemed almost rude *not* to warm up with Liza, but I wasn't sure I could get my leg anywhere near my head – I was much more likely to open my mouth and put my foot in it. There was another knock at the door, thank goodness: the friendly bear was back. We were saved by the bell.

'Miss Minnelli, your seat is ready,' beamed the security guard.

'GREAT TO MEET YOU, GIRLS!' said Liza, also beaming.

It's definitely just something I imagined, but in my head, when I think of her leaving, I can see her making jazz hands. That night, I think she went out for dinner with George. I suspect that she wasn't all that different from the teenage fans. Meanwhile Shirlie and I were delighted to be back at the hotel, where the air con was on full blast and no one was going to make us do any high kicks.

To be honest, it's only now that I realise just how crazy that moment was. We'd been on the road for months, from the UK to the US via Australia and Japan.

When I fell in love with my husband, James Crockett, one of the things that really attracted me to him was his passion for travel. As someone who studied the natural world, having worked as a geologist, he was always keen to closely observe a place and its people. It really brought home to me that I might have been everywhere but I was too busy working to really see anything. Life was a total blur of plane rides, hotel rooms, backstage in stadiums and trying to grab some sleep whenever we had the chance.

One day, feeling totally disoriented while preparing to rehearse for a TV show in Japan, I completely forgot the basics.

'Just checking,' I asked Andrew, 'where are we again?'

'In Japan,' he said, amused.

'Right, yeah, Japan. And, er, what day is it?'

George looked up and answered me: 'I think it's the tenth of December.'

The tenth of December. Why did that date ring a bell? Was there somewhere I was supposed to be, something I had to do? I turned it over in my mind for a minute before I finally worked it out.

'Oh! The tenth of December is my birthday!'

For a second, George looked shocked – 'Oh, Pepsi, I'm sorry, I feel terrible! I should have known!'

But I laughed it off.

'Don't worry, it's hilarious!'

And it was. When you're a December baby, you never expect a big fuss on your birthday, it being so close to Christmas. I'd grown up expecting very little, knowing my mum would always produce a beautiful cake and if I was lucky, a dress or some nice new knickers. Dad might make a big promise and leave me wondering whether I'd actually get a dolly, or a trip to the dog track. Birthdays used to remind me of how hard things were for my family. Now, my life was so full and frantic that I needed to be reminded of what day it was! It's a brilliant anti-ageing treatment, going on tour – you can't get older if you can't remember how old you are.

George went off with Andrew and Shirlie, and there was much whispering and giggling. A few hours later, a stunning cake was produced and these icons of eighties pop were serenading me with 'Happy Birthday'. I felt so loved and so lucky to be spending the day with my friends. In a way, it was the nicest surprise party ever – I was surprised by the birthday itself.

It was in Japan that Shirlie and I started to become more confident and independent as performers, but the results were mixed. George had an interesting attitude: in so many ways, he was quite exacting as a performer. He set the highest standards for himself and we always wanted to do a brilliant job for him, but we also wanted him to be happy with his work. Sometimes, we wished he could see himself as his fans saw him. However, there was a bit of him that loved to keep it loose. The eighties was a time for very polished, exact choreography and I think George wanted us to be set apart from that. He gave Shirlie and me a lot of freedom on stage – he wanted us to move in a way that the fans could watch and copy, just like girls in a nightclub.

When we noticed that one of the Japanese venues had a balcony above the stage, Shirlie and I thought it would be a brilliant idea to run up the stairs and dance there for a while. It would look fun, wild and impulsive – and keep the energy up while George and Andrew did their thing. So off we went and down we came – in my case, literally, as I fell down the stairs! Shirlie only just managed to keep dancing, she was laughing so hard. I was fine – I think adrenaline protected me from any pain – but when the audience roared and cheered, we saw George and Andrew grinning and waving at the crowd. They had no idea that they were cheering me, after I disappeared and suddenly reappeared again.

It's amazing just how much can happen on stage at any one time and how many things you need to pay attention to – as well as just what you can tune out, if you try. The early version of the puffball skirt that we loved, and helped to invent for our Topshop line, was a fifties-style spotty circle skirt. These were full, cinched at the waist, and a deep, reddy pink with huge black and white polka dots. I'm not sure whether Shirlie and I were supposed to look like fifties teenagers or ladybirds! These full skirts would have been perfect for moving and dancing, but they were so tight at the waist that one wrong move could send a button flying – which is exactly what happened.

I think we were dancing to 'Young Guns' on that tour when I felt a breeze and then a looseness: something wasn't quite right. Again, I immediately beckoned to Shirlie, trying to mime a plan. If we both got off the stage for a moment, we could sort it out and dance back on. I pointed to my skirt then pointed left – *You go that way, I'll go this way – it will look deliberate.* Instead, Shirlie looked at my skirt, looked at me, then worked out what had happened – and doubled over with laughter. Luckily, the brilliant Melanie was waiting in the wings, and ran out while I frantically mouthed 'Pin, pin!' Meanwhile her brother was singing his heart out, yards away, with no idea that I'd come perilously close to showing my pants to his thousands of fans. I filed that information away for the future. I didn't know it then, but one day, Shirlie and I wouldn't be able to run offstage and fix a wardrobe malfunction – we wouldn't have George and Andrew to hide behind! (Also, one day, we'd have our own range of clothes and we'd need to make sure that every button was sewn on tight.)

One place where we got to spend some time was Australia. Because we'd been working so hard, we arranged a short break, which gave us a chance to get over our jetlag. One thing that George and Andrew loved to do was to fly various family members out to join us. Shirlie's mother came along for a holiday. I'd met her a few times before and this time we bonded instantly. It was like having another Shirlie around. Maggie was so warm, loving and funny. Quickly, she was nicknamed the Agony Aunt. No matter how big or small your problem, she could solve it, usually just by listening. She'd ask you careful questions and show you that you knew the answers all along. We all felt so comfortable with her that we treated her like one of our relations.

Just like Shirlie and me, Maggie loved to be relaxed and was always looking for ways to make herself feel at home. Australia is thousands of miles from Bushey – and hot – but Maggie had brought her slippers with her. One morning, I wandered into Shirlie's room and saw Shirlie and Maggie sat up in bed, chatting and drinking tea. As I went over to join them, I saw Maggie's slippers and instinctively put them on. Shirlie laughed so hard, she was almost in tears.

'What? They just looked so comfy!' I protested as Shirlie dabbed her eyes.

'Oh, love, you're very welcome to them,' said Maggie, generously, while giggling along with her daughter.

Australia was a joy to spend time in. The food was delicious, and everyone we met was kind, open-hearted, relaxed and easy-going. There was plenty of wildlife, we could spend time at the beach and the Wham! fans loved to dance and have fun. It was a great place to play because they were always enjoying themselves. In fact, the very best thing about being on tour was that we felt privileged to be part of people's happiest memories. Every night, thousands of people came out to have fun and enjoy themselves and we were the ones entertaining them. We were celebrating youth, music and freedom so in many ways, it seemed a little strange to go from the cheerful, chilled-out crowds in Australia to China, which was still processing the aftermath of the Cultural Revolution.

In 1985, China was a mysterious place to be. We knew it had been under Communist rule, but very little information about the situation was released to the Western world. We had no real idea what life in China was like for those who lived there, but we understood that the situation was changing, rules were being relaxed and that Chinese citizens were about to start to be permitted to interact with the rest of the world, albeit in a very controlled and restricted manner.

I confess that at the time, I was so stunned by the huge honour about to be conferred on Wham! – to be the first Western pop group to play a concert in China – that I didn't give myself a moment to really stop and think about what it was like to be a young person living there. For years, listening to most pop music had been forbidden to them. Music had been my whole life, for as long as I remember being alive. During my darkest, most difficult moments, I could always dance my troubles away, or sing along to the radio. For me, the joy of music is that my body responds to it before my brain does. What would it have been like to grow up in a country with no music? For me, it would have felt like being deprived of air or water.

We were unaware of the work that had been going on behind the scenes. Simon with co-manager Jazz Summers, of Wham!, knew that getting the group to China would be a huge coup. They'd spent 18 months persuading government officials to allow George and Andrew to come to the country to play, emphasising Wham!'s sweet, wholesome image. I guess they were very careful to keep George's antics with the shuttlecock under wraps! Initially, I was excited but not overwhelmed. It seems so strange to say this now, but to me China was just another destination on a huge world tour. I was curious, I was excited, but I assumed it would be the same as always. We'd just keep our fingers crossed for a kettle in our room and some complimentary biscuits. We'd go from hotel to venue and see very little of the actual country.

How wrong I was.

Shirlie and I both loved to make ourselves at home, but she was always a little bit more anxious in a new place than me. I always did my best to look after her and keep her calm, but she was very attuned to vibes – and I think she had a bad feeling about this leg of the tour, even before we left. We started in Hong Kong, a British colony at the time. That was a shock to the system. The busiest, most bustling place I'd ever been to, it was so bright and loud and full of people, but every so often, we'd encounter something that reminded us of home. I was always happiest when I was able to sit down and have a proper meal, and in Hong Kong, the British link meant that the food was familiar. In some ways, it took the edge off any homesickness but in others it was really disorienting – it was a little bit like being in a London rush hour to the power of 10, with the thermostat turned all the way up.

Shirlie and I were both upset by the enormous gap between the wealthy and the poor. We were keen to go exploring and hit the shops but all the high end designer stores were way beyond our budget and not really our style either. When we saw a Chinese man sitting on the pavement with a gangrenous leg, it broke our hearts. He was surrounded by stores selling finery for thousands of pounds, but no one was helping.

'We've got a bit of cash, let's chuck it in his cup,' I whispered, before we ran back to the hotel.

Shirlie tried to get the receptionist to send an ambulance out for him, but she just laughed, saying, 'It's only a beggar.'

It just seemed *wrong* to walk away from those in need. George and Andrew would have helped, but we barely saw them due to all the publicity they had to do for this historical event.

Because the trip to China was so momentous, a crew were making a film about the boys called *Foreign Skies*. Directed by Lindsay Anderson, it was produced by their management team. Every so often, we were filmed too, but this was the first time that we felt that we were being separated from George and Andrew. I think this was when Shirlie started to struggle. For her, home was where George was and she could go anywhere and get through anything so long as we could all have tea and a cosy chat after the show. Now, George and Andrew were staying in a separate hotel.

The trip got harder. There was no way that Beijing could feel like just another leg on the tour. Hong Kong felt opulent, Western and familiar, but here our gloomy hotel – boarding house, really – was decorated with nothing but notices enforcing a curfew, saying we had to be in our room and in bed by 11 p.m.

At the time, Wham! were so well known that no city felt strange for long. Usually, everywhere we went, we were greeted with smiles and waves. We didn't know that in China, first, almost no one had any idea who we were, and second, most public displays of any kind had been forbidden for years. Shirlie and I were so naïve and to us, China simply seemed miserable and the culture was very different from our own and steeped in a history we knew not very much about.

For Shirlie, one of the hardest things to see was the wet market. She really loved animals and so the sight of the dogs strung up to be sold absolutely broke her heart. I saw them first, out of the corner of my eye, and grabbed her elbow. 'Come over here! Don't look!' I pleaded, but the film crew were desperate to get her horrified reaction on camera.

Later that day, they wanted to get shots by the Great Wall of China. 'Now, just George and Andrew,' said Lindsay, the director, ushering us out of the way. The resulting image was truly iconic: two performers, at the very top of their game, about to play a gig that would make history – but it really brought home to me that there was no place for Shirlie and me. We knew we were window dressing and usually that felt fine, but Andrew's old words haunted me: 'Do you want to be up at the front with us?' In China, we weren't at the front; the boys were, rightly so, the focus of this trip. I did understand – George and Andrew were living their dream and were ready to take what was on offer, they deserved it. Still, Shirlie's desolation made me determined to stay strong for her and look after her but deep down I knew she understood what the boys had to do.

At the time, food was my love language, my greatest comfort, and when I was being well fed, I felt that I could face the world. Also, live performances use up so much energy. Trying to dance on stage if you haven't eaten well is like trying to drive with no petrol in your tank. I'd always enjoyed Chinese food and I assumed that the food would be basic but wholesome – I was expecting noodles and vegetables. So I wobbled when we arrived at the Worker's Gymnasium before our big show and saw what we were being given for dinner. Several bowls of grey sludge were laid out for us – on the floor. I felt tired, hungry, anxious and almost tearful. In a couple of hours, not only would we be playing to 12,000 people – as the first Western band to ever perform in China, the whole world would be watching us – and I couldn't even get a sandwich.

Shirlie was not her usually chatty, jokey self, she looked utterly downcast. 'I miss Martin so much, we should never have come,' she whispered.

'It's OK, we've just got to get through the next few hours,' I reassured her, squeezing her hand. She always made me feel protective, I wanted to take care of her.

Over the years, I'd learned to feel a little less self-conscious about my body. Every so often I experienced a wave of anxiety when I had to pull on a tight top or a short skirt, but I was able to push it to one side and get on with the job at hand. But when we ran out on stage in Bejing, in our little leather outfits, all of the anxiety came flooding back. The crowd, in their drab greys and navy blues, were staring at us. It was like no show I had ever played before. No one was screaming or singing or dancing. Everyone seemed so miserable.

Of course, now I realise that we must have looked like aliens that had landed. No one in China had seen anything *like* us before. Doris Day could have sung a song on stage and got the same, freaked-out reaction. But we managed. We lost ourselves in the music and focused on doing the best job we could for George and Andrew. But my mind was whirring. I think that was the moment when I realised that it was time to start thinking about the future. In Wham! we'd come along for the ride and we'd had so much fun and had so much to be grateful for. But now I wanted to choose where I went, where I performed and how I was treated, and in China, at the time, no one seemed to have any choices.

Looking back, I feel all sorts of confusing, contradictory emotions about that period. I'm very, very proud of all of us. It was a huge honour to be asked to play that show and the four of us became a significant part of history. Even more importantly, I feel that we brought music to people who hadn't been able to enjoy British pop and that we were at the beginning of some major changes. I feel that music is a right, not a privilege, and everyone in the world should be able to listen whenever they would like to. However, now I know that behind the scenes the security officers were cruel to some of the crowds and people were beaten for dancing. It breaks my heart to think we had any part in that.

At the time, Shirlie told *Smash Hits*, 'People here are sad, they want freedom but they're not allowed to have it and, in a way, we're giving them a taste of something they can't really have.'

I truly hope that our work in China inspired people to pursue freedom and eventually make their own music. We realised that we'd covered so much ground – we had travelled all over the world, we were recognised almost everywhere we went and we'd played for tens of thousands of people. It felt as though Wham! was at the top of their game and for George, the only way was up.

So, what were Shirlie and I going to do next? Being in China and thinking about the role that music plays in everyone's lives had made me miss singing. Making music made me happy. I didn't know what the future held for me, but I hoped singing was in there somewhere. It was time to start thinking about life after Wham! But what would that look like? Could we perform without George and Andrew? I was excited, and I was scared. But Shirlie was always good at making her own luck and was starting to make a plan for us.

9

Shirlie – Dreams and challenges

don't think it's a coincidence that my obsession with having a baby really took hold around this time. There was so much excitement around George and what he was going to do next that I felt as though I had to start thinking about my future too. I loved Wham! and my work with the boys and Pepsi, but my gut knew exactly what I wanted, and needed – a family with Martin. However, my womb had other ideas.

Ever since I was 15, I'd suffered from completely debilitating period pains. Back in the seventies, women's health issues were rarely taken seriously. There wasn't much in the way of research or information, and anything connected with our reproductive health was clouded in secrecy and shame. My poor mum had warned that I might feel a bit rough every month when she was giving me 'the talk' – 'You might need some paracetamol on the first day and a hot water bottle, but it will pass,' she'd told me. But she had no idea what to do when my period was accompanied by vomiting and severe diarrhoea. Often, the pain would get so bad, I'd pass out. My GP told me it was 'just' period pains – 'put up and shut up', in other words.

But I didn't realise how bad these 'just' period pains would become when I got older. In the summer of 1988, Pepsi and I had flown to Atlanta, Georgia, for a small concert. We had a lovely hotel booked and while I was resting, Pepsi and our lovely assistant decided that it was a good time to go out and get a few things. I can't remember how long they took, but I think they had stayed out just a little longer than they anticipated. All I know is that when they did return to the hotel room, Pepsi found me on the floor of the loo, unconscious from the pain, sweat pouring off my body.

When I opened my eyes, I was in an ambulance.

'Can you tell me what day it is? What's the name of the president?' one of the paramedics asked.

'Um …'

On tour, it's hard to keep track of what *year* it is and international politics has never been my strong point.

Pepsi was standing with the tour manager, who was hopping from foot to foot.

'So, she'll be able to play the show?' he said.

I could hear the panic in his voice. I remember Pepsi looking at me, her eyes filled with concern. I was awake, but the pain was overwhelming. It was as though every single one of my internal organs was trying to push its way out of my body.

'I'll need some painkillers – don't worry, this always happens, it's my period,' I muttered.

One of the paramedics shook their head. 'No, no, this can't be a period, this is much more serious.'

In Wham! we had an image to keep up. Pepsi and I were supposed to be young and fun – the ultimate girls next door, without a care in the world. But offstage, I was becoming extremely scared about my body and what was happening to it. And Pepsi took my pain seriously: 'Shirlie, you shouldn't just put up with this, I really think you need to see a doctor.'

Because we'd had the odd scare with George's voice, I soon learned that there was a world of medicine beyond my GP in Bushey. Our wages had gone up too. And I realised if I was earning a bit more money, it made sense to spend it on my health. I'd fallen in love with American malls and I loved to shop around and find the best version of whatever it was that I was looking for – so I found the very best doctor! A sweet, gentle, wise woman named Ursula, who worked at the Portland Hospital in London.

I owe Ursula an enormous debt. Not only did she help me with my body and my health concerns, but she gave me confidence too. She showed me that it's OK to ask questions, to seek out alternatives and get as much information from your doctor as possible. Years later, when Martin became seriously ill, I was able to probe, push and gather as much information as I could to help him and deal with his diagnosis. When it comes to your health, there are no stupid questions and a really good doctor has the patience to help

– it's so important for everyone to know this.

After a lengthy series of tests, Ursula diagnosed me with endometriosis. Even now, very little is known about this condition, where it comes from and why it affects certain women. But then, I'd never even heard of the word before. Put simply, it means that extra womb tissue is growing where it shouldn't be, usually in the ovaries and fallopian tubes. It is thought to affect 1.5 million women in the UK – that's a huge number of women, passing out from pain every single month. Initially, I was relieved. I'd been so scared that I might be going crazy, or that my old GP was right. I was genuinely worried that every other woman was able to cope with this, every month, and I couldn't. I'd even been scared that I might have been making a fuss about nothing. It was the biggest sign I'd ever had to trust my instincts and listen to my body. However, the relief was short-lived – my diagnosis came with some devastating news.

'Shirlie, I'm so sorry to have to tell you this,' said Ursula, 'but one of the biggest complications we see as a result of endometriosis is that it can cause problems with fertility. There's a chance you may not be able to conceive.'

I would give anything to be able to go back and talk to Past Me in Ursula's office and show her a picture of my wonderful children, Harley and Roman – all grown up. Back then, I was heartbroken. I couldn't bear the idea that I might not be able to have babies or build a family with Martin. But it would be all too easy for me to look back and simply feel happy that everything has turned out OK. Now Harley is in her early thirties, I'm aware that women are still not always given the right information about their reproductive health and we're still expected to stay silent and uncomplaining. In those days, infertility really was shrouded in mystery and for me this was agony. Pregnant women were everywhere I looked. I thought about my own mother, having five children in quick succession and being forced to remain in a difficult marriage as a result. She loved us all to pieces and wouldn't be without any of us, but I thought that in a different way, she probably felt as though she didn't have full control of her body either.

Pepsi was constantly kind during that difficult period. Because I knew she wasn't ready to think about babies yet, I could confide in her openly in a way that I couldn't with the friends who were mums-to-be. But Pepsi was also brilliant at distracting me from my worries.

'Come on, Shirl, we've got to put the world to rights,' she'd say, summoning me and George for a cosy cup of tea and a gossip about the mysteries of the Universe.

I think that if I'd had different dreams, and a different set of priorities, I might have lost my head during that time. Some of the newspapers were obsessed with the four of us and what we were up to – and because of my relationship with Martin, I faced an extra layer of scrutiny. Sometimes I wonder how different it might have been if we'd all been on Instagram and other social media and able to interact directly with our fans. But the tabloids thought I was the luckiest, most enviable girl in the world. The girlfriend of hunky Martin Kemp! On stage, with George and Andrew, every night! People wanted my wardrobe! I look back now and realise that maybe I was the luckiest girl in the world but it didn't mean I didn't worry.

But I never really felt as though I was fully caught up in the glamour, or the gossip. I hated reading about myself, but when I couldn't avoid it, it seemed as though the press were describing a completely different woman. I didn't really care if people believed that my life was like a music video. It would have been nice to have lived at Club Tropicana, but my reality was the opposite of a pop fantasy. I'd always choose a perfect cup of tea over a piña colada! I adored dancing and having the opportunity to be with my friends but there were moments when I'd have given up everything just to be back at home with Martin, pregnant with his baby and pottering about. Still, deep down, I had a feeling that might not be on the cards for a while. Every so often, one of the band, even George or Andrew, would ask us a slightly scary question: 'Have you thought about what you might do after Wham!?'

Cogs in my brain were starting to turn. Part of me wanted the answer to be 'Go home, marry Martin and have five children of my own.' But I was torn. I knew I was more of a homebody at heart than Martin. He loved touring, making music and being with his band. There was no way I could take that away from him and I didn't want to sit at home and wait for him. Also, I'd grown to love so many parts of my strange life.

I'd always known that I wasn't cut out to lead a straightforward, conventional life. I had no formal exams, I'd never worked in an office and my work experience was a little offbeat. I'd had a few years of working with horses and then the rest of my professional life had been in pop. I knew how to sing, dance and be on stage, and I didn't really understand how to do anything else. Whenever I was at home, back in London and not touring, I didn't really know what to do with myself. If Martin was away, I'd go back to Bushey and stay with my mum – I'd rather do that than spend time alone in an empty flat. Pepsi loved being home alone and it baffled me: 'Don't you get lonely?' I'd ask her, confused. I wondered so much about her ability to enjoy your own company but I guess that's confidence for you. When you are secure being alone can be joyous. In fact, I love being on my own now.

Pepsi was very good at being independent, but I've always been a collaborator. She's an exceptionally talented singer. I've always loved music and singing, but I've never felt completely confident about my voice (let's face it, if your best friend is George Michael, you're never going to feel as though your own singing is anything to write home about!). But if Pepsi had the voice, I had a vision. The people from the record company weren't just being nosy about our future plans, they were curious about our next steps because they believed we had momentum on our side. Wham! were one of the biggest bands in the world. George was poised to become an international megastar – but it made sense for the fans to be interested in everything that came next. At the time, I didn't know it, but later, I'd realise I'd learned so much from George that went beyond music. I was obsessed with the arty side of pop and performance and I'd start to discover my passion for fashion and photography.

Ultimately, I've always believed that the route to your dreams isn't always a direct or straightforward one. My role in Wham! came about because I loved being with George and Andrew, and I wanted to spend as much time with my best friends as I could, so I managed to make it into a job. It was the same instinct that made me start to ponder the possibility of Pepsi & Shirlie. Every single person I loved belonged in the pop world, so I needed to stay there for a little bit longer. Maybe I could have it all – a career, and a family. I'd wait as long as I had to for the family part to happen, but that was my biggest dream of all. For now, pop was a pretty good way to pass the time.

10
Shirlie – From The Final to Pepsi & Shirlie

Pepsi and I always thought that our time in Wham! felt like student days. If it was where we earned our pop degree then Wham! The Final was our graduation. We both felt like graduates – we were proud of what we had achieved, we were ambitious and a little nervous but mostly excited for the future. We'd worked so hard and we couldn't wait to see what happened next.

I knew that I worked best as part of a team whilst Pepsi seemed much more independent than me. Deep down, I knew that she'd make a brilliant solo artist, but I wasn't ready to think about going it alone so I had to make a plan: I had to persuade her that the two of us needed to stay together, professionally. Once again, I realised that to get what I wanted, I had to manifest it. I believed in us – and I believed in Pepsi & Shirlie! I started my campaign towards the end of our huge world tour.

'So, everyone wants to know what we'll be doing next,' I told her, sipping my tea. 'I'm thinking we could do something together.'

'Oh, Shirl, I don't know. Honestly, I can't think beyond getting back to my flat in a couple of months and putting a wash on,' yawned Pepsi.

'Seriously, we've got some momentum. We've been part of Wham! – all of these people know who Pepsi & Shirlie are. It makes sense to stick together.'

Over time, I started to persuade her. I think what appealed to both of us was the idea of having some creative control. At the beginning of Wham! we were more than happy to let George do his thing. His ideas were brilliant and he knew exactly what he wanted, it made total sense to follow his instructions. But we'd seen what he could achieve and now we longed to have a go for ourselves. Even though I was nowhere near George's standards, I loved writing songs. The lyrics weren't my strong point, but I kept coming up with riffs and melodies. When you worked with George, you never stopped learning. Admittedly, his feedback was occasionally not what I hoped to hear. Once I'd played him a tape of a song I'd come up with and held my breath to find out what his response would be.

'Shirlie, it's very nice,' he responded. 'But where's the chorus?'

I *definitely* needed a team to work with! Years later, whenever George would play me his new song, I would say to him, 'That's OK, but where's the chorus?!'

If songwriting wasn't my strongest suit, styling was definitely within my skill set. I was always excited to pick out my clothes for stage and videos. For *Everything She Wants*, I thought we should be in sleek black outfits, with pearls, Audrey Hepburn style. I loved the aesthetic side of our work. Years later, I'd pick up a camera and my fascination with fashion and art would all really come together for me. But when I thought about clothes and our image, I lost myself in the flow of the work – and found myself.

Even though the beginning of Wham! took me by surprise, I was getting more focused and becoming more ambitious. Pepsi was the girl with the big boobs and the big voice, and I was the little blonde one who missed her boyfriend. But when it came to what we wore, and how we wore it, I could be so bossy that I shocked myself!

'Come over here, Peps, you need to get right in the light,' I'd say on shoots, when I wasn't instructing the photographers and telling them how to do their job. Or 'Oh, my God, you *have* to wear this dress, you'll look amazing!'

Slowly, in Wham!, our image had become sexier. Just as George had gone from sporty shorts to leather jackets, we'd stopped wearing our sweet little fifties outfits and got into tight, rubber dresses. It was very much the look of the eighties.

We were once performing at a prestigious awards show in Austria. Everyone from the pop world was there and the photographers were out in force. Martin Fry from ABC rushed over to say hello. We tried to play it cool, but inside we were all squealing. Their song, 'Poison Arrow', was one of our all-time favourites – George and I used to race each other to the dance floor whenever we heard it in a club in Watford. 'Girls, you look amazing!' said Martin. 'Those dresses are stunning,' he continued, gesturing to our skintight, black rubber numbers. 'They must be new season Gaultier, am I right?'

'Mmmmm,' I nodded, not trusting myself to speak.

The second he was out of earshot, Pepsi and I burst out laughing. 'Try new season sex shop!' She giggled hysterically. 'Not even new season,' I laughed. 'Lord knows how long they were in that Soho shop window!' We didn't mind where our stylist was finding clothes from and at the time it was impossible to tell the difference. It was a useful lesson for the future. Image was just that – a visual idea, an illusion, it didn't have to be permanent. You could be playful, you could have fun, you could use one thing and make it look like something else and you certainly didn't always need to spend hundreds of pounds. It was my way of bringing a little bit of rock to pop. Mind you, those rubber dresses were a pain to get in and out of. What we saved on designer labels, we probably spent on talcum powder.

So when it came to The Final, my mind was on the future. Dancing in tight rubber dresses was constricting and difficult, not to mention hot. I longed for freedom, in all of its forms. I wanted to express myself and I wanted to move. Pepsi and I were very similar – we could be very feminine, but we had both grown up as tomboys who loved running around. For the first time, fashion reflected our personalities and there was a way to be both. Bands like Adam and the Ants and even Spandau had juxtaposed the feminine and the masculine, and made their look a big part of their sound. Now it was our turn.

For a lot of bands, deciding when to end things and what to do next can be incredibly complicated. There's a lot of pressure on everyone to come up with a plan. Now, I think we all look back and realise that everyone should be allowed to figure out their next steps in their own time, at their own pace. But when you're young, you feel as though you should always be going onto something bigger and better – and when you've come from one of the biggest bands in the world, that can be very hard on your mental health. However, we were incredibly lucky: George was so focused, driven and ambitious, and he loved a plan. That meant that we all understood, almost from day one, that Wham! wouldn't go on forever and we had to enjoy things, moment to moment. George wasn't just thinking about his own plans, either. He was very interested in making sure that we all felt happy about what happened next – and he was quite keen to get us signed alongside him, as Pepsi & Shirlie, and supervise our management so we felt torn.

'He'd be so brilliant,' I sighed, 'But it would be really nice to do our own thing and have our own ideas.'

Pepsi agreed. We knew that George would make us a great success, but we'd reached the point where we wanted to prove ourselves, by ourselves. And we knew that no matter what decision we came to, he would always offer advice and support.

A few different labels wanted to sign us, which was very exciting. I think that gave us plenty of confidence and after being in Wham! we knew that we had to be careful about terms. We weren't just looking to see who had the biggest chequebook, we were dreaming of the chance to be creative and independent.

Soon, we were in the Polydor office, signing our very first record deal. That night, we went out for dinner in one of our favourite French restaurants on Upper Street in Islington. Pepsi brought along her boyfriend and I was with Martin – 'This is so exciting!' he cried. 'You girls are going to be *massive*! You're going to be superstars!' I squeezed his hand under the table – I felt so lucky. Ironically, if he'd wanted me to stay home and be a housewife while he travelled the world, I might not have minded, but he was always my biggest professional cheerleader. He might have been even more excited about my career than I was!

Making Pepsi & Shirlie plans ensured that the Wham! The Final felt more like a celebration than an ending. As we ran out onto the stage at Wembley Stadium on a hot Saturday evening to the roar of 72,000 fans on 28th June 1986, we gave the performance of our lives. We were happy, we were excited and we wanted everyone to remember Wham! together as a happy, joyful force. George spoke for us all when he looked out at the audience and said, 'This is the best thing I've ever looked at.' We were even joined by Elton John and Duran Duran's Simon Le Bon!

I think that I would have found this period really tough, if I hadn't had something exciting to look forward to. Ever since our disastrous trip to China, I'd become painfully aware of the growing gap between the girls and the boys. In Pepsi, I'd gained a best friend and while it was only right that George should go on to solo greatness, I felt a pang whenever I remembered the earliest days. Sometimes, we'd still get together and be properly silly, but now it seemed as though everything was very grown-up and serious. It was a privilege to play to over 70,000 people, but I would have given anything for one more weekend messing about.

Still, there was no time – we had to get to the studio. For the first time, I was going to be writing and singing. I was excited and terrified too. The label had introduced us to a really lovely man, a songwriter named Tambi Fernando. Pepsi and I loved music, but we weren't experienced songwriters and we knew that our first single needed to be chosen carefully. We were really keen to work with someone who had written a lot of music. Tambi had worked with big acts like Frankie Goes To Hollywood and understood that we needed a bold sound.

As Pepsi & Shirlie, we had a big advantage. We didn't need to be broken in or introduced in the same way as lots of other new acts – we had the Wham! fans, who already knew who we were. However, that also meant we needed to begin with a hit. When people associate you with 'Club Tropicana' and 'Last Christmas', you can't start slowly, you need to hit the ground running!

Tambi was the perfect person for us to work with. He was as kind and calm as his songs were brash and bombastic. He played us a very early version of 'Heartache' and then glanced at us shyly: 'I've been working on this. What do you think?' he asked.

Pepsi and I spoke almost in unison: 'It sounds like a hit!' we said, beaming.

However, recording the track was a little different. We started off in a studio in Westbourne Grove. Over the course of the album, we moved around a few London studios, often working late into the night because that was the only time slot available. It was tough. I think Pepsi was in her element – I think she'd always dreamed of spending time in the studio, with her amazing voice, getting to sing her heart out. But it wasn't the right environment for me. I found it slightly intimidating. We were the only women there – it was a very male space – and it made me realise how difficult it is to be creative if your surroundings aren't right. Most studios are designed to be practical. They're very dark, often they're not very clean and I couldn't even relax enough to enjoy a cup of tea – all of the mugs seemed a bit dirty. Years later, when I recorded *In The Swing Of It* with Martin, going back to the studio I noticed that things had changed. The studios were big and bright, and the cups were clean.

Back then, the worst part was feeling trapped behind glass while other people muttered and made decisions. If you'd done a good job, no one said well done. But if you'd messed up, everyone was keen to let you know about it. I'd never had a single singing lesson before. Singing, for me, was a way to express myself. Of course, I knew that I'd never be able to sing like George, or recreate that gorgeous, explosive Shirley Bassey sound like Pepsi. But singing brought me so much happiness and I felt confident that I could carry a tune.

Stuck behind the glass, I lost some of that confidence.

'Shirlie, there's a bit too much vibrato there, can you strip it back a bit?' I was told.

I didn't understand. I'd barely heard of the word 'vibrato' before, how could I take it out of my voice? My heroes like X-Ray Spex and Siouxsie Sioux were able to belt it out, but when I did that, apparently it was wrong. I needed gentleness and encouragement but I couldn't even see who was delivering the instructions: 'Cut!', 'Go again!' I think it would have helped if I could have played an instrument – or if I was able to hear every part of the sound that I was trying to put together. In fact, the one time I really enjoyed being in the studio was making 'Someday' for our second album, which George wrote for us. That was the music making experience I'd always dreamed of. George was so confident and relaxed that he was able to be collaborative and give me the feedback I needed – just things like 'I loved that line, can we see how it sounds this way?'

Still, when we'd finished with 'Heartache', we felt proud – and excited. I'd made a song with my best friend and it sounded amazing. Listening to the two of us together gave me goosebumps. I thought back to listening to her demo tape on the journey from Finsbury Park to George's house – we'd come so far!

Polydor and the studio engineers were very focused on making sure that we sounded a specific way but when it came to creating the Pepsi & Shirlie look, we found the freedom I craved. We'd explained that we really wanted an image that suited both sides of what we loved – the feminine part and the tomboy part. Life in Wham! had taught us that it didn't matter how great the music was. If you wanted to appear on *Top of the Pops* and sell records, the look was just as important as the music. We were so excited when we heard that the iconic photographer Eric Watson was coming to shoot our sleeve. He'd worked for *Smash Hits* magazine and gone on to shoot many musical legends, including Frankie Goes To Hollywood, Spandau, Adam and the Ants and the Pet Shop Boys. Best of all, Eric introduced us to the stylist Suzanne Rose.

We'd always joke that Suzanne was our secret third member. From the moment she met us, she seemed to understand *exactly* what we wanted to do. We chatted to her on the phone and told her about the looks we loved: 'We wanted to look edgy and strong, but feminine – and most of all, we need to be able to *move*,' we explained. I was inspired by some of Martin's mad Spandau outfits, the Edwardian tailoring, the Victorian lace.

Pepsi had one stipulation – no high heels. 'I need boots, if I'm going to dance' she explained.

When we arrived at the studio, I think Suzanne was just as excited as we were. 'I can't believe I'm finally getting to do this!' she exclaimed, showing us to a rail crammed with taffeta ballgowns, Wolford stockings, men's jackets and even antique bloomers. 'Don't you love these earrings?' she asked, showing us some fabulous teardrop shoulder dusters. Amazingly, they were made by Monty Don. We loved his earrings. Before he became a star of *Gardener's World*, he made some of the most iconic costume jewellery in London and we weren't the only fans – his pieces were worn by everyone from Boy George to Princess Diana.

At last, we felt happy, relaxed and comfortable. Suzanne was a really good influence on us. She made us feel calm, but excited, and we were able to really revel in the fun of our first proper solo photo shoot. Having your picture taken can be a little nerve-wracking. I'm lucky because I've always been able to think visually and lose myself in the moment – I think this stops me from feeling self-conscious. Over the course of our careers, I noticed it was harder for Pepsi – partly because she worried about her curves and partly because back then, photographers didn't take our different skin tones into account. We were a duo and most of the time it was good and right that we were treated as though we were exactly the same. But hardly anyone really thought about how to properly light black girls.

'Come on, Peps, into the light,' I'd say, pulling her under the hot lamp to make sure she didn't fade into the background.

Still, for our 'Heartache' shoot, we were having so much fun with Suzanne that even Pepsi was able to relax and really enjoy herself.

We knew that as Pepsi & Shirlie, we could expect a strong reaction from critics as well as fans. Wham! had been so visible and I understood that there was a chance we'd be judged pretty harshly by the music press. We were desperate to show the world what we could do and we'd been working around the clock – but we realised that before anyone even heard the music, they might simply dismiss us as a Wham! spinoff act. However, we weren't expecting our biggest critic to be the UK Prime Minister.

It happened in the January of 1987, before 'Heartache' was released. Usually, the period after Christmas felt a little bit flat and grey, but Pepsi and I were full of optimism and energy: 1987 was going to be our year. Also, I was in a good mood because I was spending a Saturday morning in bed with Martin, drinking tea, my all-time happy place. I was always cheerful when Spandau were home from touring. Back then, as I said, absolutely everyone watched *Saturday Superstore* on BBC1. Technically it was a kids' show, but it was the best place to catch new music and in those days, there were only four channels to choose from – you couldn't watch a box set on Netflix. Also, *Saturday Superstore* held a special place in my heart, because it was the first programme to feature Wham! If we hadn't been seen on the show, we wouldn't have been asked on to *Top of the Pops* when we were outside the Top 40 – and Martin would never have spotted me.

We might never have been drinking tea together.

But 1987 wasn't just a big year for us. Margaret Thatcher was facing a big election year and the country was torn over major issues. Many people were deeply unhappy about the way she had handled the Falklands conflict, everyone was hugely anxious about the looming threat of nuclear war and there were growing fears about AIDS and HIV, and a terrifying public information campaign that did little to allay our concerns. The fact that the Prime Minister was appearing on *Saturday Superstore* brought home just how many people were watching on that January morning.

Mrs Thatcher answered some questions from the audience about education, the nuclear threat and what she would do if she wasn't prime minister – and then she was asked to review some upcoming singles. Then they played the *Heartache* video! We held our breath. What would she think?

'It didn't sound like a heartache at all, it was all thump, thump, thump...' was her verdict.

The presenters tried to persuade her that surely she'd be able to dance to it, but she insisted, 'No, it lacked melody but the girls have great voices, strong voices.'

As soon as the programme finished, the phone rang: it was my mum.

'That silly woman doesn't know what she's talking about! It's a lovely song, with a great melody,' she grumbled.

'I don't mind,' I replied. 'You're the only Maggie who has an opinion I care about!'

Perhaps unexpectedly, Mrs Thatcher gave the thumbs up to a song called 'Beautiful Imbalance' by the Thrashing Doves. Unfortunately, her seal of approval didn't do much for their fortunes – that single reached Number 50. Luckily, things went a little differently for us ...

That Sunday, we gathered anxiously beside the radio to listen to the Top 40. Our record company had been excited about the midweeks – a few days before the official chart is announced, record companies are given an indication of what has been selling well in the shops so far. The midweeks are a decent prediction of what the final chart will look like, but they're not completely accurate and they don't take the weekend into account. If a lot of people go out and hear a track on a Friday night and buy it on a Saturday afternoon, everything can change. Thursday's *Top of the Pops* could really make or break fortunes too.

We'd been told we'd probably made the Top 5, maybe even the Top 3, but there were absolutely no guarantees. When DJ Bruno Brookes started the countdown of the Top 10 (beginning with Hot Chocolate's 'You Sexy Thing'), we started to hold our breath and didn't let go until we'd heard Number 5 ('It Doesn't Have To Be This Way' by The Blow Monkeys). We weren't 4, or 3 – but in with a bullet at Number 2! Just pipped to the post by the only person we'd ever want to be beaten by – George. He'd topped the charts with his big duet with the amazing Aretha Franklin, 'I Knew You Were Waiting …'. A Wham! reunion and a perfect moment, it seemed so fitting for us to be at the top of the charts, together. And if anyone was to be Number 1, it had to be George.

As soon as the song started playing, George called me – 'Amazing congratulations, I didn't know your record was coming this week.' He then apologised and said, 'You know you'd be Number 1 if I hadn't released my record.' I think he genuinely felt bad about it. He invited us all out to The Ivy for dinner.

I'll never forget that moment – sitting around the table, drinking champagne in the candlelight with Martin, George, Pepsi and all of our friends we'd made over the last few years. For once, I really felt like the girl the newspapers were writing about. I forgot all my cares, my anxieties about having children, my fears for the future. I was with the people that I loved the most and we'd all got to this moment together. I felt so proud of all of my friends, I belonged. At Number 2, I truly felt as though we were on top of the world.

11

Pepsi – Home Office heartache

All my life, I've loved listening to the radio. I grew up with it. In London, no matter where you go, the radio is always on somewhere. Mum would have it on in the kitchen when she was washing the dishes or doing the ironing. My brothers would play it in their bedrooms. Every single shop would be tuned into Radio 1 or Capital – and even on the street you could hear people playing the radio out of their cars. For a long time, the radio brought me nothing but joy. And as part of Wham! and then part of Pepsi & Shirlie, it brought me pride, too. I will never, ever forget those goosebumps I felt when I first heard 'Heartache' being played on the radio – and the euphoria when I learned, through the radio, that we'd reached Number 2 on the Top 40.

I never thought the radio could bring you bad news, but at the beginning of 1990, I was proved wrong. My mum rang: 'I've just heard something on the radio – and I'm really worried,' she said. 'They've changed the Immigration Act. We've got to go and register, or we have to leave the country? The Act that had allowed my parents to come to the UK as Commonwealth citizens had been superseded by the British Nationality Act. At this point, they had lived, worked and paid taxes in Britain for almost 40 years. They had spent more of their life in London than they had in St Lucia and raised a family here, yet they were expected to go to the Home Office and supply all sorts of paperwork to prove they had a right to stay in West London.

This was a true heartache. My mum had worked her fingers to the bone from the moment she arrived in this country. More than that, she was strong. She'd managed to raise a big family, take on several physically demanding jobs and stay funny, stylish and optimistic. And she'd survived the darkest and most difficult periods in her marriage. I didn't think my mum was scared of anything, but she sounded frightened now. It was nerve-wracking. She'd followed every rule to the letter, but she was worried that she wouldn't be allowed to stay in her home. She hadn't even had this news delivered to her personally. No one had taken the time to sit down with her and explain what she needed to do – she just happened to hear it as an announcement on the radio.

Also, Mum had raised me – a young woman who had gone on to contribute as much as she could to British culture. Whenever I toured with Wham! and as part of Pepsi & Shirlie, I was an ambassador for our country. Surely she belonged here just as much as I did? She shouldn't have to prove anything.

As part of the Windrush generation, arriving before 1971, my parents should have been allowed to remain in the UK and make it their home. When we talk about immigration, I think we forget that so many people, like my mum and dad, didn't just leave because they believed life would be better for them in Britain: they came to help. They were told that if they came to live in England, they could be part of the efforts to rebuild the country following the Second World War. However, the Home Office kept no records of people like them.

'Don't worry, Mum, I'll take you both down there, I'm sure everything will be fine.'

I was doing my best to reassure them, but inside I was shaking with fear – and anger too. When my dad was violently attacked and stabbed by racist Teddy Boys, it had affected the whole family. I didn't understand why they would hurt him, just because he was a black man. But my parents didn't want to draw attention to the injustice or call it out. Back then, I believed it was just one of those things. However, as a woman in her early thirties, I was increasingly aware that it wasn't acceptable.

The trip to the Home Office was long, but uneventful. I think we were all much more nervous about waiting for the appointment. I still have my dad's Certificate of Registration. I think he was proud of it, but it stirs up many more complicated emotions in me, bringing back the fear, worry and pain we all experienced – all feelings that we should not have had to go through.

In some ways, working in the music industry in the eighties and nineties made me feel very lucky. Entertainment felt much more diverse and inclusive than many other industries. We met and worked with people who travelled widely and cared about talent, first and foremost. Perhaps it was partly because of the *Top of the Pops* effect, too. As I've said, there were almost no black people on TV when I was growing up – almost the only girls I saw on screen who looked like me were singing and dancing. They say 'you can't be what you can't see' – I'm sure a wider range of people got into the music industry because it was visibly more welcoming and inclusive than so many others. Perhaps it helped that America seemed much more diverse than the UK and so many exciting sounds were coming out of the country. When Shirlie and I went over for a series of PAs, when 'Heartache' was soaring up the dance charts in 1986, everyone was stunned to hear our London accents – 'But we assumed you'd be from Miami!' one promoter said. A duo comprised of a black girl and a white girl just didn't seem very British to them! We didn't mind – we liked surprising people, we felt as though it set us apart.

To the best of my knowledge, I never experienced any overt racism in Wham!, or as part of Pepsi & Shirlie. When I thought of what my dad had been through, I was aware that everyone treated me well. No one ever mentioned the colour of my skin. However, in those days, I think we were all quite naïve. For example, we couldn't understand why, when we came back from a tour, I'd usually get stopped on my way back through airport security. Eventually I'd arrive home, my phone ringing as I walked through the door: it would be Shirlie.

'Peps, where did you go? I couldn't see you. I got home hours ago!'

'Oh, you know, they had to ask me a lot of questions and go through my bags,' I'd say.

I think we both wanted to believe that it was a 'music thing'.

'Maybe it's because we've just got back from tour and they think we've been having a wild old time,' Shirlie wondered aloud.

As you will know by now, the pair of us spent most of our downtime curled up in our giant dressing gowns with our hot drinks so nothing could be further from the truth. Also, Shirlie never, ever got stopped – it was only me.

Another issue was the problem of hair and make-up. Now, every brand is expected to be inclusive and to carry a full range of shades for a full range of skin tones. Some brands were starting to extend their ranges but many mainstream brands only carried products suitable for white skin. We were working with make-up artists who had learned their trade with these products. Often, we'd turn up to shoots and discover that this was going to make life tricky. Shirlie was very easy, make-up wise – her colouring meant that any make-up artist knew exactly how to work on her face. But for make-up artists with little experience of black skin and black hair, I was a source of confusion. Often, I'd have to tell them how to do their job and bring my own make-up along with me.

Just as my parents hadn't wanted to make a fuss about the attack on my dad, I didn't want to kick up about the fact that I didn't feel catered for, or included. The last thing I wanted was for anyone to think I was a diva. Perhaps subconsciously, I was aware of a set of double standards. I knew no one would

Our first time in America: The beginning of Pepsi and Shirlie.

Top: Receiving gifts, at home with Bob Ellis our manager in America.

Middle left: First time in America as Pepsi and Shirlie with our manager Bob Ellis.

Middle right: Maggie and Agatha, their first time on TV.

Bottom left: Pepsi, speed boating with Bob Ellis. Biscayne Bay, Star Island, Miami.

Bottom right: Pepsi, Shirlie and fashion stylist, Suzanne Rose.

Top left: Shirlie, Australia.

Top right: Pepsi and Shirlie, Australia.

Middle left: Pepsi at a Japanese temple.

Middle right: We love sushi!

Bottom: Pepsi with her limo and together in the limo, Canada.

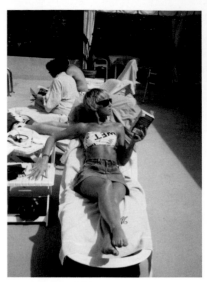

Left, right and bottom: Pepsi and Shirlie downtime at the pool, LA.

Top left: Pespi and Shirlie at a pre-show.

Top right: Maggie, dancer Dennis Elcock, Shirlie and Pepsi at Niagra Falls.

Bottom left: Pepsi and Shirlie at Necker Island, George's treat.

Bottom right: Shirlie pregnant with Harley and Auntie Pepsi.

Top and bottom left: Pepsi and Shirlie. Shirlie's early days of pregnancy in Greece for a PA.

Bottom right: Water baby.

Top left: Shirlie and baby Harley in the bath.

Top right: Shirlie singing in the studio.

Bottom left: Shirlie getting styled up for the clothes range photoshoot.

Bottom right: Pepsi's mum Agatha celebrating her birthday with Shirlie's niece Liza, Shirlie, Harley and Martin.

Top: Pepsi and Shirlie at their record company signing albums.

Bottom: Martin, Harley, baby Roman.

deliberately think this way, but there was a sense that it was one thing for a white woman to be sassy and outspoken but people would respond differently to a black woman making demands. Shirlie was always advocating for me – she would push me into the limelight, sometimes literally, on shoots, if she thought that I was holding myself back. But I was my mother's daughter and I'd always rather find my own solution than complain about anything.

As a black woman, however, my hair required extra care and attention – that was a non-negotiable. Luckily, if you wanted to find a salon that specialised in black and Afro hair, London was the place to be and I found an amazing salon on Kensington Church Street and an even more amazing stylist, an American guy called Jaye Davidson. Jaye was sweet, calm and a hair genius. He was a pleasure to spend time with – and thank goodness, Jaye introduced me to hair extensions! Sometimes, I'd go into the salon at 8 a.m. and at 6 p.m., I *still* wouldn't be finished so I'd have to go back the next day. (I've never been wildly extravagant, but I spent money on appointments with Jaye. In the eighties, my extensions could cost as much as £300 – that's over £900 in today's money.)

Jaye was exceptionally good-looking, too. 'That boy is going places!' declared an impressed Boy George.

'He better not be going anywhere, I need him to look after my hair,' I replied.

But Boy George was right. Jaye left the salon for Hollywood, starring in *The Crying Game*. He was brilliant – but my hair still misses him.

At the moment, the conversation about racism, the #blacklivesmatter movement and inclusion and diversity are raising some vital points. Part of me always felt that because I never had to go through anything as violent and traumatic as the attack my father experienced, I couldn't say that I had experienced racism but it was those subtle comments that would stick around in my head and then with hindsight, I'd realise it was a comment underpinned by an ignorance of how insensitive it was. For example, I had an experience when I was on a bus on the way home from school that still sticks in my memory to this day, I must have been about 13. An old white lady sitting next to me turned and asked me the time. I answered her, 'Yes, it's 4 o'clock.' She looked at me surprised and said, 'Oh, don't you speak well?' I then turned away and looked out the window, wondering to myself why she said that. It was only much later that I realised she didn't complete her sentence: 'You speak well for a darkie,' is what she would have said if she hadn't caught herself? I now realise that I had many moments like that, bigoted comments and actions I didn't want to complain about, that definitely indicated there was a problem.

Racism often isn't deliberate – it's the result of many, many years of toxic ideas and attitudes and layers of ignorance. When I see young stars like Little Mix's Leigh-Anne Pinnock speaking out so wisely and courageously, I'm inspired and I'm still open to learning, yet I'm not naïve to the reality of others' lived experiences and the ignorance they have to put up with in their day-to-day lives. Leigh-Anne has talked about two privileges I experience – the privilege of fame and the privilege of being light-skinned. I understand that my experience of being a black woman isn't necessarily a typical one, because in Wham! and in Pepsi & Shirlie, I was often treated like a VIP. Also, I take after my mother so my skin tone is light and sadly, many social studies have shown that women with darker skin experience more prejudice than those with lighter skin.

There are many shades of black.

As Pepsi & Shirlie, to my knowledge we weren't contrived – I believe we were brought together organically, two girls that just worked well together. I was given the chance to join Wham! because I fitted in and had a personality and talent of my own, not because I was a token black face. George and Andrew had band members who were black and white and were there because of their talent alone.

I'm also aware that my experiences aren't unique. I grew up in London and now I live in St Lucia, where the majority of people are black. I understand that many other black people in the UK are still encountering some of the attitudes and prejudices that my parents struggled with when they first moved here. Racism isn't something that only affects those who are physically attacked. We all inherit all kinds of unconscious beliefs and ideas from history, our families and the world around us, unless we stop to question them. I bonded so quickly with Shirlie because she was the first person I'd ever met who was really interested in who I was, who my family were and where I came from. She could see how we were similar, and how we were different, but never saw our differences as negative or unusual.

Shirlie is very open-hearted and always quick to question herself and learn – 'I'm so glad that you can tell me about this, it isn't anything anyone has taught us in school,' she would sometimes say. She had a point. I realised that all of my history lessons had focused on a very specific part of European history. I'd been taught about the Romans, Hitler, the First and Second World Wars, the Tudors and the Victorians but no one had ever spoken about Windrush or even what the Commonwealth was. There was a school outing when we visited the Commonwealth Institute and looked at a few models of African people living in mud huts, playing drums. I sense now an implied 'colonial saviour mindset' was being expressed through such exhibits, the unspoken narrative being one of bringing development and culture to the natives. There was nothing that gave any real context or sense of the past for me – or for any of the other children at my school whose ancestors had lived outside Britain.

I hope this is changing and I do believe that we're getting better at talking, learning and educating each other. Women of my generation, and my mother's generation too, were raised not to complain, or to ask questions. But sometimes complaining and asking questions is the only way to make sure we all develop and progress. I'm so inspired by the generation who is pushing for change. I was inspired whenever I saw a black woman singing. If it wasn't for icons like Shirley Bassey, Aretha Franklin and Chaka Khan, who looked and sounded amazing, I might not have found the courage or confidence to pursue a career as a performer.

And I truly hope there were young black women who saw me on *Top of the Pops*, working with Shirlie, and felt that there were more opportunities and possibilities out there for them than they had previously realised. In a way, travelling sometimes makes the world feel smaller – but I hope I've made it seem bigger and brighter too and given other performers the feeling that they can make it big while they're on it.

Now, I love my life in St Lucia – but I'm so glad that I was born in London. Nearly 70 years ago, before I was born, my parents made a big decision that was borne out of their loyalty to the Commonwealth: they wanted to come to London to support the UK. That decision altered the course of my life, not just in terms of my pop career, but in terms of friendship, falling in love and being able to see and experience so much. I've got so much out of growing up in the UK, and like my mum, I hope that I've given just as much back.

It's a privilege to live in St Lucia. Every day, by being there, I learn a little more about my family, who I am and what my legacy is. But part of me will always feel that London is my home and I think my parents felt exactly the same way. I'll never forget the fear and anxiety we all felt when that was questioned. Dad's Certificate of Registration makes me feel so proud of my family and of London but it also means I have a constant reminder of everything my parents had to endure, simply to belong. I believe that for everybody, feeling at home and feeling safe and wanted needs to be a right, not a privilege.

12

Shirlie – Pepsi, Shirlie Shopper and the Topshop times

Anyone who grew up in the sixties and seventies will tell you that fashion has changed enormously. Not just the looks – in fact, the looks have probably changed the least! These days, if I'm in London, I'll see people in mini skirts, maxi dresses, leather jackets, sportswear and ballgowns. Every single look of the twentieth century has been reworked and reinvented, and you can wear them all at once if you like. But fashion used to be less available. The cycles were slower, the choice was more limited and the high street could be an exciting destination. Now, you can think of something, Google it and have it sent to you the next day. Sometimes in a matter of hours. Back then, there were only a few places a girl could go. And this was my weekly ritual …

'Mum, do you want me to run you into Watford?' I'd ask.

Mum didn't drive and I was always happy to give her a lift and have a bit of one-on-one time with her. I was always looking for ways to get a quiet moment with her – she was my favourite person.

'Yes please, love,' she'd say. 'That would be lovely.'

'Great!' I'd say. 'And, er … maybe we can have a look in Miss Selfridge?'

I *might* have had an ulterior motive.

Miss Selfridge started out as the dress department for young women in Selfridges department store. When Miss Selfridge standalone shops started appearing, it was big news and I was very excited when a branch opened in Watford High Street. We didn't have much money to spare, but Mum would buy me a new outfit when she could. Rummaging around the rails was a way for the two of us to bond. It meant a lot to me that my mum wasn't like other mums. She encouraged my passion for fashion and she loved to see me dressing up.

Back then, it felt glamorous and exciting. If you lived in central London in the sixties, Biba was your mecca, but for most young women, it was hard to get hold of the outfits you'd seen in magazines. Shops like Miss Selfridge and Topshop changed all that for us. As a middle child in a huge family, I was used to hand-me-downs but punk inspired me to put my own spin on whatever I could get my hands on. I loved vintage, I loved repurposing different bits and pieces, but looking at brand new clothes and seeing how the displays changed every week was so exciting and inspiring. So, when Pepsi and I were approached to create our own range for Topshop, I was *thrilled* – and I knew just how much those Saturday high street shopping expeditions meant to teenage girls – I'd been that girl.

A few years later, when Pepsi joined me in Wham! I remembered all over again how shopping with a new friend can be such a big part of bonding. George and Andrew nicknamed me 'Shirlie Shopper' because if I had some time to myself before a show, I loved to explore the shops. For me, it was the best way to get to know a new place in a short amount of time.

Pepsi and I had a similar style. When we first met, we both had a bit of a tomboy look. More often than not, we'd turn up to rehearsals and interviews and realise we were wearing matching Levi 501s. For us, movement was the most important thing. We wanted to look good, but we didn't believe anyone should have to suffer to look beautiful. Or, to rewrite the old saying, every woman should be able to look beautiful while wearing clothes she can laugh in, dance in and run for the bus in.

For Pepsi, buying clothes was something she was able to do when there was a special occasion. Her lovely mum was incredibly clever and creative, and very good at reusing and repurposing bits of fabric and making old things look new. Pepsi told me that the only really fashionable new thing she could afford to buy was *Vogue* magazine. There was a famous model called Pat Cleveland, who used to walk the runway for Halston – she was one of the first African-American models to appear in fashion magazines and Pepsi found her hugely influential and inspiring.

In the eighties and nineties, the line between fashion and art was becoming seriously blurred. On the one hand, fashion was becoming slowly more democratic and affordable. But on the other, expectations were changing for women and there was less pressure to look 'ladylike'. You could wear Doc Martens with a taffeta ballgown – and this is the look that we, as Pepsi & Shirlie, embraced.

Like Miss Selfridge, Topshop was originally a 'young' offshoot of a ladies' clothes shop, Peter Robinson's department store. It started as a stand-alone shop in the early seventies and was one of the first places that young women could buy clothes made by the iconic sixties designer Mary Quant. What I remember most about Topshop was its atmosphere – it felt more like going to a club or a concert than to a clothes shop. There was always the newest music playing, amazing lighting and cool murals and pictures on the walls. The best thing about the Oxford Circus branch was their vintage section – you didn't need to worry about being caught wearing the same outfit as everyone else if you were prepared to rummage around and find some fabulous one-offs in the basement.

The idea for our Topshop line came from our manager, David. He had lots of friends in the business end of the fashion industry – a line of work we used to call 'the rag trade', the much more commercial side of high fashion, where huge amounts of clothes were produced for big shops. David was very inventive and creative, and I think he saw how Pepsi and I really came into our own when it came to styling and developing our image. He could also tell how quickly young girls were trying to imitate our outfits after seeing us on *Top of the Pops*. Before we knew it, we were in a meeting room, having meetings with David's friend's company, picking out fabric and materials. We liked to listen to music while we worked – everyone from Madonna and T'Pau to Sade and Phil Collins. We wanted to think about how people might move while wearing our clothes, not just how they would dance to our songs.

Making the range was great fun and simply felt like an extension of our styling sessions with Suzanne Rose. We didn't feel that we were under any pressure to make it a huge success, perhaps because nothing like it had ever been done before. I'm proud to say that we were the very first pop act to collaborate with a brand. Now, we're used to it and everyone from Beyoncé to Kate Moss has created a Topshop line. But we just relaxed and let our imagination guide us. I don't think we really understood the scale or significance of what we were doing until the clothes were on the rails.

When we went to the Oxford Street store for the launch, there was a huge poster of us in the window. It was a bit of a 'pinch me' moment and I didn't quite know what to do with myself. I remember thinking Pepsi looked amazing. It's only now that I realise how much she pre-empted Amy Winehouse's style. In fact, I think I remember reading an interview where Amy spoke about seeing pictures of Pepsi when she was a young girl and being inspired by the way she dressed. Still, it was daunting. I think we felt a bit self-conscious: could we live up to our poster? However, we loved the atmosphere in the store. A DJ was playing a live set – I think it was a young Pat Sharp! It all felt very fun and friendly, and every so often, we'd be welcomed to the store:

'Don't forget, Pepsi & Shirlie are here! Come and check out their range!' Soon, the Pepsi & Shirlie puffball dress was the number one selling item in the shop.

The puffball skirt is a controversial eighties fashion classic. It was not a look for everyone, but we loved it because it had volume, but was perfect for dancing. It was invented during a styling session for 'Heartache' when Suzanne Rose made a skirt for Pepsi. The plan was to combine the masculine and the feminine. Suzanne had brought dinner jackets along for us to wear and she'd made a tight skirt for Pepsi, presumably to show off her curves, Azzedine Alaïa-style. The skirt was a cream satin tube.

'Step in it, Peps,' said Suzanne, tweaking and shifting the material.

As a pencil skirt, it was a little too loose and too long. As Suzanne pinned, the skirt started to change shape and puff upwards and outwards.

'Hang on!' I exclaimed, just as Pepsi was saying, 'Oh! Actually, I think it looks really good like that.' We loved it. The skirt referenced the fun, fifties look we sometimes wore on stage in our Wham! routines. It had the Edwardian, exaggerated theatricality that we loved in Vivienne Westwood's tailoring and some of the Spandau stage outfits but it also seemed bang up to date, utterly contemporary and of its time. We knew we had something special and it was so exciting – we weren't being dictated to by existing fashion trends, we were paving the way for something new. So it seemed incredible that what began as a lucky accident and a bit of an experiment was being bought and worn by Topshop shoppers. In a way, it felt just right. After all, ever since we were teenagers, we were exploring and discovering our own style.

When we started to earn some money, we occasionally invested in designer pieces. I loved the art of fashion and designers like Alaïa, Westwood and John Richmond. At that point, I wasn't a typical Topshop shopper. What I wanted was to make the looks I loved accessible to teenage girls. Most of all, I think Pepsi and I hoped that they would do what we had done and shape the outfits, add their own accessories and experiment. We didn't want to see Pepsi & Shirlie clones walking around, we just wanted to inspire people as we had been inspired.

I don't really have any regrets from that period – only the things I didn't do. I wish I'd become much more involved in the fashion side of the business. At the time, we had so many balls in the air. We were some of the luckiest women in the world and we were offered some truly incredible opportunities. The pace of life was frantic, and dizzying. I said yes to almost everything, with a smile on my face, but I really wish I'd made more of an effort to understand the finer details of our Topshop collaboration. It was the most brilliant fun. We loved the work, we were proud of the collection and we enjoyed working with everyone. But if I could go back and do it again, I'd like to give it a really good go and maybe change direction a little bit. I knew my pop career wasn't going to be forever, but I think I could have worked in fashion for a while.

I do think that women in all entertainment industries have an increasingly strong understanding of what their personal brand means and how they can use it to empower themselves and express themselves creatively while succeeding as businesswomen. Of course, for Pepsi and I, one of the best things about creating our own clothing line was that we got to do it together. The looks were inspired by the fashion we love and our work with Suzanne, but they were also an expression of our friendship. We were similar, but we weren't the same, and I hope that the clothes we created were a celebration of our differences as well as a way of sharing the things we had in common.

Looking back, I'd be the first to admit that I could be slightly bossy during parts of the collaborative process. I never, ever meant to bully Pepsi, but I cringe a little when I remember some aspects of creating the range. We never had any disagreements about the clothes themselves, but I was always trying to get Pepsi into shorter, brighter, tighter looks. But then, I think that's a major part of friendship too. A friend is a person you can be absolutely yourself with – but a friend is also the one who can look past your anxieties and insecurities and wants you to be your best and most beautiful self.

There's one promotional picture of the pair of us that I adore. I'm in a black, off-the-shoulder sweatshirt, and black capri pants, she's in a white T-shirt. We're both wearing wide black belts and the most enormous tutus. We're lifting our skirts and looking at the camera. I'm sure that was a typical shoot. I imagine we were both hot, tired and exhausted from having to lean back and stand on one leg. I'm certain we were wondering where our next snack was coming from and how soon we could get hold of a cup of tea. I'm sure we were both longing to put our jeans back on. But when I look at our faces, I'm overwhelmed with joy and pride. Nearly 40 years later, I'm able to say that we both looked beautiful. But more importantly, I think we looked really happy.

Fun and friendship was always at the heart of everything we did together – in that way, I think Pepsi & Shirlie really honoured the Wham! legacy. In everything we did, we were determined to work hard and make music – and more! – that was as good as it could possibly be. But not many people can say that they launched a bestselling clothing line with their best friend and I think even fewer can say that the friendship outlasted the clothes! Even when we were both feeling truly on top of the tree, we instinctively put each other first. We might have been surviving on fizzy drinks and snatched hours of sleep, but if we hadn't loved being together, we may not have got past the first Wham! tour. I believe we were both talented and ambitious, but we never prioritised the pursuit of our ambition. A lot of our success was down to the fact that we were always looking for ways to help each other to shine. Ultimately, I think that's one of the things that is so wonderful about fashion, shopping and dressing up. It brings women together. We dress for each other and we all want each other to look and feel good.

13

Shirlie – For better or worse

At the beginning of the eighties, I'd come back to Bushey with no job, no prospects, no money and no friends – all my belongings were stowed in the boot of my tiny car. By the end of the decade my life had changed beyond all recognition. I had my own music career, I'd been part of one of the most successful acts of the decade and now I had a lovely house in Highgate, North London. But much more importantly, for me, I had the baby I'd spent years longing and trying for. I was finally married to the love of my life and he was pursuing his dreams too, transitioning from pop star to film star. From the outside, it looked as though my life couldn't possibly be any better. I should have been giddy, but I was starting to realise that even though I did have it all, I wasn't sure that I wanted it all.

It was a complicated time for women in the workforce. For my mum and plenty of other women, working outside the home was something you did because you urgently needed money to support your family – it couldn't be avoided. But there was suddenly a lot of pressure on all women to have a *career*. Of course, it was wonderful that attitudes were starting to change and that slowly, most women were able to explore more choices and options but I was finding it harder and harder to reconcile the demands of my career with my desires. I knew I was at my happiest when I was at home, with baby Harley.

Unlike those early days with Wham!, being in the studio didn't bring me any joy and travelling made me miserable – I felt stuck. For Pepsi and I, it was really important that we used our work and our image to share the ideas we truly believed in. We wanted to show the world that women could be confident and bold, that they could do anything they wanted to do and make their own rules. My heroines had talked about creative expression, being daring and doing their own thing.

On the one hand, stepping out of the limelight and giving up Pepsi & Shirlie to take care of my baby seemed absurd. Even now, I know it's very hard for new mothers who want to work – many workplaces are very old-fashioned when it comes to giving women the flexibility and freedom they need to make their paid jobs compatible with motherhood. But 30 years ago, it seemed pretty much impossible. I got the impression that no one understood why I couldn't simply leave Harley at home with a nanny, but that was unthinkable to me. I wanted to be with my daughter. But record companies want you to do everything as fast as you can. Every minute you spend in the studio costs them money, they don't factor in half an hour here or there so you can comfort your crying child.

Thank goodness I had Pepsi. She was always kind, patient and prepared to cheer up Harley and make her laugh. 'She's our third member,' Pepsi would giggle, as Harley gurgled and squealed. 'She's a really good kid, too.'

Considering how busy our schedules were, Harley was always so well-behaved on planes and in studios. But she was a tiny child and it was a difficult environment for her to be in. We were expected to drop everything and do whatever the record company needed us to do. Harley looked like a little doll, but I think a few of the people from the label struggled to understand why she didn't behave like one.

I guess it took me a moment to realise that my priorities had shifted. When Pepsi & Shirlie began, we were both in Wham! mode. We thought it was normal to work all the time, to fly across the world for a single PA and to spend every night either performing or appearing at parties and events. For performers, there's a blur between work and fun. Pepsi and I were never party animals, especially not on tour. We loved going out dancing with George and our friends, but as time went by, and we got busier, our social lives changed. I missed hanging out in nightclubs and knowing people were staring because they liked our dancing – *not* because we were those girls from Wham! But the more successful we were in our industry, the more boring the parties became. We couldn't really relax and have fun. We always loved seeing our friends and catching up with them, but there was sometimes an atmosphere and an attitude that Pepsi and I both struggled with. So we'd be invited to events, and we'd go along to keep the record company happy, but we'd both be looking forward to sneaking away somewhere quiet for a proper chat. It's ironic – I spent so many nights surrounded by all the champagne I could drink, gasping for tea.

Initially, I loved it and I knew how lucky I was. I was prepared to work hard and give it my all. As Pepsi & Shirlie, we had a huge opportunity in front of us and I needed to seize it – I owed it to Pepsi, to George and Andrew, and to Martin. All of these people believed in us and wanted to see us soar. However, by 1991, when we were starting to make our second album, *Change*, my world had transformed. I'd achieved my ultimate ambition, motherhood, and at that point, music simply didn't feel compatible with it. The world had changed too. Back in 1986, when we had a hit with 'Heartache', our sound was right for the charts. But the pop of the eighties was falling out of fashion. Everyone adored dance music. DJs were dominating the charts and there was less room for acts like us. Record companies loved it most of all, because dance music was so cheap to produce. When everything could be done electronically, it was much less costly for them. It made less and less sense to send your acts out to America, when emerging DJs were making Number 1s in tiny bedroom studios and sending videos over there, without having to pay any airfare.

It didn't help that there was another recession on its way. During the eighties, people were starting to feel as though they had a bit more money in their pockets and they wanted to rush out and buy records. But now, they were worrying about their job security and they were anxious about spending their cash. I think those big periods of upheaval often lead to changes in the music that people like to listen to. After all, when George and Andrew started writing songs for Wham!, they were talking about the dole, unemployment and the anxiety that young people had about finding work. Now, we'd come full circle.

Polydor, like so many record companies, really tried for us. But we seemed to be working twice as hard, without really getting anywhere. We were having increasingly depressing meetings about how to keep the budget down. For our second album cover, *All Right Now*, Pepsi and I thought a bright pink would be the perfect colour: 'It's fun, it's feminine, and it will really stand out on the shelves!' we told a team of executives. They frowned at us. 'We've run the costs and the pink ink is just too expensive,' we were told.

At the beginning, the part of being in Pepsi & Shirlie that had excited me so much was the opportunity for some serious aesthetic expression. This was mad! We had our own Topshop line and we weren't allowed to choose the colour of our record sleeve? The budgets were getting tighter and I felt that the record company was losing faith in us.

Another blow came when our amazing stylist, Suzanne Rose, was getting married – and we weren't allowed to go. We'd been so excited when she'd told us about the wedding.

'Of course, I want you both to be bridesmaids,' she'd said.

'We can't wait!' said Pepsi.

At the time, I had a few good girlfriends that I'd met through Martin and Spandau. I'd become very close to

Steve Norman's partner Gayle and I had a tight-knit bunch to bond with. Pepsi and I were best friends, but we were colleagues too, and I knew that Suzanne's friendship really meant a lot to her as it did to me. Of course we would have walked down the aisle with Suzanne in our old Fila outfits, but because she was a super stylist, we knew we'd get the best outfits to wear.

However, shortly before the wedding was due to take place, our record company had some bad news: 'You've got to go to Japan for some promotion,' we were told. The dates clashed with Suzanne's wedding.

'There must be a way to change this,' I pleaded. 'If we can just put the trip back by a couple of days, we can be at the wedding too.'

Everyone shook their heads. Japan was non-negotiable and there was absolutely nothing we could do. Understandably, Suzanne was devastated and I think quite hurt. We understood. She had done so much to create Pepsi & Shirlie, she was such an instrumental part of our success – it felt seriously wrong to miss her big day.

During that period, Pepsi was my rock. She had stayed by my side when I was in the grip of baby fever, dreaming my way through boring meetings and imagining my future in a beautiful house, with Martin, cuddling my beautiful baby. And then she stayed focused while I was getting increasingly distracted and frustrated, wanting to be with my baby. She asked the right questions, stayed alert and really kept our careers going. But even though Pepsi was on the ball, the signs seemed to be pointing to an exit. I knew my heart was no longer in it, but most of all, that it wasn't fair to rely on Pepsi to keep our momentum going. I was so lucky to be working with such a brilliant, talented woman and I wanted to see her fly. It wasn't fair to her to keep on the way I was, with one foot in music and my head and heart at home with Harley.

Still, I was worried. How could I tell Pepsi that I wanted to leave when all this had been my idea in the first place? I was the one who suggested that we do this after Wham! On one hand, I was certain that she would go on to even bigger, better things. She was gorgeous, she had her fabulous, big Shirley Bassey voice and she had real range. She could keep making pop records, or create music with a soul or RnB sound – or do something completely different. I believed in her, totally. But I knew how much effort and work she had put into our joint careers over the last few years. Surely I'd be letting her down? In a way, it felt worse than dumping someone. More than anything, I wanted our friendship to survive. I couldn't bear not to have Pepsi in my life anymore, but I couldn't face any more travelling or recording and being away from my family either. What was I going to do? I had to find the right moment and the right way to talk about this – and there was never a good time.

We were at yet another glamorous party, surrounded by celebrities, loud music, shouting and cheering. Everyone was having fun. I knew I wasn't in a good way because I'd never felt less like storming the dance floor in my life.

'Peps, I have to tell you something,' I blurted out, grabbing her elbow and dragging her into the bathroom. 'I can't do it anymore. I can't be in Pepsi & Shirlie, I need to be with Martin. I'm so sorry ...' I started to tear up.

Pepsi gave me the biggest hug: 'I know, Shirl. I get it. I was expecting this to happen. You need to go and be a mum,' she told me.

I couldn't believe it. I was so scared that Pepsi would be upset, but I think she knew me better than I knew myself. She got it, she got *me*. I thought that Wham! ending was the least acrimonious music split in pop history, but this might have the edge. Just two girls, crying in the loos at a party, hugging each other and wishing each other luck.

I was worried that we might have to finish promoting the new album, but I think by that point, the record company didn't mind calling it a day either. Perhaps, if my heart had been in it, we would have fought a little harder, but our sales had been declining and to be officially relieved from my pop duties felt like a relief. Martin and Gary were celebrating the success of *The Krays*. The eighties had been our music decade and now it was time to take a break.

After 10 years of working to the schedules of tour managers and concert promoters, now I could work to the schedules of two of my favourite people: Harley and Martin. I could do normal Mum things. I loved walking with Harley, pushing her around Highgate Village in her stroller, seeing her delighted response to the wildlife on the Hampstead Heath. She was so happy and sweet-natured.

I don't think she missed trips to the studio. But Martin's acting career was really starting to take off. He had actually acted before Spandau started. He'd worked with Anna Scher – his parents had scraped up the money to send him to her famous Islington after-school drama club – and showed real promise, earning roles in acclaimed TV series like *The Glittering Prizes*. It made sense for him to return to that world and his performance as Reggie Kray was getting him all sorts of exciting auditions.

Martin was regularly flying in and out of Los Angeles, and whenever we could, Harley and I would go out there to be with him. George had a house in the heart of Beverly Hills and we loved to stay with him and relax. George's career was going from strength to strength. At the time, he was taking America by storm, so it was handy for him to be based out there. But when you're as famous as he was, it's hard to make new friends. Of course, he was close to lots of people in the music industry, but I think he really liked having me bring a little bit of Bushey Meads energy to Hollywood. We could just chill out and be together. George adored Harley, too. He knew how much I'd longed for her and he was a loving, doting uncle. (One of my favourite funny memories is of Harley, when she was a little bit older, being taken to see a George Michael concert at Wembley. 'But how do all of these *other* people know him?' she asked, confused.)

I'd been to America more times than I could count, but this felt like the first time that I was really, really experiencing a place and enjoying how much fun it was to hang out in the land of swimming pools and sunshine. When I was back in London, I missed Martin like crazy. I was so proud of him, and so excited for him, but sometimes I felt frustrated too. My plan had been to quit music and be at home with my husband and my baby but we were still sometimes separated by oceans and spending all of our money on flights and phone calls! (Another shock was that when we had record contracts, we never actually saw phone bills or hotel bills. Ultimately, any money a group makes has to pay for these things, but the record company takes care of the bills in the first instance. When Martin was auditioning, he had to pay his own way.)

So, life wasn't exactly normal, but it was close enough. I felt as though I was finally growing up and getting everything in order. In 1992, everything changed again. Even though it had taken me years to get pregnant with Harley, it felt as though I blinked and Roman was on his way. It was the loveliest news. Understandably, I think Martin had been a little bit nervous about fatherhood the first time around but during my second pregnancy, we were both glowing and beaming. It felt as though our little family would soon be complete.

Roman liked Los Angeles so much that he decided to make his first appearance there. Martin had some work out there and we wanted to make sure that he didn't miss the birth, so I came out with him. We were planning to stay with his brother Gary, who'd just starred in the smash hit film *The Bodyguard*. We got off the plane, into the California heat, and prepared to wait in the Immigration queue. Even if you're just coming for a holiday, it's a long, uncomfortable wait. Martin was coming to work – and although he had all the right forms and permits, that meant he had extra queues and extra questions to deal with. He also had a wife who was eight months pregnant and hiding her bump under a vast pile of coats and cardigans. Usually, I never sweat. I could dance on stage for three hours and not end up with so much as a drop of perspiration on my forehead but pregnancy alters your body chemistry and I felt seriously sweaty and uncomfortably hot.

Martin says he started to worry when we were called up to the booth and as I walked – well, waddled – a bead of sweat rolled down my face and fell off my chin. He squeezed my hand.

I just have to get through the next 10 minutes, I thought to myself.

I always found American airports and immigration intimidating – God knows how it feels when you are actually guilty of something! The 'have a nice day' policy doesn't apply when you're in the queue for interrogation.

Years ago, George and Andrew had teased me about my Bushey accent and tried to teach me to 'speak posh', just like they did. I loved how they spoke and I was always conscious of not pronouncing my Ts. If I could 'speak posh' to the Immigration officials and dazzle them with some British charm, maybe I could get out through the other side.

Fortunately, the official didn't notice that I'd gone a funny colour or appeared to be floating in a cloud of coats. However, he did seem to be reading Martin's forms very, very slowly. I'd found reading hard at school – perhaps I should have felt some sympathy for him! But it was a struggle. I just had to remember to breathe. I could see the whites of Martin's eyes. We were both trying to stay calm for each other, but I *knew* I was having a contraction.

Finally, we were stamped and waved through.

'Martin, I think it's ... I think I'm ...' I muttered, as I felt the blood drain from my face.

He could see I was struggling and he was getting worried, telling me to take deep breaths. We made it to the nearest taxi and went straight to Cedars-Sinai, the celebrated Hollywood hospital. Many famous people gave birth there, so Roman and I would have been in *very* good company, but my son wasn't ready to make an appearance just yet. I was having Braxton Hicks contractions – something that happens, often towards the end of a pregnancy, when your womb starts to prepare for the birth with some practice contractions. It's something many women go through. (Now I've learned that dehydration can trigger them and it's typical to feel dehydrated after a long flight.)

Poor Martin! We both thought all of the drama would be limited to a studio set – it wasn't meant to start before we'd left the airport! Roman incidentally is a born performer – technically, I suppose he was performing even before he was born. Luckily, he arrived 10 days later when we'd both had a chance to rest and recharge. It felt magical. The four of us were together, staying with Gary, and with George just down the road. We were surrounded by people we loved and Roman's first days were filled with sunshine. Still, after my son's birth, I was looking forward to life calming down a little. Following our dramatic airport experience, I was hoping that was the last time I'd have to do any dramatic dashes to the hospital. As always, you should be very careful what you wish for ...

A couple of years later, we'd more or less settled in California and our life felt idyllic. I was at my happiest when I was driving with Martin, cruising down a freeway in the sunshine. I was always relaxed. Usually, I prefer to be the person behind the wheel, but I was always happy to be in the passenger seat when I was beside my husband. We'd been married for six years, but I still felt like a newlywed – especially because living in LA really agreed with Martin. Because of the demands of his work, he had to look good. I thought he *always* looked good, but now he was tanned, fit and visiting the gym almost every day – he'd never looked better. We both felt happy and healthy too, thanks to all of the swimming and sunshine.

Even though I've never been a person who goes in for big public displays of affection, when the two of us were alone in the car, I behaved like a teenager. I always wanted to put an arm around him, or I'd reach over to rub his head. And that was when I found the lump.

'That's weird, that wasn't there before,' I said when I felt something small, but solid at the top of his skull.

'Maybe it's an insect bite or something?' wondered Martin.

'No, it's hard, it's as though the bone has changed. Maybe you should get it checked out?' I said, slightly concerned. I was the worrier in the relationship, but even I knew that after Wham!'s awful trip to China, my anxiety levels had skyrocketed and there was a good chance I was fretting over nothing. Martin told me he'd get it checked out, but I think it slipped his mind. He felt happier and healthier than ever – surely his head couldn't just change shape?

We came home to London for Christmas, to spend time with our family, and I kept an eye on the lump. Was it growing, or was it just my imagination? It was hard to tell whether Martin's head was changing, or whether the changes were all in *my* head! And there was so much to feel positive about and be grateful for. Frank and Eileen, Martin's parents, were staying – sweet, kind, gentle people who I adored. Harley and Roman couldn't work out whether they were more excited about seeing their grandparents or being visited by Father Christmas. It was a magical moment and I didn't want to spoil it by focusing on my fears. Surely there was nothing to worry about?

Martin was filming *The Outer Limits* in Canada, so he flew back out, while I stayed in London. It was nice to be home again and get into a routine. Harley and Roman were both young, adorable and constantly getting into mischief. Harley was at school, making new friends, and she'd come back full of questions and pictures for the fridge. Roman was now walking, talking and climbing around, treating every piece of furniture in the house as an opportunity for an adventure, or an assault course. This was the family life I'd dreamed about and I loved it – but I felt exhausted. As long as I was focused on making sure the kids were clean and fed, I didn't have time to worry about Martin.

However, when he was filming, Martin had realised the bump on his head had become unignorably, alarmingly enormous. He came home and saw his GP.

'This sort of thing is usually a calcium growth but we'll refer you for a scan,' the GP explained.

So when the phone rang, on a chilly, grey afternoon, my head was full of thoughts of dinner, and the dishes, and doing the school run. I was a typical busy young mum, always attempting to do several different things at once. Roman was chatting away to himself and I had one eye on him, hoping he wasn't going to attempt any acrobatics or escapology.

'Hello?' I said, briskly, hoping it wasn't a telesales caller.

'Shirlie, it's me. The scan showed that I have a brain tumour. I need to see a brain surgeon,' I was told.

A brain surgeon.

Martin and I spoke on the phone constantly when we were thousands of miles apart, but even though he was just up the road, in another London postcode, he had never sounded so far away. Was he completely spaced out, or was I in shock? It was probably both. The next day, I drove him to the hospital. Martin's parents stayed at our house to look after Harley and Roman. I still don't know how I managed it – my whole body felt numb. Did I even remember to lock the front door?

215

At the hospital, the consultant explained that they needed to schedule surgery as soon as possible and that Martin had been booked in for the following Monday.

'Surely we need a second opinion? Why don't we go back to California and see a doctor there?' I said, thinking of the GP who had told me that my endometriosis was 'just period pains'. Doctors weren't always right, this had to be a mistake. Now I realise that with shock came denial. I simply couldn't believe what was happening. Not to my family and our life I'd been dreaming about. Martin was the love of my life. I knew I was destined to be with Martin – but I never thought that our destiny involved this hardest and scariest test.

Waiting for Martin's operation might be one of the greatest challenges I've ever experienced as a mother. I focused all of my energy on staying as calm as I could for Harley and Roman. Inside, I was screaming and crying, but as long as I was awake, I had to pretend that there was nothing to worry about. Even though they didn't know it, they helped. They were so funny, curious and love-filled that they forced me to live in the moment, with them. I didn't want to think about a future when Martin didn't come back from hospital, but a tiny part of me was trying so hard to make sure that our little family had a good weekend together. They knew Daddy had hurt his head, but the clever people at the hospital were going to make him better.

I think the shock of the news was still producing plenty of adrenaline and that allowed me to carry on and go into autopilot. I couldn't bear to think about the worst-case scenario. How could I begin to tell Martin just how much I loved him and how much he meant to me? It would have felt like tempting fate.

That Monday was one of the longest days of my life. Unable to concentrate on anything, I couldn't read, or watch TV, or eat. I just paced the kitchen, trying not to stare at the phone, waiting, hoping and worrying. Martin had gone into the theatre first thing in the morning and at five o'clock, just when I was losing my grip, the phone rang.

'Martin is conscious,' said the consultant. Relief coursed through my body like lightning. 'But the operation took much longer than we expected it to.'

The surgeon had removed a tumour the size of a grapefruit.

Thank goodness for Frank and Eileen, who came to the hospital with me. I knew they were heartbroken too. They were so very proud of their sons. Like me, Martin came from a working-class background. His parents had raised him with lots of love, and not much money, but they had always recognised his talents and done everything they could to support him. In the early days of Spandau, Eileen had run up the elaborate, Edwardian-style shirts that Martin and Gary wore on *Top of the Pops*. They had cheered for their sons every step of the way and they were Martin's biggest fans. The three of us were devastated when we saw our gorgeous, golden boy, grey and hooked up to a series of beeping monitors. But Frank and Eileen made me feel that it was OK for me to fall apart for a bit – I'd been trying so hard to be a brave mum and they let me be a scared little girl.

However, I think I grew up so much in those moments. Up until that point, parts of my life had been chaotic and crazy. I'd had so many opportunities and I'd made so many difficult choices, but I thought stress and anxiety were mostly about work. I thought that one of the toughest things I'd ever have to go through was leaving Pepsi & Shirlie, or feeling miserable on tour in China, or even just feeling down in the dumps towards the end of a tour, after months of not eating or sleeping properly. But this was serious, this was the most frightening situation I'd ever faced. And I knew that it was a pain and a heartache that no amount of fame, success or money can protect anyone from.

Martin spent weeks in hospital. And even when he came home, his recovery was far from over. The scan had revealed a second, smaller brain tumour underneath the first one. Whenever I had a spare moment, I was reading and researching, looking for information in order to find out whether there was a way of operating that didn't involve cutting Martin's head open again. The surgery had left him with severe cognitive impairments. He struggled to find his way around the house and to tell the difference between right and left. Sometimes he had seizures in the night. What's so crazy about that time is that I shut everyone out of my life, even George and Pepsi. I knew that they were really worried about me but I couldn't face them at that time.

We had to sell our house. Martin wasn't able to work and I had no idea what to do. Apart from making pop music, I wasn't qualified for anything and now I had two children and a very sick husband to look after. I wouldn't know how to go about applying for a job. How would my CV read? 'Experience of horses, young children and pop stars, can dance for hours regardless of jetlag, good at running up phone bills and finding shops that sell strawberry milkshake.' Also, I think Martin and I both found it really hard to ask for help. We were proud. For years, we'd been able to share our success, pick up bills and treat the people we loved. Pepsi and I had some of our happiest moments when we ordered our mums huge fridges and freezers – really too big to fit in their kitchens. Our work was what had allowed us to be generous and to be the helpers.

Now, I felt horribly vulnerable. I didn't have any success to share anymore. I knew Pepsi was doing some temp work and I felt that she was incredibly brave. I still got recognised everywhere I went, even with a baseball hat and dark glasses on. The tabloids were fascinated by Martin and ran lots of stories about his illness. It was hard not to think that they would have a field day if 'Shirlie from Wham!, wife of tragic Martin' was spotted taking dictation or stacking supermarket shelves. Even though I would have done any of those jobs in a heartbeat if it meant keeping my family safe.

George came to the rescue. He wanted to help – and he was joining me in my research quest, always looking for solutions that might make Martin better. But he knew that the last thing I wanted was a handout. So, for the second time, he gave me a job: 'Shirlie, I've been thinking about fan clubs. I want to go online, the internet is the future,' he said. It was the early days of websites – people were starting to get the internet at home and at work, but we were a long way from the smartphone addicted world we live in now. Honestly, I wasn't convinced it would take off, but George persuaded me to run the website, arranging for subscribers to get exclusive access to tour tickets and new music. Never having sat at a computer before, I had to learn everything from internet to what each icon meant. This was actually great for me as it was a welcome distraction from the worry.

At first, the role was mostly administrative and I was surprised to discover that I had a knack for it. Just as I loved getting into the fine detail of Pepsi & Shirlie shoots, I learned that my interest in visuals was proving useful and I was able to oversee the different elements of the website, ensuring George's fans could access the information they needed in the most appealing way. But then, something unexpected happened. The website featured a forum, where fans could speak to each other, and it was my job to moderate and write replies when necessary.

I knew that he was beloved and that his many fans were intense, passionate people who were moved by his work but it was utterly humbling to discover just how much they cared and also that George's music was helping them through the hardest parts of their lives. Some of these people turned to his work for comfort during their darkest days.

To my surprise, I realised that I was fast becoming the website's unofficial agony aunt. Martin's illness had changed me. I'd always tried to be kind and empathetic but sometimes, when you're in the public eye, you see the worst in people. I was always busy, always rushing and often feeling as though I had to protect George from the people who were only drawn to him because he was so famous. Also, as I mentioned earlier, Pepsi and I were often approached by people who saw us as the way to get to George and Andrew. I felt shy and easily overwhelmed, and sometimes it was easier to put up a barrier. However, I'd been the recipient of so much genuine kindness – from close friends and family, but also strangers. In hospital, the relatives of other patients had always been ready with a smile, a glass of water, or a reassuring chat, and it wasn't because I was Shirlie from Wham!, it was because I was a woman worrying about her sick husband. I didn't have to do anything or be anyone special in order to deserve their kindness.

So, I did my best to pay it forward. People using the forum were confiding in me and I was stunned to discover that I had answers for them. Separately, they felt vulnerable, but together, we could find strength in each other. Again, it made me realise that I was growing up.

It helped me realise that there was no family in the world like mine. Maybe I'd wanted to have my own family so desperately because I wanted to rewrite the past. I'd think about my noisy siblings, my shouting dad, worrying about my mum, worrying about money and wishing I could live in a calm, beautiful, flower-filled house, where nobody shouted. I'd been so sure that I was alone and that other families were 'normal'. It took Martin's major brain surgery to make me realise that there is no such thing as normal. Every single person we pass on the street has something difficult that they are dealing with. Empathy is the most powerful tool we have. We might not be in exactly the same situation as someone else, but we can understand that they have felt pain, fear and sadness in the same ways that we do.

My son Roman has made *Our Silent Emergency*, a BBC documentary about mental health struggles – especially how men and boys in particular aren't encouraged to talk about their feelings and the impact this can have. In 2020, his lovely friend Joe Lyons died by suicide. Joe came for dinner, shortly before he died. I remember thinking how glad I was that Roman had such a kind, funny friend and wishing we could find a great girlfriend for him. Usually, if someone is sad or upset, or struggling, I can spot the signs and pick it up – but nothing about Joe's demeanour made me worry. This really brought home to me just how much we encourage people to hide their feelings and bury them.

I honestly believe that talking can save our lives. Many people have told me that hearing me talk about Martin's illness brought them comfort and relief when their loved ones have been ill. I think social media can be a complicated tool. On one hand, I realise that for some people, it makes them feel the way I did when I was a little girl, looking out at the world and seeing everyone else's 'perfect' lives. But on the other, it connects us in a way that we have never been connected before and gives us a way of offering comfort and support to each other when it's hard to ask.

Miraculously, George found an American surgeon who was able to treat Martin's second tumour using a stereotactic radiation machine – a sort of laser. Even better, the machine wasn't in America, it was down the road in St Barts Hospital. Physically, Martin was on his way to making an unprecedented good recovery. I liked to think I could manifest the good things in my life and make my own luck, but this scary situation had been beyond anything I could manifest and I felt so lucky that Martin was getting better. However, mentally, we were both shaken. All of my loving, nurturing instincts were stirred, but I knew that no amount of loving and caring could give Martin what he'd lost – his confidence. It would come back, over time, but this experience had changed us both and made us much more aware of our vulnerability. However, I never stopped believing that Martin was my destiny, or that we were meant to be together.

Looking back, I wish I could tell Past Shirlie to be a bit kinder to herself and to give herself a bit of a break. I tried so very hard to be strong for everyone and to hold everything up, but it was just as important to let myself be sad and scared. I didn't have to know all of the answers, I just had to take every day one minute at a time.

14

Pepsi – In the Eye of the Storm

For 10 years, my life was go, go go! I circled the globe. I loved being busy, I always had somewhere to be. Sometimes it was stressful, sometimes it was overwhelming. It was always exhausting. But I've always been a grafter and work is my happy place so looking back, it's no wonder I struggled so much when everything stopped.

Shirlie and I both believe that anyone who has a pop career should be given some sort of mandatory therapy. Most of the people in the music industry experience their biggest successes when they're quite young. When I went on my first ever tour with Wham! I was still growing up. In some ways, those experiences forced me to mature very quickly. I learned to get on with everyone, to squeeze a last hour out of a day when I was completely drained of energy and to say 'hello' in umpteen different languages. But I missed out on some of the important basics. I knew how to put a wash on and how to pay my council tax, but getting into a routine of normal adult admin was a shock to the system. I always relied on our management to deal with these mundane but important issues. After a tour, I'd crave my own company because it was such a novelty to me – and even then, after an hour or two of being home alone, Shirlie or George would ring to make a plan for the evening. For years, I'd been so busy, I could barely hear myself think, but when Pepsi & Shirlie was no more, I suddenly had endless alone time and I felt lost.

I'd been so excited about recording our second album, *All Right Now*. We started to make the record out in Los Angeles, a city I loved. At the time, LA was filled with Brits who were hoping to make it in Hollywood. As well as seeing George, who was doing really well out there, Shirlie's husband Martin was out and about auditioning, as was his brother Gary. There was a lovely energy and a sense of community. Also, many of the actors were at the beginning of their careers and we'd leave them sunbathing by the hotel pool, waiting to hear about auditions. We had work to do and that felt like a privilege and a sign of success. I didn't mind being stuck in a dark studio, missing the sunshine – I was making music, which is all I had ever wanted to do. However, I could tell that it was hard for Shirlie – and Harley. Harley was such a good, sweet-natured baby, but she struggled with the heat, the time difference and the long days. She was only a toddler and Shirlie and I both believed we could make the set-up work. After all, there were two of us and I could always tag in when Harley needed a cuddle, but we were stressed and I think poor Harley picked up on some of that stress.

At the time, we were friendly with a producer called Ian Prince, who was based in LA and had done some work with George. Polydor, our record company, were keen to send us out to work with him. Ian was great, but I think he was under a lot of pressure to keep costs down. Shortly after we started recording, there were growing murmurs about an upcoming recession and everyone became very budget conscious – so we finished mixing the album in Shepherd's Bush.

I tried hard to stay positive and optimistic and to make the music sound as good as it could be. It was so important to me to keep our energy up and I've always believed that creative people usually produce their best work when they're happy and relaxed. (That might not be true of classical painters, but I think it's definitely true when you're making pop songs!) However, I think the label's money anxiety really put a dampener on things. We had a brand new A&R man called Glen Skinner and I know he was determined to do his very best for us but he was caught between a rock and a hard place. When we were told that we couldn't do what we wanted because the label wouldn't pay for it, Glen was the bearer of the bad news. And when we were upset and frustrated with the label, we gave him an earful.

For me, it's always been incredibly important never to be a diva. I've always understood that when you work in pop, you're surrounded by people who work just as hard as you do. A Pepsi & Shirlie record wasn't just a Pepsi & Shirlie record – from the songwriters to our amazing stylist, Suzanne, there were tens, maybe hundreds of talented people making vital contributions, even though we were the ones with our names on the sleeve. I know that if I'm tired and fed up, everyone else is probably tired and fed up too. Whining and complaining has never been my jam, I like to get my head down and get the job done.

I will admit that I've had occasional diva moments, but I can count them on the fingers of one hand. One diva upset happened in a New York diner when I was with Shirlie. We'd been busy with interviews and appearances all morning and dashing from place to place without time for so much as a cup of tea. Even though I'd been feeling fine, I went from zero to *starving* the second my body registered the fact that it was long past lunchtime. 'Oh, look! Welsh rarebit!' I said, pointing at the menu. My body was flooded with longing. Home felt very far away and I craved cosiness. All I wanted in that moment was some melted Cheddar and a dash of Worcester sauce. My need was so intense, it felt as though I was experiencing a brand new emotion. However, when it arrived, it wasn't in the same family as Welsh rarebit. Not even third cousins with it. It was strangely fluffy – a cream cheese, Philadelphia-type spread. Technically, it was cheese on toast in the way that a tomato is technically a fruit.

At this point I'd been to America a few times and I should have known better. The joy of being in the US was having the chance to eat all of the food that was hard to come by back home. Waffles and maple syrup! Hershey's Kisses and Twinkies! All the Pepsi I could drink! We knew that British classics were usually served with a 'twist' and not to pin all your hopes on getting a mug of Tetley's tea with normal milk, or beans on toast. But then, the sight of the American Welsh rarebit was enough to reduce me to tears. I didn't storm out or flip the table, I just pushed my plate aside and muttered, 'I want to go home.' I knew my mum would be horrified if she heard that I was wasting food. Right then, I would have given anything in the world to be back in her kitchen and have her tell me off. This diva moment might not seem much, but it's those simple things that can push you off the edge – hard cheese, not soft cheese!

But those moments were rare and usually, they were simply a symptom of being on tour, tired and miles from home. The studio was my happy place. Still, it was becoming increasingly clear that the second album just wasn't coming together as we'd hoped it would. There seemed to be mounting pressure and tension, less room to experiment and have fun. Did we need to update our sound to reflect the DJ-led chart trends, or did we need another 'Heartache' – a banger of a single – to recreate the impact of our biggest hit? I was trying so hard to see the good, but Shirlie and Glen seemed to think we'd lost the magic in the mix, almost before we got started. When I heard them gloomily listening to a playback and saying, 'That doesn't sound great, I wish we'd tried a different tempo,' I was so fed up that I walked out of the studio – they were so critical.

Admittedly, when I think of a 'diva moment', I think of an icon like Billie Holiday, or my beloved Shirley Bassey, getting out of a limousine while an assistant fetches their fur coat. Divas have power. But then, I didn't feel as though I had any power at all. I'd been singing my heart out and working as hard as I could, and even Shirlie seemed to be losing faith in us. We've talked about it since – she doesn't remember me walking out – but now I know she felt so torn and was struggling to meet the demands of music and motherhood that she was struggling to find any positive energy. If the music industry itself had been different, and the label was able to really get behind a pop act, we might have been carried along by waves of momentum. Because we'd been part of Wham!, we'd been spoiled a little bit. We knew how it felt to be on an upward trajectory and be surrounded by people who believed you could only get bigger and better, but, just like many of our pop contemporaries, we now had to deal with a downturn.

For a while, I did my best to keep us both buoyed up. Shirlie wasn't just my best friend, she was a sister to me – she was my family. Harley was my family, too. I'd been there, fretting, when she was suffering from endometriosis and passed out with pain on tour. I'd held my breath and held her hand for every period, and every hopeful moment, and watched her despair and eventual joy as she waited to have Martin's baby. When she finally rang to tell me she was pregnant, moments after taking the test, I felt so euphoric and delighted that I ran around saying, 'We're pregnant!'

Shirlie had always been the one to make sure I never missed out on any of the limelight. On shoots, during interviews, she'd be the first to share the stage and the space with me. Once Shirlie is on your side, you have a friend and an advocate for life. Admittedly, she could be a tiny bit bossy, but never, ever ego-driven. When she bossed me about on shoots ('Wear this! Show off those lovely boobs! Look at your tiny waist!') it was because she wanted me to shine.

So when she was juggling the stress of work with being a new mum, I wanted to pick up the baton. In meetings, I'd do my best to show up for both of us, knowing it was my turn to keep things afloat, making sure that I asked all the right questions and trying to make sure we retained our original vision and identity. We could be pretty, pop and punk at the same time, representing something for all the girls who loved music, dancing and dressing up, and wanted to feel feminine without necessarily wearing high heels.

But over the course of recording the second album, everything felt harder and harder, and my energy ebbed away. Originally, we'd wanted to make Pepsi & Shirlie happen because we'd been offered so much creative control. Now, it seemed as though fate was stepping in and starting to dim the lights. Everything came to a head at one of George's end-of-tour parties. Shirlie took my hand, and said, 'Peps, there's something I need to tell you.' I think I knew what she was going to say before she said it. The two of us were almost crouched in George's tiny loo, the door locked, while the bassline of the music pounded around us.

'I can't do Pepsi & Shirlie anymore!' she blurted out.

When I looked at my beloved friend, I could see the stress and anxiety on her face. We'd been on the most incredible journey together but now it was time for us to try different paths, at least for a little while. I hugged her hard. I think I'd known it, on a cellular level, for some time, and I knew it was nothing to do with me, or with us. Her life had changed dramatically and she needed to be with her family. I knew she had been unhappy for a while. The best gift I could give her was to accept the news with grace.

With hindsight, it's easy to be philosophical about the way life ebbs and flows. The trouble is that when your life has been nothing but flow for a while, it's really disorienting when everything ebbs. Our parting with Polydor, our record company, was almost as straightforward as my split with Shirlie. They were happy to let us call it a day. We continued doing PAs and we now had a feisty female manager – Cheryl Robson – who managed to get us bookings. There was a song off the album called 'Someday' that was written by George which we promoted and before our departure, the record company had invested in a video for the track. We had a couple of sweet dancers who joined us on stage.

It was actually fun doing these shows for a while. We had one of the most memorable performances at a British Army barracks. The audience got so excited to see us, they could not resist jumping the stage. Cheryl had to get us off because the soldiers that decided to get up onstage started para-crawling on their tummies. It was the most extraordinary sight, but we had to get out of the way. The promoter had to calm the crowd down but after a while we went back on and had one of the best PAs ever – the paratroopers couldn't get enough and roared and roared for more Pepsi & Shirlie – it's always nice to leave stage with the audience wanting more.

For almost all of my adult working life, someone else had been in charge of my time. If I had a break, I'd be able to make the most of it because I knew that there wouldn't be long before I had to get back to work. As a musical act, we'd done everything we could to establish some independence. We wanted to be in charge of who we were and what we stood for. As professional women, we were used to being told when to get on a plane and when to go to a studio. I went back to my little apartment and I didn't know what to do with myself. The days blurred and I felt lost and numb. I started to fall into a depression, struggling to structure my days. Who was I? I'd been part of Pepsi & Shirlie. Now Shirlie was Mum – was I still Pepsi? Could I be?

I think that any major loss or ending comes with a kind of grief and perhaps that's what I was experiencing: I felt shocked, confused and burnt out. I was trying to find my feet and make a plan to make music when I got a big, practical shock: Pepsi & Shirlie was, officially, a business. And we had been declared bankrupt.

We had always been quite careful with our money. Shirlie and I had both grown up with next to nothing, after all. We'd seen people spend lavishly and recklessly but while we both loved an occasional trip to the shops, we weren't big party people. When we did go out, we'd dance all night, so it wasn't as though we were racking up enormous bar bills. The most extravagant thing we'd do was buy washing machines and fridges for our mums. But I had been advised to use the money I was making to buy property. Ever since I got my little council flat when I was a teenager, I'd loved knowing that I had a home of my own. My first proper apartment wasn't that much posher – but I was a homeowner. I'd been able to buy somewhere to live, doing what I loved, and that made me feel so proud.

However, the same recession that was causing such trouble for the music industry was creating problems elsewhere too. Changes to the UK economy meant that thousands of people were falling into negative equity and interest rates made it hard to keep up a mortgage on a home that was no longer worth what you'd paid for it. And once Pepsi & Shirlie had been declared bankrupt, that home had to be sold to pay the bills.

It was painful and devastating. Shirlie worried and wanted to help, but I knew she had enough to worry about. Martin had just been diagnosed with a brain tumour and was recovering from a major operation. I think we both felt a complicated mixture of shame and pride. I felt too low to be useful to her and too guilty to help – my problems seemed insignificant, compared with what she was facing. So we stayed in touch, but almost superficially. I think I tried to be strong for her, I didn't want to give her any more to worry about.

Going bankrupt forced my hand. I couldn't afford to stay at home – I had to go out and look for work. I was nervous about my prospects, I hardly had a typical CV and I dreaded being spotted. I could imagine giggling schoolgirls, spotting Pepsi from Wham! behind a reception desk. But I'd just have to deal with it. I was proud of my pop heritage, but I was also too proud not to work.

I stumbled into a temping job at Phillips the Auctioneers in Bayswater. At the time, it was a world I knew little about.

Initially, I was behind the till in the gift shop. During quiet moments, I was allowed to leaf through the beautiful catalogues and books. I learned about art, the natural world. It was fascinating. I had the chance to learn something totally new and I was wholly absorbed. Years later, when I met my husband, James, I'd discover that these new passions of mine were one of the things that connected us. Perhaps this is what happens when you're friends with Shirlie – you start to manifest your future, whether you mean to or not!

In the shop, I rediscovered my confidence. It was a temp job, no one really asked much detail and no one recognised me as 'Pepsi'. Perhaps pop fans didn't tend to visit auction houses, or maybe no one saw me because they didn't expect to see me there, and just thought, 'Oh, she looks a bit like that girl from Wham!' If ever I went out with Shirlie, people knew exactly who I was, but on my own, I had some freedom from my 'famous' life. However, I was shocked to realise that I was good at the work. Because I loved to read about the auctions, I picked up knowledge quickly. If anyone came in with a question, I knew the answer. And I knew how important it was to be on form – energetic but calm, quick-witted but flexible. Years of PAs and interviews and meet-and-greets had taught me how to talk to absolutely anyone and connect with them quickly. Soon, I was promoted!

I was asked to work on the main reception desk for the building. There was something really liberating about being able to lose myself in the job, knowing that I wasn't going to be doing it forever. I think that made me better at it, I was able to relax. I wasn't especially anxious about

'One of my happiest days ever!'

Top left & right: James and Pepsi, our wedding day.

Above: Pepsi and James in New Zealand.

Above: James, Pepsi, Shirlie and Martin, St Lucia.

Below: James, Pepsi and Martin.

Top: Harley, Shirlie and Martin aboard Good Expectation, Jus'Sail, St Lucia.

Bottom left: Shirlie and Martin aboard Good Expectation, James and Pepsi's boat.

Bottom right: Shirlie and Martin renew their vows.

Above: Roman, Martin and James.

Shirlie, Martin and Pepsi.

True friends become
your family.

making mistakes, so paradoxically, I didn't make very many. I was truly rubbish at typing, but I was always upfront about that and I quickly realised that being good with people was much more important – that was the biggest part of the job. Again, maybe a little bit of magical manifesting was at play. I think my acting career didn't necessarily start on stage, but behind the Phillips reception desk, where I played the role of Capable Woman Working at an Auction House.

I must have been convincing in the part, because I got promoted again! I was asked to attend a live auction and take telephone bids.

'I'm not sure that I can do this,' I told my boss. 'These people are bidding hundreds and thousands of pounds! What if I make a mistake?'

'You'll be fine,' he replied. 'You're a good communicator and a good listener. We trust you.'

The day dawned and I tried not to let my imposter syndrome overwhelm me. The room was packed, the atmosphere unlike anything I'd ever experienced before. It was nothing like playing to a stadium, it was much more nerve-wracking. You could tell that everyone was filled with nervous energy and excitement, but there was a strange quiet that dominated the room.

My telephone bidder was brusque. 'Hello, how are you?' I said, introducing myself and trying to be as charming as possible. I got a gruff reply of 'Fine.' But soon, I lost myself in the work, waiting for the bidder's lot to be called. He was bidding on painting 22 and the bidding was starting at £5,000 – that's a lot of money today but it was a small fortune in the nineties. I knew that all I had to do was listen carefully and stay as calm as possible. Eventually, the auctioneer banged his gavel: 'To the lady in red, for £45,000.' The lady in red was me! We had won! I got the most brilliant buzz – to be honest, it was much more fun than spending my own money. (Well, I'd been declared bankrupt, I could barely scrape together £45!)

The confidence boost that job brought me was invaluable. One of the strangest parts of leaving a pop career was realising that in some ways, I'd become helpless. I think a lot of artists get used to having everything done for them. Shirlie and I never, ever wanted to become spoilt or assume that people would look after us. In a way, we were lucky with Wham! As the band got bigger and bigger, people were desperate to give George and Andrew the star treatment, but even after we'd played to 50,000 people, we'd still be washing our own knickers in the sink, halfway through the tour. Shirlie and I wanted to keep ourselves grounded and down to earth. We weren't easily swayed by the glamour of it all and wanted to retain some sense of reality. You have to wash your knickers! (It's your mum's worst nightmare, because quite often there *is* a bed-making fairy and you *do* treat the house like a hotel because it is one!)

I didn't miss being looked after, but I did realise that I felt out of depth in so many areas. I had a very specific set of skills – singing and dancing – and I wasn't sure that they translated to anything of value in my post Pepsi & Shirlie life. It meant so much to me to discover that I could be good at something entirely outside pop. I felt my self-esteem start to come back and cut through the fog of depression – I had survival skills, I was going to be OK.

Shirlie was very supportive and very impressed too – 'I can't believe you're doing so many different things,' she said, admiringly. That meant a lot – and while she was supporting Martin, through his illness, I didn't want her to have to worry about me. At the time, I think she had the worst of both worlds. There was lots of tabloid interest in Shirlie and Martin as a couple and perhaps an element of tall poppy syndrome. Shirlie and I had been golden girls, travelling around the world with Wham! In the nineties, George was hounded by tabloids in the UK and the US, with people desperate to speculate on his sexuality. The media interest in his private life was starting to overshadow the interest in the music he was making. It's tragic and toxic, but I think that if you've experienced any kind of success, there's a real collective public *schadenfreude* when you're perceived to be 'failing'. So George experienced horrible gossip. In the tabloids, Martin went from being a pop star and a film star to being a man with a brain tumour. And the end of Pepsi & Shirlie, and our bankruptcy, fitted this depressing narrative.

However, even though our shared career might be over, or at least on hold, our friendship was intact. We all knew that we needed to come through and support each other, and no amount of grubby gossip could stop us from being there for each other. I had my dark days, but there was plenty to put them in perspective. George was mourning Anselmo Feleppa, his partner, who tested positive for AIDS and had died of a brain haemorrhage. Anselmo was a kind, gentle man and George missed him desperately – and immediately after he passed away, we were all worried that Shirlie was going to lose Martin. It's only looking back that I realise how very young we all were to be dealing with that volume of grief and anxiety. I did feel lonely, and I did struggle with my mental health, but at the back of my mind I knew I was lucky to be alive.

Another dear friend who supported and was kind to us all was Connie Filippello. Connie had been Wham!'s publicist and worked with George for the rest of his career. (So many of the people who started working with George in the eighties carried on working with him for decades. I think that says so much about him. He had a gift for choosing talented people to work with and everyone who loved him wanted to be around him; he wasn't given to pop star tantrums and he inspired a lot of loyalty.)

Back in the Wham! days, it was Connie who first introduced me to Buddhism. A kind woman with a gentle spirit, she was always eager to help us in any way and always encouraged us to be our best in any situation. During our downtime, on tour, Connie would teach us how to chant and how to meditate. Buddhism never quite stuck with Shirlie, who was a little more drawn to Christianity. (Perhaps because she had a crush on Robert Powell in the film *Jesus of Nazareth*!) But I'd been to church when I was a little girl and although I loved the singing, I found the experience strict, stuffy and boring. Mass was my mum's thing and it never really clicked with me.

But in Buddhism, I think Connie found calm among the chaos. It's a faith that is ultimately about losing your sense of self and trying not to be controlled by your ego. In the eighties and nineties, it became quite fashionable. Lynne Franks, the legendary PR guru, was famous for practising Buddhism, inspiring Jennifer Saunders' character Edina Monsoon on the BBC comedy *Absolutely Fabulous*. For a lot of people, I think that somewhere along the way, Eastern spirituality became conflated with eighties and nineties materialism but in the world of pop, there was sometimes a little too much focus on the ego. When you're on magazine covers and playing to enormous audiences, it's natural to become dangerously wrapped up in your sense of self and your identity. Gently and quietly, Connie used her Buddhist practice to show us that there was an alternative and that we could navigate this strange landscape without becoming too self-obsessed. Also, Connie understood that life after Wham! and Pepsi & Shirlie was going to feel a little strange.

There are some people who fall away, once you're out of the public eye, but Connie was constantly checking in and making sure I was OK. Often, she'd invite me to parties and events, encouraging me to get out of the house. I tried, and went out every so often, touched by her kindness but most of the time I couldn't face it, or I wasn't in the mood – 'Sorry, I'm tired,' I'd say, but thinking, *and I don't want to be the sort of person who would go to the opening of an envelope*. I didn't love the parties when I was busy working in the music world and now I couldn't face the idea of becoming the sort of person whose only connection to that world was through the parties.

Still, I always loved hearing from Connie and one day she rang with a suggestion: 'Pepsi, they're auditioning for *Hair*, the musical. I know we've talked about acting, why don't you go along?'

I was excited and terrified – 'I've not really done anything like that before, I'm not really sure what *Hair* is,' I protested.

But Connie was very good at playing things down. She knew that if she made a big deal out of the audition, I might be too scared to go – 'It's all very relaxed, just go along and be yourself, give it a try. It's not a traditional musical,' she explained. Strangely, my lack of experience bolstered me a little. My naïvety gave me a little bit of courage. I had no idea what to expect, so all I could do was go along and see. After all, I'd managed to survive – and thrive – as a temp. Connie had confidence in me so I could find some confidence too. So, I headed to the theatre, cautious, confused – but quietly optimistic …

15

Pepsi – Treading the Boards

ENTER, STAGE RIGHT

'PEPSI' – A young woman in her early
thirties takes to the stage. She's
trepidatious. She's performed in
front of huge audiences all over the
world, but this is new. She doesn't
know what to expect. Still, as she
crosses from one end of the stage to
the other, she finds her feet.

DIRECTOR: Do you have any experience
in acting?

PEPSI: No, nothing. Absolutely none
at all. I'm not really sure what I'm
doing here.

Connie had said that it wouldn't be a big deal. She'd told me that I might as well go along and see what the producers wanted. She'd explained that *Hair* is a big ensemble show and that every single production varies, so it wasn't necessarily a case of me being right for a particular part. She believed that if the director saw something in me that they liked, they would want to work around it.

It had been over 10 years since I'd turned up to audition for Wham!, singing my heart out with my bag on my shoulder. Did I feel confident, mature, older and wiser? Not really. In fact, all I had going for me was Beginner's Mind. If I'd gone in as Pepsi the Pop Star, I might have lost my nerve and felt too self-conscious and awkward to audition. In that moment I was Pepsi the Grafter, Pepsi the Girl With No Acting Experience But Tons Of Enthusiasm. I was able to relax and see how it went. I wasn't pinning all of my hopes on being discovered, I just wanted to try something new and see whether or not it was for me.

I must have been a little nervous, because even though I prepared a song, I have no memory of what it was. Also, hilariously, I discovered that I was a very bad dancer. Dancing had been my job in Wham! and a much bigger part of my work than singing. When it came to feeling the beat, improvising with Shirlie and generating chemistry with George and Andrew, I was a total pro. But the idea of following very strict instructions, the 'one two three *step*' that the choreographer was looking for, I was hopeless. Still, I did my best and I really enjoyed meeting everyone who worked on the show. I went home feeling really proud of myself for trying something different – at least I could tell Connie that I'd made an effort.

Sometimes I think that when we really, really want things, we get so obsessive and caught up in our longing that it's harder for us to get them. Shirlie's manifesting is different, I think – she can be so calmly convinced of a future wish or goal that she's able to relax when she thinks about it, she's not desperately trying to force anything. As a Buddhist, I try to practise the philosophy of detachment, which means not obsessing over particular outcomes. Buddhism is clear on the principle of cause and effect: if you want to understand your future, consider your thoughts, words and deeds in this moment. The actions you take now or how you speak to yourself in your mind will have a tangible impact on the path ahead. In Nichiren Buddhism, a Japanese Buddhist movement in the Mahayana tradition, there is no grey area: the battle to win over your fundamental darkness, that inherent negativity which we all have, is a battle of light and dark – it really is all in black and white. So, when it came to the audition, I simply went in there and did my best, enjoyed the process and then left the energy of that experience in the room. Because I gave it my all, I had no attachment to the outcome so I wasn't obsessed with getting a part in *Hair*. I wasn't constantly craving a big break and waiting around for the phone to ring – and I think this might be why it *did* ring.

I was called back for a second audition. And again, for a final audition. Even though Connie had done a really good job of making everything sound casual and relaxed, it was becoming increasingly apparent that theatre was a serious business. People I recognised from TV were auditioning alongside me. Paul Medford, who had been in *EastEnders* from the very start (Kelvin Carpenter), was trying out for a role. As was Sinitta, who ended up playing the role of Dionne. Sinitta had a theatre background and seemed very wise and experienced. I remember talking to her while I was waiting to go in during the audition process. She'd ask me, 'Pepsi, do you *really* want to get the part? Do you *really* want this?' She knew how tough and competitive the theatre world was and she was passionate about getting the part. I shrugged – 'Well, you know, if I get it, I get it,' I replied calmly.

I wouldn't be there if I wasn't keen, but I didn't want to lose my mind over it.

Deep down, I knew I was going to give it my all – but I didn't have anything else to give, so there wasn't any point in worrying. The dance auditions were difficult and I remember one girl stumbling out in tears, totally distraught. I went to comfort her. 'I just want the part so badly,' she sobbed. I was so moved to see that the theatre brought out this much passion in people, but I realised too that this hunger and this desire could make them dangerously unhappy. Because I didn't have a theatre background, I was unaware of how hard it was for so many actors. (Later, I'd learn an old joke: There are only two times when actors complain. When they're working, and when they're not working.) But I was so, so overjoyed when I finally heard that I got the job.

Hair is pitched as something between a traditional musical and an onstage 'happening'. First performed in

1967, it's all about free love, harmony, drugs, protests and counterculture. It was also revolutionary in that even though it was first performed off Broadway, it became one of the few early Broadway/West End shows to include a racially diverse cast. The structure of the story is loose and because it's designed to be performed at any time, all over the world, producers and directors have the freedom to rewrite the story and even create new cast members. So, Connie's prediction came true: I was cast as 'Pepsi' and I really had the freedom to make the role my own. I was also asked to understudy the female lead, which I loved. It gave me such a confidence boost, without any pressure to be perfect. Once again, I embraced the opportunity to learn – and I learned so much.

I loved the rhythms and rituals of rehearsals. Every day, I had a routine and a purpose. Physically and mentally, I was completely engaged and challenged, and I could lose myself in the work. Because so much of *Hair* is about togetherness and performing as an ensemble, there was a real sense of camaraderie among the cast too. Theatres are magical places and The Old Vic is an iconic theatre to work in. It's been a theatre, in one form or another, since 1818. I was working in the same place that Laurence Olivier and John Gielgud had performed! In a strange way, it took me back to that very first Wham! tour too. Being backstage, waiting in dressing rooms, admiring old posters and being enchanted by the unique mix of the shabby and the grand.

Famously, *Hair* features full-frontal nudity. I knew that this was going to be a challenge for someone as body conscious as me, but there would be nothing grubby or creepy about it – everyone has to get naked in the show. This is a huge part of the philosophy of the musical, celebrating equality and the beauty of the human body. Still, I felt nervous. Figuratively, I was millions of miles from the workmen who harassed me on the street when I was a young girl, but on difficult days, I could still hear their voices in my head.

However, the directors worked so hard to establish genuine intimacy and connection among the cast. As well as practising our lines and dance steps, we spent a lot of time learning T'ai Chi, a form of 'moving meditation'. This made sure that we were in our bodies, rather than our heads, and it helped us to communicate with each other physically. T'ai Chi was a great leveller and every cast member came to it as a beginner, more or less. I think it made me realise that experience is not the be-all and end-all: trying something new can inspire you to approach everything in your life in a fresh way.

When the day arrived, my nerves were tempered by excitement. Every day of rehearsal had been different and I kept discovering new sides to myself. This was a chance to honour my curiosity. I had no idea how it would feel to get fully naked on stage. I'd never, ever done it before. But I was a different woman to the one who had walked in and feared her lack of experience might hold her back. I felt strangely brave. Also, I wanted to honour the spirit of intimacy that the ensemble had built together. The stage was set circular, so there were seats at the back of the stage, so I decided to turn my back on the audience out front in the main auditorium and let some of the cast and the seated audience at the back be my audience instead. It made me feel powerful and part of a collective. A sheer, silk curtain fell almost immediately and the lights went down. So we didn't really see much of each other – but the audience did get a glimpse of my boobs and bum!

To my surprise, it wasn't scary at all. It felt cathartic, I could be totally free. It was everything I needed at that point in my life, and the release felt joyous. Maybe it's because, when I worked in pop, I was aware that there is so much window dressing, pretence and artifice. Shirlie and I never really fell into that, but we were aware of all the bluster and swagger that so many people hid behind. On stage, there was nowhere for anyone to hide, but it wasn't exposing, it was liberating.

I'd been on a long journey with my body and I'd finally come home. I had the loveliest response from the audience, too. I felt strong, powerful and confident, and I think that's what they responded to. They sent me letters, telling me how beautiful I looked up there, and I knew it was my attitude and energy they were seeing. Some sent me little ornaments shaped like the Statue of Liberty – I think that's what my posture and stance reminded them of. And, because *Hair* is *Hair*, quite a few of them left me envelopes with reefers in them! I've never been a smoker, but I loved the gesture and I was delighted they came to celebrate free love, self-expression and the spirit of the sixties.

For me, it felt like an evolution and a revolution so it was so important to me that my friends came to support me on the first night. I wasn't really nervous about the show going well, or remembering lines or stage directions, but I really, really wanted my group of friends, which included Shirlie, Martin and George, to come along and enjoy themselves. I'll never forget seeing their faces beaming on the front row. I was so proud of the work we'd made together – it was our legacy – but this was a Pepsi moment. It was the first thing I'd done by myself, without Shirlie and without Wham! I longed to make them proud of me. Without a doubt, those three clapped the loudest, and for the longest.

The next day, George and I were on the front page of the *Evening Standard*, with a story about how he'd come to watch my performance. That made me so proud, too. Shirlie and I had always joked about our role in Wham! and being 'the cherries on the icing on the cake', but when I was in *Hair*, I was the cake! I was starting to establish my own identity and I didn't feel lost anymore. I was beginning to figure out who I was – a strong, confident woman, who was ready to show herself to the world. Literally.

As my confidence returned, I felt ready to go back out into the world again. I even started to enjoy the parties, making a brand new set of friends. For years, I'd been part of a very close-knit group of people who knew us best. We'd been travelling together so much that our colleagues and crew became very close to us. We were never really in the same place for the same time for long enough to break away and make new friends.

Certainly, in Wham!, people were so fascinated and captivated by George and his fame that Shirlie and I felt quite anxious about new people getting to know us. Sometimes they saw us as a path that led directly to him – they didn't want to get to know him, they wanted to 'collect' a celebrity acquaintance. Instinctively, we kept the circle closed. I think Shirlie also felt this way about Martin, at first, because of his fame and then she wanted to protect him from the public when he was ill. He then took on the role of Steve Owen in *EastEnders* and I think that millions of people felt as though they *did* know him, because he was in their living rooms, several nights a week.

But when I started acting, I had the space to meet new people and to be friendly and curious about them. Shirlie was still my closest friend, but she was busy bringing up her young family. It was time for me to enjoy a little freedom and independence, even using the skills I'd honed at Phillips. I realised that in order to work on different productions, with different casts, it was really important to establish quick connections with everyone. My Wham! gang would be my friends for life, but I started to appreciate other kinds of friendships too. You can become very close to people over a short period, because life throws you together during a particular time; you usually stay in touch, but you don't remain in each other's lives in the same, intense way. And that's OK.

One acquaintance I made during those times was the Australian-British singer and actor, Natalie Imbruglia. She'd moved to London and we had lots of mutual friends, so we were always bumping into each other. She was great fun – kind, generous and always up for a laugh. She wasn't starry or intimidating at all, but I became slightly shy when she started dating David Schwimmer.

Like pretty much everyone who had a television in the mid-nineties, I loved *Friends*. It was my favourite programme. Shirlie and I both adored it and we'd talk on the phone and share our favourite lines – it really made us laugh. Although we'd seen plenty of American sitcoms on TV, we'd never seen anything that we'd related to quite so hard. It really captured the essence of being young and wanting to have fun, while worrying about what the future might hold. Every single scene set in Central Perk made me so happy, because it reminded me of our early days of Wham! and how we'd tease each other and have endless debates. Andrew was the cynic, Shirlie was the spooky one, George had all kinds of clever, contradictory theories – and I'd be the peacekeeper. Watching *Friends* felt bittersweet, because it made me feel so nostalgic for my own youth, but it also gave me a chance to travel back in time and remember some of my happiest days.

So when Natalie brought David to the Groucho Club, I was completely starstruck. This was something that rarely happened to me. I'd performed onstage with Elton John and been out to the same clubs as Boy George. Jaye Davidson, my old hairdresser, was an Oscar nominee. I wasn't easily phased, I usually kept my cool, but a little voice in my head kept whispering, 'Ross is in the room! Ross is sitting on the sofa! Ross is getting up to go to the bar! Ross!'

'Natalie,' I murmured, trying to sound relaxed, 'could you introduce me to your boyfriend?'

When David came over and said hello, he was every bit as funny and charming as I'd hoped. 'I *loved* Wham!' he told me, before asking me questions about George and telling me some of his favourite songs. I was so thrilled that he knew who I was. Everything was going really well until things started to wind down: 'It was really nice to meet you, Ross,' I beamed.

How embarrassing! But David really did sound like Ross. Obviously, their voices were the same, but all of his expressions and mannerisms were so very Ross-like. In a way, I was too excited to feel awkward about it, but I was nonetheless mortified. Needless to say I've had a few intense encounters with fans and I remember how awkward it sometimes felt. At least now I knew what it was like to be on the other!

Acting came with its highs and lows. As my theatre career started to take off, I had the honour of being cast as Josephine Baker on a nationwide tour of the UK. It was a demanding juicy dream role. Josephine was a truly remarkable woman. She's remembered as a singer, dancer and entertainer, but she was also a French resistance agent and a civil rights activist. There was a topless scene, but after *Hair*, I wasn't afraid – I felt powerful and the staging and lighting were so beautiful and thoughtfully done that I knew the scene would have a big impact.

Initially, everything went really well. I loved having the

chance to use my voice to its greatest capacity. When I worked on *Hair*, I'd learned so much about theatrical choreography that even the dancing wasn't too challenging. (You'd think that it would be easy for me to play a professional dancer, after years of actually doing that job, but it was still a bit of a workout for my body and my brain.) For once, I felt completely confident. I'd worked so hard, I'd pored over my lines and I believed I could play Josephine in my sleep. But then it all went horribly wrong …

It happened during one of my most dramatic scenes. In the play, Josephine Baker is speaking to the people of Cuba about Eva Perón, the First Lady of Argentina (and the inspiration for her own musical, *Evita*). Josephine was inspired by her, and Perón's work had a big impact on what she achieved as an activist. It's an incredibly significant scene and I'm supposed to be rousing the audience with passion and fervour, as though they are the crowd who have assembled to hear my rallying call.

The trouble was, I started to think about what to have for dinner.

It only took a second of lost concentration, that was the terrifying thing. I believed I was so well-practised and rehearsed that I could go on autopilot and let Josephine run the show. I should have known that when my stomach starts to get chatty, it can sometimes shout over my heart and brain. I stood, dazed and frightened, trying to think of my first line. We didn't have anyone prompting us. But the more scared I felt, the more blank my brain became.

What was I going to do?

In that moment, the audience saved me. I've always known that when I'm performing, I'm nothing without an audience – I feed off their energy entirely. If people have come to see me, I want to serve them and to make sure they have the best night of their lives; I've always got so much from them, I want to give back. However, this time I didn't need to do anything. They saw me, lit up, in a power pose, registered my panicked pause and started applauding. They were prepared to pretend it was all part of the show – in fact, I daresay a few of them *did* think that. I felt so humbled, and grateful. Their kindness and generosity dissolved some of my shame and filled one of my hardest moments with love. However, I was aware that I was causing consternation backstage.

'She's forgotten her lines,' I heard the stage manager murmuring.

The great thing about theatre is that you're all working together and a whole team of people were rushing around behind me, preparing to get to the next scene, in order to make my mistake appear seamless. But the worst thing is that you're all working together. When I performed, I wasn't just doing it to make myself proud. I'd act my heart out for the whole ensemble and crew. When I shone, everyone shone. But if I made a mistake, I wasn't the only one who had to deal with the consequences. I wasn't embarrassed for myself, I felt absolutely terrible because I had let everybody down.

My wise friend, the actress Nicola Grier, was also appearing in the show and after the debacle, she came to see me. Not one of my colleagues had mentioned it, but I was spending the day alone, feeling desperately ashamed and humiliated. I think I was in shock, stunned that my brain could let such a thing happen. It wasn't as if I was a new performer, seized up with stage fright. This had occurred when I felt sure of myself and my work, and that was scary. Nicola's no-nonsense, tough love approach was just what I needed.

'Pepsi, you need to get over this,' she told me. 'You're not a doctor, no one has been hurt. This isn't a matter of life or death. It's just a job and you need to get back on the horse.' To reassure me further, she added that every single actor she knew had experienced this at one point or another. I realised that I'd been going through the motions and become too comfortable. Never again would I get distracted on stage, I was committed to delivering the experience the audience had come for.

The fun of theatre was starting to feel a bit stressful, due to the moving around from theatre to theatre. When I'd appeared in *Hair*, I felt carefree, and I was starting to get nervous about the fact that I'd have to start thinking about looking for a new job before the current one was ending. Auditions are a necessary part of the process, but they're no fun and they were starting to suck the life from me. My first big job came because the producer liked me and wanted to build a role for me but that wasn't typical. What *was* typical was not to get a part because of something completely outside your control, like your height.

Here, I have to give credit, again to my old Wham! bandmate and Buddhist mentor, who happened to also be

Connie's partner, Hugh Burns, for introducing me to the musician Mike Oldfield, who was looking for someone to perform the vocals on his upcoming Then and Now European Tour. Hugh had told Mike that I was perfect for the part and luckily for me, he agreed. It was amazing to get back on stage and perform to stadium-sized audiences again, this time as a frontperson. Although Mike was obviously the star of the show, he gave me the space and the opportunity to hold centre stage for certain parts of it. It was a European-wide production that came with its own troupe of team members, another tight-knit family on the road together; familiar, fun yet different from my days with Wham! It was very much a professional commission, this was no youthful high jinx. I took my role very seriously and never underestimated the responsibility that Mike had placed on me.

The tour commenced in September 1998 with a big performance at Horse Guards Parade in Central London. I was over the moon that Shirlie came to see me and stood in the rain while I performed one of Mike's biggest hits, 'Man In The Rain'. In December 1998 I would lose my mother to breast cancer so coming into a new year without her was very hard for me. My last show with Mike in 1999 was on New Year's Eve at the Brandenburg Gate in Berlin, where we brought in the New Millennium. It was a magical night and felt like a proper rock'n'roll ending to the 20th century but my heart was broken with the loss of Agatha, my mother.

After my run with Mike Oldfield, I was offered an opportunity to appear in *The Lion King*. My head said, 'This is a big deal, it's a huge West End show a great chance for you, wonderful exposure ... you'd be crazy not to take it.' But my heart said no – or maybe, 'This doesn't feel right.'

Another role presented itself: a musical called *Leader of the Pack*, a jukebox musical that was going on tour. Maybe it was the idea of travelling again that appealed to me. I was used to moving around from place to place, and after months of feeling lost, I hoped that I could find myself if I stopped sitting still but alas, I was in a relationship too and going on tour was a way of distracting myself from the fact that it wasn't really working. Like every relationship I'd been in, it was good – but not right. I worried that maybe I'd become too independent over the years. Maybe it was me. Shirlie was always so open, and open-hearted, about her quest for love and finding The One. I'd always loved my own company and ever since I was a little girl, I struggled to work out why other girls got so overexcited about boys. I didn't believe in The One – certainly, not for me. But losing Mum had unlocked a yearning for closeness. I'd never envied Shirlie, but I was starting to wish for a relationship with the tenderness and ease that she shared with Martin.

Leader of the Pack is a musical based on the life of songwriter Ellie Greenwich, who wrote songs for the Ronettes and worked with Phil Spector who produced the song 'River Deep Mountain High', my big number in the show. It gave me another chance to play an inspirational, iconic woman. I don't think there can be a performer alive who hasn't been influenced in some way by Tina Turner – her incredible voice and the way she moved onstage. Perhaps there was a special resonance for me when I thought of everything my mum had gone through. Tina had left a violent, abusive marriage and her honesty and courage had given hope to thousands of women in that same position. I really don't know whether seeing Mum's experience of marriage had an impact on my relationship choices but night after night, singing 'River Deep, Mountain High', I reflected on whether I was ready to stop protecting myself from pain and hold out for Big Love. I remember being at the theatre in Newcastle, my head swirling with big feelings and emotions: 'Universe, I really am ready to know what true love is', I whispered to myself.

The Universe was listening. And it had an answer for me in Norwich.

The set required a moving stage. I was singing with two other singers, performing a Darlene Love number. We were on my own little platform, stage left, and a stagehand or technician had the job of moving a series of ropes and pulleys in order to bring us into the centre. In Norwich, I looked over to make sure I was about to be towed – and was stunned to see a handsome blond god in the wings.

Who are you? What are you doing here? I thought.

Usually, the crew of a theatre is made up of pale guys who don't look as though they see much daylight (understandable, when they're working during evenings and matinees, they don't get to go out and see the sun very often!), but this man was *buff* and didn't fit the mould. I learned when we started to chat on the side of the stage that he was between contracts as a yacht captain in the Caribbean.

I'd learned my lesson after the Josephine Baker moment – no man was handsome enough to distract me. So, I'd sing 'River Deep, Mountain High' and give it my all. But my castmates could see that I had an audience in the wings. The Shangri-Las giggled and nudged me. One of them told me, 'That man cannot take his eyes off you.'

Initially, I tried to ignore it. After all, I was in a relationship. It wasn't going brilliantly, but I did have someone waiting for me at home. But the buff stagehand kept watching – and he kept appearing in my dreams. Not wanting to take any chances and confused and frustrated, I asked the Universe again: 'What is going on? What do you want me to do? You'd better show me!' As soon as the thought left my head, there was a knock on the door of my dressing room.

There he was.

'You did a really good show this evening, it was a fantastic performance,' he told me.

I gawped at him. Usually, cast and crew were kept very separate, backstage. I knew it wasn't very easy for him to come to my dressing room, he'd taken a risk. But what did it all mean? He asked me if I wanted to go for a drink. But I freaked out – I couldn't, I was with someone.

'Well, what are you up to tomorrow?' he persisted. 'I'm from Norwich. I could show you around, if you like.'

Now that was fine. A harmless, platonic, sightseeing tour of Norwich. What could possibly go wrong?

We met up at lunchtime the next day and James showed me the beautiful cathedral. He told me about his life. We had plenty of unexpected connections. He had just come back from the Caribbean. As a geologist, he was working for an organisation that was taking American high school and college students on educational yachting voyages through the Caribbean islands. He was, in the best possible way, a geek. He'd just found out that his PhD funding wasn't coming through, so he was stuck for a plan and thinking about going to New Zealand. He'd been out of the country, working in remote, beautiful places, for years. He had zero interest in pop. And for quite a few years he worked abroad so he was unaware that Pepsi & Shirlie had been any part of Wham! He initially didn't know who I was – he just loved hearing me sing 'River Deep, Mountain High'.

Immediately, my connection with James just felt right. As well as being one of the most handsome men I had ever laid eyes on, he was kind, he was curious, and I loved that he came from another world. I loved acting, but I was falling out of love with all the rules and pressures surrounding it. It was so refreshing to connect with someone who saw the world in a totally different way. That was it – he saw the world. When he talked about the beauty of nature, and what he'd learned after years of study, I felt totally transported. I wanted to see it with him and explore it with him. And I hadn't realised how being 'Pepsi' had affected me. For years, nearly everyone I'd met had come with a preconceived notion of who I was. No matter how kind or friendly they were, my pop history created a tiny barrier, a little bit of awkwardness. I hadn't really noticed the effect this had until I met James, who was able to connect with me directly and didn't bring any showbiz baggage with him. This was what

I'd been asking the Universe about – it had been worth waiting for.

Acting had been something I adored. It brought me new opportunities, new friends and growth. It gave me the chance to develop my independence and discover a side of myself that took me by surprise. I'm so grateful that Connie encouraged me to explore that world – and so proud of myself for what I achieved. Not necessarily just the starring roles, reviews, applause and plaudits, although they were lovely things to experience. I'm proud of myself for picking myself up when I was at my lowest and being brave. I'm proud that I managed to stumble through those difficult dance rehearsals and persevere, finding a way to be brave when my new life felt challenging and scary. And I'm proud of myself for getting to know myself well enough to realise I was ready for a change.

Giving a live performance can be scary, it requires gathering a lot of courage. But for me, what took the most courage was what came next. I knew that James was the man for me and so I decided that I was going to live with him in Norwich. However, one of the things I love about him is that he lives to explore and go on adventures. Long after most people go backpacking, I did just that and went to New Zealand with James.

I'd been to Australia before, as a wide-eyed twenty-something on a tour schedule, but this was totally different. Now in my early forties, the idea of travelling with a backpack and sticking to the bare essentials was a shock. James couldn't stop laughing when he tried to lift my backpack and found it was too heavy to pick up. Still, I got into the rhythms of backpacker life, exploring the world with the man I loved and seeing natural wonders through his eyes. It reminded me of my very first trip to St Lucia, with my mum. When everything is stripped back, and you're worrying about the fiddly extras that get in the way of your typical day, you're forced to go back to basics – and you realise just how many riches surround us all, if you stop to look. I'd lived a life filled with premieres and parties, but nothing was quite so exciting as visiting a remote beach and watching a turtle make its way across the sand.

We made a home in New Zealand, a stunning country with some wonderful people. We lived in Wellington, the capital city, where we bought our first house together. It was a small and cosy wooden clapboard place, built in the classic Kiwi style. It had a lovely north-facing aspect, elevated on a hill in the southern suburb of Island Bay. It was a real haven for us, and it was ours. It felt special to have a place of our own. I got a job working with a natural beauty company called Living Nature. I quickly dove into the responsibility of creating vivid and alluring window displays at their flagship store in the centre of the city. I felt it gave me an outlet for my creativity and I loved that the customers got such great results from using the products. On the side I did some singing with local musicians and even enjoyed a few jingles gigs with a local producer that I would knock out on my lunch break in a single take.

We were married in the picturesque seaside town of Kaikoura on the South Island. James and I had decided to send invitations out to our friends and family but were not sure who would be able to make it to New Zealand due to the distance. However, we had friends who lived in Australia, and my dear friend Nicola Grier who performed with me in the Josephine Baker production and our fabulous photographer pal Nick Haddow were visiting Australia, and they accepted the invitation to come. Nicola became my bridesmaid. My family were not able to make it but James' mum Mary decided she had to be there. Unfortunately Shirlie and Martin were not able to attend but they gifted us a beautiful standing mirror which we still have today. Incidentally, Martin and Shirlie had their wedding in St Lucia which I couldn't attend. We both got married on the other side of the world. I suppose at the end of the day wanting to get married is about two people. So for us having some of our special friends and family celebrate our special day was a beautiful bonus.

We loved the pace of life out there, had some good friends and enjoyed visiting exotic Pacific islands such as Tonga and Samoa for our holidays, yet it never quite felt like home. A couple of incidents made us feel very far from those we loved.

James had even been an extra in the *Lord of the Rings* movies and I had performed at a few festivals with local musicians. Yet in early 2004, after three years, we felt our time there had run its course. It had been an adventure but it was time to move on. The year before we left New Zealand I suffered a miscarriage, which left me somewhat scarred with the pain of the loss. I had questions: *Who am I if I'm not a mother? What is my purpose in life now? Or are these just labels we give ourselves?* I had to rediscover myself.

It was hard to talk to anyone about it and up until this day, I don't think I have ever shared this experience with Shirlie in depth. So many women go through this experience and suffer in silence and feel ashamed, I sure did.

With James' support, I managed to move on with my life and we decided to live our life with purpose – but what was it? I now knew I would never be a mother. Soon after my miscarriage, I entered early menopause and all the extra challenges that came with it. At the end of it all, it had given me strength and a real appreciation for life. Watching Shirlie go through her desire to have children, I have come to realise having children is a miracle because not every woman is granted the blessing of becoming a mother, it's a big responsibility not to be taken for granted.

The idea of living in London after the pace of New Zealand did not appeal so we moved to James' hometown of Norwich, where we had met. When we lived in New Zealand, James discovered the power of infrared saunas, which transformed the back pain he had suffered for many years. He found them so effective that he wanted to bring them back to the UK – a business we ran for six years together until 2010 when we moved to St Lucia.

This next chapter in our life was one of serendipity and a leap of faith. One day, I popped into our nearest branch of Hotel Chocolat for a Friday treat and noticed something interesting on the label: 'Cacao from St Lucia'.

That's where I'm from, I thought.

I felt a huge swell of pride as I shared that fact with the bemused sales assistant.

16
Pepsi – Finding Home

What does home mean to me? Growing up, I was never quite sure. Was it West London, a house filled with noise and chaos, constant comings and goings? A place where everyone knew my name – at least, everyone knew *one* of my names – but I was never sure that they really knew *me*, where the rhythms of my father's drinking dictated the days?

Was it the feeling of peace I found in my first little flat, content in my own company as I waited to find out what the world had in store for me? Or was it in a hotel room, with Shirlie curled up beside me, snoring softly? A tour bus, a seat on a plane, a smart apartment? Backstage in a West End theatre? Backpacking on a tiny yacht in the remotest island chain of the kingdom of Tonga, my first house with my husband in New Zealand?

Shirlie and I bonded almost instantly over the fact that we could make any place feel like home. Instinctively, we could see any space and work out how to make it cosy. I thought home is a feeling, not a particular place. Yet, when my husband James and I talked about leaving the UK and where we might live, I was surprised to hear what came out of my mouth: 'I think I want to go to St Lucia, I want to go home.'

Although now, the neighbourhood has changed almost beyond recognition, Notting Hill and West London were a lot like the West Indies when I was a little girl. Of course, London could be cold, grey and gritty, but the Windrush generation had brought the sounds and scents of their island with them. The beautiful, musical patois, with elements of African and French, was the soundtrack of the street. Our local shops sold imported fruit and spices, alongside Walkers Crisps and Fry's Chocolate Cream. And of course, I was surrounded by family. Every other face belonged to an auntie, an uncle, a cousin. Many of the younger ones were born in Britain, like me, but there were plenty of people, like my parents, who had moved to the UK and knew about the warm sea, soft sands and gentle breezes.

The last time I had visited St Lucia, I was in my teens and it loomed large in my imagination, a magical place that didn't seem entirely real. Of course, I wanted to go – but it was like wanting to go to Disneyland, or the moon. I didn't think it was possible. So I couldn't quite believe it when my mother summoned me and said she had some important news: 'Listen to me, I have something to tell you. We're going to St Lucia. You need to meet your family, your grandmother, your Auntie Emma. Your daddy's going to pay for it.'

I frowned. *Really?* My father's track record wasn't great. I was used to him constantly promising trips and treats, only for him to end up in the pub, drinking his money away. This was a man who couldn't get me a new dolly or remember to take me to watch the dog racing. Was he really going to raise the money for a very expensive plane ticket? My hopes weren't high. Worst of all, I didn't want him to disappoint my mum – I was used to hiding my sadness when Dad didn't come through, but I hated to see her hurt.

Still, for once even Dad seemed determined to keep his word. He also had a talk with me: 'This ticket is expensive. I won't be able to pay for you to go again, this is the very last time. I want you to meet the family and I want you to enjoy it!' Because money was so tight, he could only afford a ticket for Mum and me. At the time, my younger brothers didn't seem to mind that I was getting on a jet plane with Mum. Our older sister Tecia and older brother Charleston who were born in St Lucia were busy getting on with their lives in the UK and were happy that I was finally going to see the island they had left behind.

I was so excited – not just about the holiday, but about spending time with my mum. Our relationship was pretty typical: we worried about each other. She just wanted her kids to be clean, kind, decent people who didn't get into trouble – 'As long as you never bring the police to my door, I'm happy', she used to say. I worried about her worrying, especially when it came to my father's drinking, and did everything I could to keep my own worries away from her. Mum had an unreliable husband, young children to worry

about and several cleaning jobs to get to. She didn't even
have time to come and visit my school on parents' evening.
When my mother said she couldn't do something, she really
meant it and I learned to accept it and take it at face value.
All I wanted was for her to be happy and not to cause her
any extra trouble. But now I finally had an opportunity to
see her relaxing with the rest of her family and to really get
to know her.

Mum was in her element as soon as we arrived at the airport.
'You always take new panties on holiday,' she had told me
confidently, and even though there wasn't much cash to
spare, she'd filled our suitcases with brand new underwear.
Queen Elizabeth II was my mum's fashion icon. This was
partly because St Lucia is part of the Commonwealth and
Mum had grown up admiring and idolising the royal
family. Looking smart and suitable mattered a great deal to
her and it was important that we travelled in the greatest
style possible. Honestly, I can't quite remember what I wore
– probably my smartest skirt and a clean jumper – but Mum
was in her good navy suit, a crisp white blouse and a flowery
hat. It was a far cry from the leggings and trainers we wear
on planes today.

Now, Heathrow looks like a smart shopping mall, filled
with glossy brands and bars, but in the early seventies, there
was not much to do at the airport. Still, it was a fascinating
place, full of promise and purpose. I'd never seen so many

people – and quite a lot of them were dressed like my mum! I remember the buzz of murmured conversations, the possibility and excitement in the air. No one took travel for granted, everyone was preparing for an adventure.

Mum was thrilled by every detail of the journey, down to the crockery we used on the plane, square white plates filled with chicken in a creamy sauce. We never went to restaurants as a family, so this was part of the treat. 'No washing up for me,' she smiled and I started to realise just what this break meant to her. Mum's life was defined by duty, but for the first time since she landed in London all those years ago, she could relax and have fun. I was happy dozing and daydreaming about the next six weeks, captivated by the fluffy clouds – and then stunned by the way the blue sky seemed endless. To think that was there, all this time, above the grey.

The excitement fizzed in the pit of my stomach. I was expecting to be shocked by my home country, I thought I might find it strange – like visiting a different world. I wasn't nervous, but I was curious. When the plane finally hit the runway, charging down the tarmac at top speed, I had to bite my lip to stop myself from squealing with joy. It felt like a rackety roller coaster at the funfair. My mum's face was changing, the worry lines at her temples softening and disappearing. I stood up and followed her through the plane and out of the door.

Home.

The first thing I noticed was the scent: earthy, fresh rain and verdant vegetation, coconuts, perhaps. A sweet, creamy flower – new, yet not unfamiliar. It was fresh, but warm, carried on a soft breeze. I didn't know a breeze *could* feel soft, but this felt like a velvet glove against my face. Even though I thought I'd left my cares behind in London, I felt the last bit of city stress drop away.

'Laurie, look! There's your uncle! Your cousins are here!' said Mum, sounding unusually giddy and girlish. It might be a trick of my memory, but here I picture her, still fresh in her blouse and hat, gliding down the steps and waving with her fingertips, just like the Queen.

Everywhere we went, we were welcomed. Our family were so excited to see us. We stayed with my Auntie Emma, my mother's sister. Her house was very simple, but comfortable. She didn't have a TV, so we'd sit together in the evening and listen to the radio. Occasionally, I'd hear voices: 'She's here! She's here!' Then, the island did not get many visitors, and so our arrival was a big event. Local children would come and sit on Auntie Emma's doorstep and simply gaze at me. It's strange – in London, something like that would make me feel very self-conscious, but in St Lucia, I didn't mind at all. In fact, I felt like a princess. I loved that people found my differences exciting. They were kind and curious, and they wanted to celebrate.

Another really special moment happened when I was asleep. Because there wasn't that much space, Mum and I were sharing a bed at Auntie Emma's. It was easy to get used to the arrangement, and in a lovely way, it reminded me of being a little girl spending lots of special time with my mum. When I was tucked up with Mum, I felt safe and warm. One morning, after I blinked open my eyes and as I started to rub the dust away, I noticed that she was gazing at me with real love, tenderness and fascination. It was as though she was at an art gallery, looking at her all-time favourite painting. Of course, I reacted like an obnoxious teenager (well, I *was* 15): 'What, Mummy, *what*? Why are you staring? What's going on? Have I got something on my face?'

She did not break eye contact: 'You were talking patois. In your sleep, chattering away.' She was so proud. Even though I'd been around people speaking in patois from the moment I was born, I never felt sure that I understood it. The gorgeous language sounded like rolling, breaking waves. I knew the beats and the melody, but I didn't think I'd ever be able to work out what the words meant. Yet, after just a few days of being home – in the home I never realised I'd had – it turned out I'd known the language all along.

More importantly, if I got to be a princess, my mum was the true queen. We became the best of friends and great travelling companions. One of my favourite memories was seeing her rush into the ocean, floating and smiling. I know she was kicking up her heels underwater: 'See, Laurie, the water is so warm, it isn't like Margate,' she smiled. Perhaps once a year, we'd all get on a coach and go on a day trip to the Kent coast, with lots of other West Indian families who were missing home and had to make do with the freezing North Sea. Mum loved the chance to have a proper fish and chips supper, but it didn't really compare with the chance to swim in the crystal-clear Caribbean waters.

Seeing my mother relaxing and having fun had a huge impact on me. I'd always been a dreamer, and always hoped and yearned for a life that felt different from hers, and from what I could see around me, growing up. It seemed that you either struggled, worked and did your best to make do – or, if you were lucky, you settled. I had big dreams, and a huge imagination, but no space to express my feelings, and no real role models. No one out there was showing me what might be possible but watching Mum in the water, I felt as though I was seeing joy for the very first time. I didn't have to live a life like hers but if, in the right setting, she was able to put her problems aside and experience happiness, I knew I could do that too. And I needed to make sure that I chose happiness whenever I could, rather than waiting for a once-in-a-lifetime holiday.

Anyone who has ever spent any time in St Lucia will know that time seems to move at a strange pace on the island. In the moment, it stands still. Nothing is hurried, nothing is rushed, every day seems long enough for everyone to do everything they need, with plenty of time to relax. There's always tomorrow and you can trust that the sky will be blue and the sun will shine. But then, you blink and a week, a month or a year has gone by.

When it was time to go, part of me felt as though I'd lived there all my life, but the other part was thinking, 'We just got here! I only landed yesterday!' Still, I wasn't sad to leave and I carried some of the magic home with me. In St Lucia, for the first time in my life, I'd felt special – and I kept feeling special. I'd been on an adventure, I'd been with my people, and I'd been seen and heard. I'd left London as an awkward, dreamy teenage girl, confused, not so confident, yearning for excitement but not sure how to look for it, or where my life would take me. I returned, still feeling like that princess. Not grand or boastful, but relaxed and self-possessed. I admit that I also tried to keep my St Lucian twang for as long as possible and I really wanted to speak like my family.

St Lucia was the beginning of my global journey. I didn't know that I was about to start travelling all over the world but I always vowed that one day I'd return. Over the years, I waited and hoped, as tours and concerts took me across both hemispheres. Every so often, I wondered about going for a holiday – but after coming back from Australia or Japan, the idea of coming home and then getting on another plane seemed like the least relaxing vacation idea. I was so excited and delighted when Shirlie and Martin got married out there, almost in secret, in 1989. Later, we found out that the officiant was a distant cousin of mine, so I had a representative there.

After I met James, I rediscovered travelling and adventure. As a geologist, his work took him all over the world – but when I travelled for work, I was either on stage or in the hotel. To me, Las Vegas looked like Liverpool or Lanzarote. But James' work was different and it took him right into the country, meeting people and studying the land. For him, this was such a great passion that he wanted to keep doing it in his own time too, travelling and exploring as much as he could.

I think I really knew that James was the one when I realised he was the first man I wanted to share St Lucia with. I couldn't have imagined myself there with any other boyfriends. Perhaps, subconsciously, it was connected with family. The island was full of people who loved me and wanted the best for me. On some level, I knew that if I came to visit with a partner who wasn't perfect for me, they would worry. But when it came to James, I felt sure that they would love him too.

At first, we went for a holiday. We loved the sea, the warm breezes and being with my family. When we came back, we planned to go back out as soon as we could. Still, planning another vacation didn't feel right. Before our holiday to St Lucia, James was studying for a master's in Responsible Tourism and with the course you get informed about internships around the world. On our return from our holiday in St Lucia, he was surprised to see a six-month internship position had become available in St Lucia. It was hard to ignore this amazing piece of synchronicity, considering while on holiday we had talked about living in the Caribbean – talk about manifesting your dreams, this was a dream come true.

Soon after moving to the island we created our business Jus' Sail, a heritage sailing company which uses an authentic locally built wooden trading sloop called Good Expectation for laidback sailing charters for tourists. We lovingly restored her and she wows our guests with her grace and authentic island style. However, during the quieter summer months we created a training programme for unemployed youth as part of our commitment to give back to the island. We have trained hundreds of students, arming them with the soft skills they need to navigate life and supporting them as they gain practical knowledge and qualifications needed to find employment. With our local partner organisations and supporters, we provide them with training sessions in swimming (despite living on a tropical island most St Lucians cannot swim and there is no formal training in the curriculum), first aid/CPR, an introduction to customer service and an internationally recognised sailing certification.

Years ago I completed my life coaching diploma in Norfolk so when I was seriously questioning myself about my future and those thoughts of 'if I am not going to be a mother or a performer?' I found my life's purpose. Putting that skill to good use, and helping mentor these young people to gain the clarity and confidence to take their lives forward in a positive way gave me so much energy. We now have graduates who have sailed across the Atlantic, hopped on vessels across the Caribbean Sea to Panama, circumnavigated the Caribbean to deliver a pirate ship to its new home in Honduras, and each time I bump into one of our many graduates and see their smiling faces with their bright and shiny work uniform that they wear with such pride I feel joy. And it hasn't gone unnoticed, we receive amazing feedback from employers thanking us for our efforts in investing in their dreams and future.

It is not easy to raise funds. It takes time and preparation to put in place the right programme. But it has ALWAYS been worth the effort. When we take our students offshore to sail say to neighbouring Saint Vincent and the Grenadines, I am always so happy to see the students' reactions when they see the iconic Pitons come into view through the haze as we sail back home. The appreciation that they express for seeing their home island is something very special. St Lucia is a special place and these young people often really grasp this fact when they see her from the bow of our boat. On a visit to St Lucia over Christmas 2019, Andrew learned about our training programme and our beautiful little training vessel Spica of Dart. He was taken by our efforts and was determined to help in some way. On learning that the boat needed an engine, he helped us and encouraged his friends to do so as well. Along with the generosity of others, we were able to secure a new engine. It's so great when an old friend sees what you are up to and immediately jumps in to support your endeavours.

Now, over 10 years later, we're still there. Every morning, I wake up with the sun. The breeze ruffles the curtain and feels soft on my face as I lie beside the man I love. The air smells sweet and creamy – and now I can identify the flowers, jasmine and frangipani. At last, I know I'm exactly where I should be.

I'm home.

17

Shirlie – Always be yourself

think everyone has a complicated relationship with creativity. We all need to express ourselves and I believe that sometimes we make things that urgently need to be shared with the world – and sometimes it's the act of making and sharing that saves us.

One of the greatest privileges of being so close to George was watching him at work. He was a genius, and to me, it seemed that he was 'downloading' music from the Universe. He made songwriting look effortless, but there was more to it than that. Music was the way that he expressed himself and he had the sort of latent talent that comes along maybe once every hundred years if you're lucky. He didn't just hear a melody or get an idea for a lyric, every single instrument and aspect came to him. I know he worked very, very hard but also, I don't think he would have been able to stop writing music, if he wanted to – the creativity simply poured out of him.

My relationship with creativity is a little different. Growing up, I guess I never saw anyone making art. My soul cried out for some way of expressing itself and I've spent my life searching for ways to satisfy that creative craving. I've been very lucky and found it over a series of happy accidents.

When I was a little girl I had such an amazing imagination. Creation comes from your imagination after all. I realised very early that the first step to unleashing your creative spirit is learning that you don't need to be like anyone else. When I think of how kind and supportive my lovely mum was, shouting back at the boys who made fun of my green hair, I realise she was giving me the confidence to be myself. Being able to respond to your own ideas and emotions is very freeing and that's what she gave me; there were no rules or regulations that stopped me from being creative. And that continued over the coming years: no matter what I did, creativity just kept finding its way to me. It wasn't something I did constantly, but every so often, I'd get a melody stuck in my head and I'd have to get it down.

When Pepsi & Shirlie started, I was so excited to have a creative outlet. When we made the first album, working in the little studio in Kensal Rise with Pepsi and our songwriter, Tambi, I felt that I was coming into my own. One thing that helped me to get into the flow was the fact that we were just left to get on with it. Working in the studio meant that we weren't travelling and I loved being able to go to the same place, at the same time every day, and I didn't have anyone to answer to. No one was constantly accounting for my whereabouts. Now, I realise that this was so vital to discovering that feeling of flow. I loved that it felt collaborative and that there were no right or wrong answers. It was about trying, exploring and seeing what emerged.

It's the same feeling that I discovered when we worked with Suzanne Rose. When I was growing up, I had no idea that there was such a job as stylist, but that's what I found myself doing. Suzanne was so much fun to collaborate with. Some of my favourite memories of Wham! were the times when I was involved in choosing our outfits and picking a 'look' for Pepsi and me. Most of the time, I didn't feel especially confident or talented, but when I was given a creative outlet, I was totally absorbed by the task. I felt completely happy, relaxed and connected with what I was doing and the part of my brain that sometimes felt anxious or self-conscious was silenced.

Martin is a very creative person too. Of course, when he was ill, it was hard for either of us to make any time for art, music or self-expression. We were simply trying to get through a very dark period of our life, one day at a time. Still, Harley and Roman inherited our creative genes. When you have young children, your house is always filled with imagination and they inspired me to start to get into photography. We always had cameras around, because we wanted to take as many pictures of our babies as possible but also because when I was growing up, many people didn't have cameras. I bet that my mum would have been too scared to pick one up even if she had one so, there were hardly any photos of me as I was growing up.

I drove my kids nuts as I couldn't get enough pictures of them. Also, Martin's illness had really brought home to me the importance of memories. Life was fragile and I wanted to capture every happy minute. In fact, my obsession with photographs began when I was little. Whenever I went to someone's house, I'd ask to see their photo albums. I'd be desperate to know what their parents looked like when they were younger and find out as many details as possible about their lives and where they came from. Perhaps I was looking for a blueprint for family life. One day, I dreamed of having a home and family that felt quiet, peaceful and loving – the opposite of everything I had grown up with it. In other people's pictures, I could look for clues and start to work out how to do it.

But as well as the usual pictures of baby steps, birthdays and messy mealtimes, I was filled with an urge to do something a bit different: 'Come on, kids, I've got an idea,' I'd say, herding Harley and Roman outside. My obsession with vintage clothes hadn't gone away. I'd dress them up as Victorian children, sometimes adding wings for a fairy feel. It was a game we all loved – Harley was a budding artist and Roman was a born performer. However, in the blink of an eye, your children turn into teenagers. Even when they are still quite young, they pick up an adolescent attitude and say, 'No, Mum, I'm not coming to the woods with you and dressing as a Victorian ghost!'

Photography was a passion that would not leave me alone. I put my camera down and got distracted by life and its demands – I'd take plenty of pictures of friends and family, but that was as far as it went. Still, one day, I noticed an advert for a photography course at a local college and it ignited a spark in me. Because I'd had such an awful time at school, I felt quite vulnerable and insecure about my lack of qualifications. I still had an awful memory of my brother telling my mum, 'She's just stupid, she'll never get it,' and feeling as though I *couldn't* learn and couldn't try. Well, I really wanted to try. I loved the idea of surprising everyone, studying a subject I already knew I loved and becoming a professional photographer.

The course I'd chosen was for beginners, but unfortunately, the teacher was unavailable and it was cancelled at the last minute. 'There's a foundation course that the art teacher is running, we'd be happy to transfer you onto that,' said the administrator. I didn't know what a foundation course was – a much more intense way of learning that is supposed to prepare you for a degree – but I was really keen to give it a try. After a few classes, I started to struggle though. Every lesson, we'd be given a theme and I'd be so excited to interpret that theme and bring some creativity to the idea. But the tutor didn't seem to like my work. Everything came to a head when the theme was 'boxes'. I'd worked so hard and I was so proud of what I'd made – a truly expressive, Tracey Emin-style image that channelled some of my punk history.

'This is good, but it's not what I asked for,' frowned the tutor.

I felt awful – then listened to him praising another student, a young, pretty girl who had taken a picture of a cigarette box that she had made a lipstick mark on: 'This is excellent,' he told her.

It didn't matter that I was a mature woman, a mother of two children, a person who had grown up and lived an exciting life. In that moment I was five years old again, back in the classroom, fighting back the tears as I struggled to understand what was on the blackboard, feeling confused, frightened and left out, waiting for the teacher to start shouting at me.

Utterly overwhelmed, I walked out. Somehow, I managed to drive home, but when I parked, I couldn't leave my car. I stayed in the front seat, sobbing my heart out. All I'd wanted was to boost my confidence and capture that glorious feeling of losing myself in my passion. I'd believed that I could be arty and I wanted to feel good about what I was making and make it in an environment where there were no wrong answers. I felt panicked, excluded and ashamed. I couldn't go back to college, I wasn't even sure that I could get back into my house.

Suddenly, there was a gentle knock on the window. Martin and Roman had found me in the car. Understandably, they thought something truly terrible had happened.

'They … didn't … like … my work…' I sobbed, thinking about the cigarette box again. I just couldn't fathom why that was 'good' and my work was 'bad'.

With great love and patience, Roman and Martin coaxed me out of the car. 'We think you're brilliant,' said Martin. 'I'm sure that the people at college really think you're brilliant too.'

Not long afterwards, the college called. They had found a tutor who was able to teach the beginners' photography course. 'The art teacher wants to apologise,' said the administrator. 'He thinks you're really good – he was critical because he thinks you have so much potential.'

However, I'd since realised something important: I *wasn't* a scared little girl who had to be forced to go to school, I was a grown-up, a mature, experienced woman who could choose what felt right. And learning in that environment didn't feel right at all. I had to make room for my creative spirit and a classroom simply wasn't the right space for me. My fulfilment would come if I pursued it independently. I was never someone who learned by listening, I had to learn by doing.

I decided that I needed to teach myself how to take the kind of photographs that I liked so I started to play with my camera, experimenting with all of the settings, concentrating on how the images made me feel. They were all quite soft and filled with light. I remembered something I've always known: I need to trust my instincts. During difficult or stressful times, we sometimes stop communicating with our intuition, but it's always there to guide us if we stop and listen for it. It's the most valuable, effective tool we have. Thanks to Instagram, I was able to share my work and the feedback I got from followers made my heart sing. People often observed, 'Your photographs make me feel happy.' This was just what I wanted to achieve. In fact, my love of photography comes from the way that beautiful images make me feel. My world has sometimes felt scary and uncertain, and if I can add more beauty and happiness to it, that brings me joy as well.

Looking online, I discovered the work of an American stylist. I loved her pictures. They had that ethereal, fairy feel – the look I was trying to capture when I was dressing Harley and Roman as tiny Victorians. As a fan of hers, I got in touch and she invited me to come to America to shoot for a magazine with her. She loved my work too and her approval and kindness gave me so much confidence and faith in my ability. Knowing that she liked my pictures dissolved the shame and fear that had built up after that bad experience at college.

As parents, Martin and I both knew that it's vital for children to be able to express themselves creatively, whatever that form takes and we had a responsibility to nurture, encourage and support them. We realised that we never wanted to put any kind of pressure on Harley and Roman to do or be anything and that creativity takes many forms. We didn't want them to feel that they had to go into music and performing. In fact, I don't think any parent who has experienced the music industry would want to push their children in that direction. We never wanted our children to put themselves under any pressure, or to force themselves to succeed at the expense of their sanity. However, we also hoped that they were going to inherit our creative genes that they could tap into to help them in whatever career path they would choose.

Roman and Martin are very similar and Roman has always loved to talk and entertain. He adored school because he could make the teachers laugh. However, Harley is a lot like me. She's so creative, but she doesn't seek out the spotlight and she struggled with school, just as I had done. Although my school experience was an awful one, in a way, I'm so glad that I'd been through it because it enabled me to understand Harley better and give her the help she needed. I could always see how smart she was and explain that she was like me and learned the most when she was doing something, not sitting still, trying to get her head around theories.

I think lots of parents put their children under an enormous amount of pressure to go to university because it's the done thing. We think that we're giving our kids the best start in life that they can have, if they have a degree. But with Harley, I knew she'd be much happier if she started out doing the work she loved as soon as she could. After leaving school at 18, she was a little lost and we had to have lots of chats about the things that she liked or loved doing. Harley had no interest in going to university but like any parent, we were concerned about what she would do in the future. I always told my children that it doesn't matter what you do, as long as you find something that you love doing and do it well. She thought about becoming a photographer and so I got her a camera to start her on this journey. Martin and Harley spent hours together working the camera.

I used to think that if I could give my children anything, it would be confidence. Now I realise that self-belief comes and goes. Some people might be born confident, but most of us have to cultivate it over time and we learn how to do this over the course of a lifetime, having been through all kinds of highs and lows. Something I've learned from Martin is that sometimes, creative confidence follows the creative act. Roman is similar. I don't think either of them leaps out of bed every morning thinking, *I'm feeling so confident that I'm going to do this today.* But their urge to make something, or try something is so overwhelming, the idea of not doing it seems more anxiety inducing than having a go.

A couple of years ago, Martin found himself back in a studio, working with producer Brian Rawling. Martin had been combining his love of music with his love of acting, even starring as Billy Flynn in the West End production of *Chicago*. But my love of music was strictly confined to singing in the house. Also, we had a rule about leaving work outside the front door. Martin's job is demanding – he's never worked a nine-to-five schedule and sometimes he's coming back late from a theatre, or away filming for weeks at a time. We really value and appreciate our family life and being able to relax and enjoy being with our friends and family (and our gorgeous dogs). Our home is our sanctuary, and as soon as we start to get involved in each other's projects, it's not just that it isn't a nine-to-five affair – it becomes a 24/7 obsession. So, when Martin asked me to join him in the studio, it would be an understatement to say that I was reluctant.

After Pepsi & Shirlie officially ended, my experiences of music had been mixed. Some had been really positive. With Pepsi, I'd sung backing vocals on Geri Halliwell's Number 1, 'Bag It Up'. After Geri left the Spice Girls in 1998, she turned to George for advice and we ended up becoming friendly. In fact, I was on holiday with George in St Tropez when Geri left the group. Geri flew to Paris and I met her out there with Kenny Goss, George's boyfriend at the time, to give her a bit of moral support.

Harley had been a massive Spice Girls fan and was so desperate to meet them that I'd asked George as he was appearing on the show, 'Can Harley and I come to *Top of the Pops* with you and you could introduce us to the Spice Girls?' Both he and I were excited for Harley, remembering that feeling of what it feels like when you meet your pop idols. One of my biggest regrets is that I didn't take any photos of Harley with the girls. At that point, they were the most famous group in the world. Because I remembered how intense everything felt at the peak of Wham!, I didn't want to bother them by pointing a camera in their faces – or look like a mad fan myself! Then, thanks to a series of weird coincidences, Harley and I ended up appearing in the video for their single 'Mama'. The director was looking for mothers and daughters to take part and it turned out my cousin was building the set *and* it was being filmed in my friend's studio. At the time, I wanted to be behind the camera, not in front of it, but Harley was thrilled. And I suppose it makes up for the fact that I didn't take any pictures of *Top of the Pops*. So, Harley got to feel like a Spice Girl and we have a beautiful record of that day.

Still, I remember looking at the girls and worrying about them. It all seemed scarily familiar. I think a lot of pop bands burn out so quickly because that level of success seems to generate more and more work, and the pressure on them becomes unbearable and life feels like a trap. What was once this wonderful ride turns into a roller coaster of other people's expectations. So, when Geri left the band, I had a lot of empathy for her. I think George was really touched and flattered that she wanted his advice about what to do next – and Geri seemed very focused.

Not long after that, Geri had asked if Pepsi and I would sing on her latest single that she was working on. I called Pepsi and asked if she wanted to record vocals for Geri and she'd never said 'I'd love to' quicker! It was going to be fun being back in the studio with her, I thought. So, when we went into the studio to record 'Bag It Up', the pressure was off. It was Geri's moment to shine, we thought the single was great and happily, it reached Number 1.

A little later, Pepsi and I were asked to work together again. There was a boom in eighties nostalgia and we were invited to sing at 'retro weekenders' – usually events at holiday camps, where pop acts would come and perform some of their biggest hits. It was a bit of a shock to the system, to say the least. Pepsi and I had always loved performing because we got such a high from the audience response. We'd almost peaked early. Wham! hit the ground running, our audiences seemed to grow with every gig and everyone we saw was screaming with joy, singing along and exploding with happiness because that's the type of band that we were.

When you've played Wembley Arena and the Hollywood Bowl in LA, it's a bit different to perform on a little stage for an audience who are a) so drunk you can't work out how they're still standing up and b) wearing fancy dress. I remember one night especially, we were told everyone was so excited for us girls to be on and Pepsi and I were expecting for everyone to be in eighties gear or at least our T-shirts but we couldn't believe our eyes when we saw rows of people dressed as carrots and Superman – it was more of a fancy dress than an eighties night out. I can honestly say that I saw many things in the eighties, but not people dressed as carrots. Pepsi was a rising star of the stage. She'd been in big plays and musicals, and she was a huge talent. She didn't need to sing our old songs to a room of drunken carrots! For me, it changed my relationship with performing. I was so proud of our work and had so many happy memories of the concerts I had performed at, but when we did these 'gigs' it made my heart sink as it seemed a million miles away from where we started.

After that, I decided that music might not be in my professional life ever again – or at least not for a while. I'd always love music and the music my friends made and singing along to the radio, but I had no desire to set foot on stage or in a studio. Still, you know what they say, the rhythm might get you!

There was no one more surprised than me when Martin said to me, 'Why don't you come in the studio to sing a song with me?'

'You don't need me,' I told him. 'You need to go and do this on your own.'

But he insisted, 'Come on, definitely come to the studio and let's try a song together.'

So, I found a song that I loved, 'You Make Me Feel So Young', and we practised it in the kitchen first. We then sang it to Harley, because I thought if anyone is going to be honest then Harley will. And her reaction was golden: 'That's fantastic. Oh my God, you *have* to go into the studio, Mum,' she said.

And that's just what we did.

Early 2019, Martin and I arrived at a studio in Surrey. I had absolutely no expectations and just thought, *Let's see what happens*. And it was quite a nice feeling to know that it was something that we could take or leave. Martin introduced me to Brian, the producer, and he said, 'Come on then, what are you going to sing for us?' Suddenly, I felt like I was on *The X Factor* or something. But Brian reacted the same way as Harley did, he just said, 'That's wonderful, let's record it!'

Even though I'd been in two huge bands, there's always that little insecurity when you enter a recording studio. This time I loved the fact that I didn't have to sing to create a Top 5 single, it was all for pleasure. That day we recorded one song and the producer sent it to the record company. To my surprise, they said that they wanted Martin and I to do an album together. Originally, it was meant to be just Martin on his own. Believe it or not, I had a day or two to think about whether or not I wanted to do it because I was so not sure that I wanted to put myself back in the limelight again. But the record company left the creative input to us and we could choose what we wanted to sing; it was a once-in-a-lifetime opportunity to do what we wanted to do.

In The Swing of It is full of old-fashioned love songs and it's an unapologetic celebration of passion and romantic love. However, it's also a love letter to our family. As well as taking the cover photograph of Martin and me, Harley wrote two of the songs – 'Like We Used To Do' and 'When We're Apart.' When she was a little girl, I thought I had to choose between a career and motherhood. Being a mum felt fulfilling, but there were moments when I really missed music and making things.

Pepsi has always supported and encouraged me at every turn. When I left Pepsi & Shirlie, she understood, completely, that I wanted to be able to be with Harley and be a mum. It wasn't a difficult decision at the time, but it was a heart-wrenching one. Neither of us had any idea what the future would hold and neither could we have possibly predicted that my beautiful baby would grow up to write brilliant songs and that I would be able to sing them.

18

Pepsi – Love, loss and light

When you've spent some time in the limelight, and everyone you meet has preconceptions about you, it's hard to make new friends easily. However, over time, your old friends aren't simply your friends anymore: they become your family. Life changes so quickly – people have families, major career changes and move across the world. It becomes increasingly important to spend time with the people who have known you from the very beginning. That's how it was with George and me: he was a brother to me. He had teased me, laughed with me, fought with me, celebrated with me and grieved with me. I loved him – I never dreamed I'd have to grieve him so early.

It's impossible to overstate just how important family was for George. His brilliant, beautiful mother Lesley inspired so much love in all of us. She was Wham!'s biggest fan. The group, and George, have some of the most adoring, enthusiastic fans in the world, but Lesley was a true force of nature – she had believed in him fiercely ever since she let us dance on her white carpet.

Lesley left us all far too soon. She was only 59 when she died from cancer, in 1997. She was immensely kind, warm, loving and real. Ever since Wham! were soaring up the charts, every aspect of George's life had been subject to intense scrutiny and press intrusion. There was always a photographer or two lurking around outside his house in Hampstead. Lesley was a force for good. I think she kept George down-to-earth. Without her, I think he felt desperately vulnerable.

When she passed away, we were all united in our grief – and even though George had always been sensitive and deeply compassionate, I think the loss unlocked something profound in him. I'll never forget his kindness and tenderness when my own mother, Agatha, passed in 1998.

Mum was in a hospice, where a wonderful team of nurses were looking after her, doing their very best to make sure she spent her last days as comfortably as she could. She'd drift in and out of sleep, exhausted, but once, she opened her eyes to a group of visitors.

'Mum, look who's come to see you,' I whispered, gently.

Mum spotted Shirlie first. 'Hello, Shirlie. It's so good to see you,' she said, with real joy in her voice.

'Mum, there's someone else here too.'

I pointed to George, sitting at the foot of the bed. 'Hello, Agatha,' he waved.

Mum beamed – she was utterly delighted. Even though

she had next to no energy, George's presence had revived something in her. She was like a fan at a concert.

We knew George was living with grief. He never stopped being sweet, generous, chatty and open-hearted, but I honestly don't believe he ever got over losing his mum. When I lived in London and Norwich, I was also so touched when he would make the effort to come to my birthday parties – it was always such a pleasure to see him. Away in St Lucia, I maybe saw him every other year or so, when I came back to London for a visit. I knew Shirlie saw a lot of him, and we kept in touch remotely, as best we could. I often thought about how lucky we were to be connected so quickly. When my parents moved to the UK in the fifties, it would take weeks to send a letter home. Thank goodness for video calling. Mostly, I knew to ignore the gossip and rumours I heard about George or read in the papers. There was always something doing the rounds, and usually without any truth to it.

For me, Christmas 2016 was an unusual one. James and I had only recently set up Jus' Sail, our heritage sailing day charter company, and Christmas week was our busiest time. People were coming over from the UK, Canada and the US, craving some December sun. We could have sold the boat charter five times over on Christmas Day but we always insisted on giving ourselves and the crew that day off – it's important to keep some days sacred for family.

I remember the morning being magical. Christmas in St Lucia is a unique experience. The bright sunlight glittered on the water. Instead of wearing coats and hats, people wander the island in shorts and flip flops, calling season's greetings to each other and toasting with rum punch. What's weird is that everywhere you go, traditional Christmas songs are being played. I'd go to the supermarket to do my Christmas food shopping and hear 'Last Christmas' being played over the tannoy. I was always happy to hear that song, because it brought back so many memories of our glorious trip to Saas-Fee in the Swiss Alps to film the video. I could be drinking a cold beer in a beach bar and be transported back 30 years and thousands of miles to drinking hot chocolate with Shirlie.

Some local friends were coming over for a Christmas visit, but we deliberately kept the day low-key. I remember feeling a deep sense of gratitude to have had a great day overwhelmed with happiness. I loved the peace and quiet. I remember thinking, *This is how Christmas should be. No drama, just calm*.

We were doing the usual last-minute preparations – plumping cushions, putting out snacks, checking on the turkey in the oven and deciding whether to play a Nat King Cole or Michael Bublé Christmas medley on the stereo, when my phone rang: Shirlie. I saw the caller ID and picked up immediately – I was expecting a call from her as we always rang to wish each other a happy Christmas.

'Oh, hi, Shirlie! Merry Christmas! Are you having a lovely day? How's Martin? How are the kids?'

'Pepsi, it's Harley.'

'Oh, Harley. Happy Christmas! It's so good to hear from you, how are you?'

I've been close to Harley since she was a baby. Every so often, we'd speak on the phone and talk about what we'd do when she came to St Lucia for a visit. It was a little strange that she'd be ringing before Shirlie did, but I didn't really think anything of it – she was probably just making a festive call.

'Pepsi … I … Pepsi. Pepsi, this is …' Over and over again, Harley said my name. She sounded breathless and upset.

I started to panic.

'OK, Harl, where are you? It's OK. Where's Mum? Where's Dad? What's happened?'

My first thought was Shirlie. Something must have happened to her, or Harley was in some kind of trouble. I had to stay calm for her: 'Is Mum there? Can you put her on, or your dad?'

'Pepsi, Mum can't talk to you.'

Oh, God.

'She's too upset. She can't come to the phone … She's … it's …' An agonising pause. 'Yog has died.'

I couldn't possibly have heard her properly. I must have said 'Pardon?' because she said it again.

The room was beginning to spin. Even James, who couldn't hear Harley, was starting to realise this wasn't a normal Christmas phone call: 'What's going on? Are you OK?' he asked, as my legs buckled from under me. He took the phone just as I fell to my knees. James has told me afterwards that I wailed. I have no recollection of that moment. None. Just a dark hole in my memory, still too painful to acknowledge.

No. No, no, no! Not my friend. Not Yog.

I had a very clear picture of George at Christmas. He should be beside an enormous tree. He should be preparing for his big annual party. He should be beaming at his sisters, Yioda and Melanie, watching them opening fabulous gifts, surrounded by firelight and fairylights. A world without him in it was unimaginable. A Christmas Day without him, his absolute favourite time of year – utterly unthinkable.

As the awful, awful news started to sink in, there was a knock at the door. Our Christmas Day guests had come with pumpkin pie and festive cheer. They had no idea about the terrible news we'd just received. I didn't know what to do, I simply couldn't get up. James had to greet them – and send them away again: 'We're so sorry, Pepsi just heard – we've had the most terrible shock. There has been a family emergency.'

That was the only way to put it.

James had to be my rock. He had loved George, too. And George had adored him. Unlike Shirlie, who met the love of her life when she was still so young, it had taken me a little while to find The One – and George knew that. He'd watched my boyfriends come and go – all perfectly nice guys, but not quite right – and then he saw, in James, someone whose spirit matched mine. Like me, James was shocked, stunned, heartbroken. And like me, James knew George as a friend before he thought of him as a celebrity.

Because he had been away from the UK during many of the Wham! years, he saw George as I did – kind, complex, huge of heart, generous to a fault. James had those qualities too and he kept my life together over the next few weeks, as I felt as though I was about to fall apart.

George, Shirlie and Andrew, we all grieved for our mothers, together – but even though those losses felt almost unbearably painful, at least we had a little time to say goodbye. We could be there for the precious final few weeks and days. But George's death came entirely without warning. Any kind of shock causes the body to produce a huge amount of adrenaline. It's known as the 'fight or flight' hormone and it's supposed to protect you. But our bodies don't always know the difference between physical and emotional attack. The shock stayed with me for days, before the grief really started.

Also, when I lost my mum, I was able to grieve her intimately and privately. I could share my feelings with my closest friends, but no one was out there, giving their opinions on her life or her work. There was no speculation from strangers. But even in St Lucia, George's death was big news. I was hugely grateful to be away from UK press intrusion, at least. My old London number didn't work, so no one was calling me, although some dogged journalists did track me down via the Jus' Sail website. James fielded their calls with the same simple message, 'Pepsi has no comment at this time.' I could ignore all of my emails but I knew that Shirlie and Martin were being hounded. Their phones were constantly ringing, journalists had even been turning up outside their house. Still, every newspaper I saw seemed to have a picture of my beloved friend on the front. And the supermarkets *still* played 'Last Christmas'. My happiest memories became unbearable – I thought of George, gorgeous and joyful in Saas-Fee, and wept and wept.

Grief is so strange in the way that it plays tricks on us and manipulates our sense of time. Every day feels the same and every minute feels like an hour. I desperately wanted the sadness to end, yet I couldn't bear the idea of moving on. I wondered whether I should go back to London and be with Shirlie and her family, but leaving the house was hard. The idea of going out to the airport seemed utterly unthinkable. But then, something happened to force my hand.

Every year, at the BRITs, there is a tribute to a truly legendary artist. And in 2017, it seemed only fitting that the artist should be George Michael. Any tribute would need to be delivered by Andrew, Shirlie and me. Of course, we'd all been together at various gatherings and private parties, but this would be the very first time that we'd be united, as Wham! in public, since 1986.

I received a call from one of George's oldest friends and manager, David Austin: 'Hi Peps, it's David.'

My heart skipped a beat with fear – there was more bad news?

'Hi David, everything OK?'

'Yeah, Peps, everything's OK. I've called to ask you a favour ...'

I was starting to feel really nervous.

He went on: "You know The BRIT Awards? They want to honour Yog and we wondered if you would be up for flying to London for the ceremony. But it's top secret, you can't tell anyone anything, they said. Not even your family.'

I had only one condition: 'Of course, that's fine – but there's no way I can do this without my husband James,' I said.

The idea of getting on the plane without him simply wasn't an option.

It's very strange, living in St Lucia and flying back to the UK for a couple of weeks. It feels like a holiday in reverse. It doesn't seem right to leave the sea, the sun and the palms and get off the plane to rain and grey skies. Still, it definitely wasn't a holiday. The flight seemed never-ending. I couldn't pay attention to any of the films, my mind raced. What would it be like when I arrived? How would Shirlie feel? How would it be to spend time with her and Andrew under these circumstances? Could we pull it off together? In a way, I couldn't wait to be with my best friend, but in another, I knew that seeing her would unlock another layer of pure grief.

We were taken from the airport straight to the hotel. In a funny way, keeping things 'top secret' really helped. While it was definitely odd to be back in London, and not even allowed to let some of my closest friends and family know where I was, it was good to have a project to focus on – it distracted me. When you're struggling with grief, shock and loss, it can be hard to be around even the most well-meaning people. Over the next few days, I'd be spending time with the only other people who understood.

When we started rehearsing, it was a shock. There was a lot of hugging, a lot of 'you look great' and a lot of reminiscing. I'd grown used to my friends, getting older. Shirlie was a glamorous grown-up woman, a mother, someone who had weathered all sorts of tragedies and disasters, nursing Martin when he was seriously ill. Andrew had lived a life too, even becoming a professional motor racing driver before moving to Cornwall. We'd all become grown-ups, yet when the three of us were together, I couldn't help but see our young ghosts – the kids we were, so full of optimism, enthusiasm and hope.

I know lots of people who say they revert to their teenage selves, no matter how old they are, when they see their siblings and visit the family. Well, for us, it was exactly the same. Andrew was the perfectionist, witty, charming, cracking jokes to help lighten the tension of the moment – but always wanting to do one more take and get it right, determined to honour his chum with the most personal and moving eulogy.

'We need to do it exactly how we're going to do it on the night!' he'd cry, slightly exasperated.

And Shirlie's slightly sulky, punky streak – dormant for over 30 years – re-emerged. 'You know I'll do it properly when it's time,' she'd say, after another low-key run-through. That has always been Shirlie's style. On stage, she absolutely sparkles with energy and flair, but she's always holding it in reserve. She wants to share her best work with an audience.

Me? I became the moderator, the peacemaker: 'Andrew, you know Shirlie's going to be brilliant, on the night,' I'd say. 'But, Shirlie – maybe we do both need to do one more run-through ...'

Putting the tribute together was a challenge but in our hearts we knew what we wanted to convey, but what can you possibly say about a man who left us far too soon, but who has creatively lived a thousand lives? How could we reconcile George Michael, the megastar with millions of fans, the iconic singer and songwriter that the BRITs audience loved so much with Yog, the man we all loved so much? How could we celebrate everything we adored and cherished about him, while protecting some of the most special, significant memories for ourselves? Luckily, the autocue helped. It seemed so strange, watching our words rolling out in front of us and projected on a screen – we were seeing our thoughts come to life. Which made us giggle nervously when we tripped over the words.

'I don't know how it's possible to stumble over this sentence,' I laughed. 'It came out of my head – I *wrote* it.'

Still, on the day, I felt nervous. With George – and with Andrew and Shirlie – I'd played to countless crowds all over the world and I'd loved the excitement and the anticipation. I was always desperate to get out on stage and entertain. But this felt different, and utterly overwhelming. I had moments of feeling strangely numb, as though I was floating – and moments of feeling sick. We were invited to say hello to Coldplay in their dressing room, they were going to perform George's classic ballad 'A Different Corner'. The members of the band were very gracious and we wished each other well in our tributes onstage.

When we walked out onto the stage, the roar of the crowd took me by surprise. *That* was when it sunk in. I'd forgotten that no one had been expecting us. We'd been so fixated on getting to this point that the tribute had been the only thing on our minds but the audience were reacting to seeing Wham! for the first time in three decades.

Andrew spoke first. Nervously, I tried to focus on his words, rather than the people in front of us. Even though I'd heard this speech so many times, I really wanted to pay attention to this moment.

'It felt like the sky had fallen in … a supernova in a firmament of shining stars has been extinguished.'

It was just right – a beautiful, lyrical description for a beautiful, lyrical writer of songs. And to me, it *still* felt as though the sky had fallen in. And to this day it still does. I still feel it when I hear George's voice, it's still painful.

Shirlie's words were simple, but perfect: 'I will never forget my wonderful friend,' she said, tearfully. Her raw emotion resonated around the world. No one was in any doubt over the significance of the role that George had played in her life – or that the megastar was also a deeply kind, loving human being.

Now it was my turn. For a moment, I hesitated. The enormity of where I was and what I had to do was hitting me hard. How could I do my friend justice? The audience blurred before me. Everything seemed strange, and yet strangely normal. I was onstage, with my closest friends; we were together. This was exactly how it used to be – how it *should* be. But nothing was normal, nothing was OK. We were here *for* George, but he should be right there with us. Again, I realised how weird the world felt without him in it. Grief shook me up once more. But then, he *was* there, wasn't he? We were all here, united in our love for him, for his talent, his spirit, his energy; he would never really leave us.

As I tried to collect myself, the audience clapped and cheered. For as long as I have been a performer, the audience has been my friend. At that first ever Wham! Capital concert, it was the response from the audience – the *love* from the audience – that got me hooked on this incredible life. Even when I faltered and had one of the most difficult moments of my career – freezing up and forgetting my lines when I was playing Josephine Baker – kindness and support of the audience got me through. I was reminded of the most valuable lesson I'd ever learned: the audience wants to see you succeed, they are on your side. And as they clapped, I felt them encouraging me, showing me that they wanted to hear what I had to say. They had loved George too. They wanted to celebrate him, and they wanted to hear what I had to say about this miraculous man.

Like Shirlie, I kept my words simple: 'There's no doubt whatsoever that George and Wham! changed my life,' I said. 'His beautiful voice will live on forever as a gift to us all.'

I wanted to blend the two sides of this beloved man, who it had been such a great privilege to know. George changed my life in countless ways. My destiny was set as soon as I received that phone call and went off for an audition, when Wham! were just 'those white boys who rap', as far as I was concerned. And then, on a white carpet in Radlett, when George watched me dance, and watched Shirlie, and decided. Thanks to George, Andrew and Shirlie, I'd gone from Paddington to St Lucia and travelled around the whole world in between. But it was their friendship that changed my life, ultimately. They took me – a dreamer, a lonely girl, who only really wanted to dance – and gave me a second family. They made me laugh and he made my world bigger and better.

But I wanted to leave the audience with hope, too. *My* George wasn't there for me anymore, as a friend I could call up, or go out for dinner with. But the megastar had left a magical legacy. George's truly astonishing voice would live forever. It was a real gift that would keep on giving. There were children who had yet to be born who would grow up, fall in love with it, be inspired by it and write songs of their own.

The world was watching and I'd spoken from the heart. In some ways, a lifetime wouldn't be long enough to talk about how much I'd loved George and to explain just what his friendship had meant to me. But I'd kept it simple, straightforward and pure – and delivered the best tribute I was capable of giving.

When I had finished speaking, the crowd roared with love and approval. It seemed so strange to be saying goodbye – but then, it wasn't a goodbye. And I knew that together, we'd done him proud. In our grief, in our heartbreak, the three of us had united to create something bigger than all of us put together. As we came off the stage, I was so moved to see so many familiar faces. Martin, Harley, Roman and James were there, as well as so many of the people who had worked with George over the years. Ronnie Franklin, the man who had worked as George's security detail for many years, had come and we hugged hard – 'I still can't believe it,' he said. At the time, I reflected on how very hard it must be for him. His job was to keep George safe – and even though it was a practical role, I think he felt that he should have been keeping him safe at all times.

Back in the dressing room, we opened a bottle of champagne and toasted our wonderful friend. We could hear Chris Martin starting to sing 'A Different Corner.' We felt tearful, but triumphant. I think we had given him the best possible send-off.

For the next few days, our phones were exploding. I had so many notifications that my handset couldn't process them all. I was so touched, and so moved. The tabloid interest and speculation in George had been hard to bear, but no one was calling to gossip – everyone was sending love, offering their condolences and wishing us all well. But the only person I really wanted to talk to was my beloved little brother Robbie. Up until that point, I hadn't even been able to let him know that I'd arrived in England. Still, right before the ceremony, I'd given him a call: 'Listen, I can't tell you any more than this – I wish I could. But please make sure you're watching the BRITs on TV tonight.'

'What's going on? What are you talking about?' Robbie was confused, perhaps a little concerned.

He'd tuned in, and I didn't have to keep the secret anymore: 'You were wonderful, you were all wonderful. You said the perfect things,' he said.

Of course, I wanted to do George justice for his fans and for all of our friends – but I think Robbie's approval meant the most to me.

Being asked to come to the BRITs was a huge honour. It made me aware that we were keeping a pop legacy alive. Whatever the three of us went on to do, we'd made something that would go down in history. Even though we were working in truly heartbreaking circumstances, I'm still so proud of our tribute and what we made together. It's only right that George should be remembered by some of the people who knew him best.

Christmas is still bittersweet. On the one hand, every Christmas Day will take me back to that terrible phone call and the shock, pain and anguish that coursed through my body when I heard the awful news. One of the strangest things about grief is the way it fades and grows at the same time. Initially, the pain is so intense, it's physical, but it lessens. I've learned to live with it. It's a wound that slowly heals yet it remains tender and every so often, something will remind me of the pain and it will come flooding back and floor me again.

However, even though Christmas Day is the anniversary of one of my saddest, hardest memories – made all the worse when George's wonderful sister Melanie, who shared so many of the ups and downs of life on tour with us, died three years to the day after her brother – Christmas time is filled with my very best memories of George. He just loved it! December gave him the opportunity to do all of his favourite things – throwing parties, buying presents for people, decorating and dressing up. My birthday, on 10 December, marked the start of George's Christmas calendar. We'd always get together and do something special and it was the moment when he 'allowed' himself to get into the spirit of the season and start feeling really festive. Hampstead, the area of North London that he called home, turned into a fairyland. White lights twinkled and glistened in the trees and you could smell the excitement and anticipation in the air – OK, to be honest, it was probably the local bakeries, using extra cinnamon in their mince pies. But Christmas brought out George's best sides – his boyish enthusiasm and his legendary generosity.

When I lived in London, I'd usually have a birthday gathering, but as I got older, I stopped having big parties and started to plan cosy, intimate meals in my favourite pubs and restaurants. And it didn't matter where we were, who came along or how many bottles of good wine we got through (usually a fairly sizeable number), every single time I got up to pay at the end of the meal, George would beat me to it. He never even told me he was doing it – I'd just make my way to the till and hear, 'Don't worry, the gentleman has already taken care of it.' This was in addition to a birthday present. George lived for this sort of gesture. Every time, I'd say, 'Thank you so much, it's so kind of you but you really shouldn't keep doing this.' And he'd always say, 'No, please, let me, I want to. It makes me really, really happy.'

Maybe that's the very best lesson he taught me. I learned so much from him, constantly. He showed me how to be a performer, how to constantly work, strive, develop and improve, and how to make sure that I always delivered the very best work that I was capable of. Shirlie, Andrew and George taught me about friendship. Thanks to them, I discovered that I wasn't destined to be lonely and that the love we have for our best friends is just as true, deep and meaningful as any romance. They taught me to open my mind, embrace every opportunity that came my way and that life can be hard, but it's also hilarious and we must always see the funny side when we can. But most of all, they taught me, by showing me, that giving is every bit as wonderful as receiving. It's a platitude, and I've heard those words thousands of times, but Shirlie, Andrew and George are the three that have truly lived it.

And it's only fitting that George's greatest present to the world was a song. 'Last Christmas' really is a gift that keeps on giving. It's become as much a part of Christmas as mistletoe, the lights on Regent Street and jokes in crackers. It doesn't matter where you live, or even when you were born, it's a song that will evoke the spirit of the season in so many different ways, for so many different people. Many people might hear it and think of being with their family, a special Christmas kiss, or perhaps an office party that got out of hand! For me, it's about being 24, on the trip of a lifetime, having a proper winter wonderland experience, *living* that video, having the best Christmas ever with my best friends in the world.

I'll never stop missing George or missing the memory. I was so, so lucky to have that magical experience and in some ways, I wish I could go back in time, just for fun, and relive every single second. But most of all, I'm grateful. I'm filled with gratitude for having the opportunity to be part of something that means so much to millions. I'm grateful that someone like me – a school leaver from West London who nearly spent her life working for a travel agent, ended up having the opportunity to see the world instead of sending other people across it. I'm grateful to have known George, the megastar, and Yog, the mate – and that I was there to be one of the first to hear so many of everyone's favourite songs. I'm grateful every time I hear 'Last Christmas' because, as I said, his beautiful voice will live on forever – it's the most generous gift to us all.

Still, I'd do anything to simply have one more dance with my wonderful friend.

19

Shirlie – To love and be loved

I f anything has defined my life, I think it has been my capacity to love and to be loved. Love has defined my choices, my friendships and even my work. In everything I have chosen to do, love has come first. Love is what has made my life so bright and happy, but perhaps the only difficult part of loving the way I do is living with the grief that sometimes come with it. I love my friends and family with my whole heart – and so losing those I love causes me the greatest heartache.

George – Yog – wasn't just a friend, he was my family. We grew up together. He was the one who was brave on my behalf, bringing Martin and me together. He witnessed every single significant moment of my adult life. When my children were born, he shared my joy and celebrated with me. When Martin was seriously ill, George was one of the first to help, practically and emotionally. George was *always* looking for ways to help. He was famously generous, he could be very lavish but his generosity went way beyond wealth. He went out of his way to see people, and understand them, and honour their humanity. He is one of the greatest singers the world will ever know, and one of the greatest listeners that I will ever know.

When I close my eyes and think about my friend, I don't see a superstar in a leather jacket.

In the winter of 2016, George came over for a chat. Christmas was looming. It can be a tricky time. It was George's favourite holiday, and he loved to celebrate the season. But as we get older, the prospect of Christmas can bring sorrow and joy. It's a time of memories. We look forward to celebrating with the people we love, but it's hard not to think about those we've lost when we've shared so many special Christmasses with them in the past.

Winter is hard for me, not just because I love the sunshine but because of those dark, short days which increase my anxiety. I love being outdoors and winter takes those opportunities away. I always thought I didn't like winter because I grew up in a house with no central heating and as a builder, my dad wouldn't be able to work as much if it rained or snowed – which meant he wouldn't get as much work, which in turn would make him more angry. But for some reason our house came alive at Christmas: the coal fire would be roaring, Dad would decorate the house, not leaving a piece of wall free from shiny tinsel and decorations.

Christmas became much harder for us after Martin and I lost both of our parents. It changed the dynamic. Not only that our children grew up and no longer wanted to get up at 5 a.m., but you're now trying to wake them up at 11 a.m. when they have stinking hangovers!

For Martin, I sometimes think the legacy of his illness makes him feel especially anxious. If he isn't as busy as he likes to be, he associates it with the period of time when he was recovering and felt stuck because he wasn't able to work at all. Martin's solution is usually a practical one – he makes work for himself. He doesn't look back, he always has his eye on the next day. It's remarkable how he just gets on with it, with little pity or nostalgia. He just keeps moving forward.

Anyway, I hadn't seen George for a while. As with Pepsi, we could go for months and months without seeing each other but deep down we knew that it would only take seconds to reconnect. He sent me a message, asking if he could pop over. I said it would be great to see him and Martin was away, which was perfect as it was always nice to have company. I said I'd make some dinner for us and not to get to me too late as by now I loved to get to bed early. George arrived on time and we had dinner. As always, it was lovely to see him. We sat on the sofa and went into one of our old lengthy chats. He kind of had that ability to get you talking. He was one of those people, a bit like my mum, with the gift of making you feel comfortable and safe even when you're telling them your deepest secrets.

Towards the end of our conversation, I posed a question I'd never asked him before: 'Have you enjoyed your life? Have you liked being famous?' I have no idea what inspired me to ask him that. We never really talked about his experience of fame. Maybe it was because I was curious about the contradictions within my friend – that a man who really was quite sensitive and private was able to share so many intense emotions in his music, and that he was expressing himself in a way that captured the feelings of millions of people.

George smiled, with real warmth in his eyes: 'Yeah. Yeah, I have. It's been really good.' I knew there had been so many times when it hadn't been easy for him but he was able to do the work he was put here to do and he had inspired so much love in so many fans.

That conversation brought me a little comfort, weeks later, when I thought the sharp shock of grief would never, ever stop.

Nearly every single thing George did, and a lot of things he did *not* do, ended up becoming front-page news. His death was no exception. It was so hard to process privately the pain and sadness of losing someone I had loved so much. At home, as a family, we grieved together. No one could stop crying. We were all in shock and we were doing our best to support each other, but the sadness was overwhelming. When someone as famous as George dies, everyone was grieving. There was a collective, global grief for George. If I went for a dog walk I would be stopped by a well-meaning person to say how sorry they were. If I went to the supermarket the same would happen. The worst thing was that we couldn't go for a walk or leave the house and give ourselves a little bit of space to process the pain.

There was simply no way of being able to escape the bad news. I couldn't look at a shop window or hear a car radio without seeing some news – or cruel gossip – about my beloved friend. Usually, one of my favourite parts of December is constantly hearing 'Last Christmas' in restaurants and taxis. We had such a wonderful time making that video in Saas-Fee. It was a party, really. George and Andrew brought their rugby-playing pals, who were great fun and determined to make the most of the hotel bar.

Pepsi and I were in our element. We were at our happiest when we were comfortable and cosy, and there's nowhere on earth that is cosier than a hotel in an Alpine village over a winter weekend. To be honest, I'd never seen such perfect, picture-book snow. I think Pepsi's fans imagine her wearing Azzedine Alaïa dresses, or puffball skirts, but my favourite image of Pepsi is one where she's wearing an outfit that didn't even make the 'Last Christmas' video. I heard a knock on the door of my hotel room and when I got up to answer, there was Peps, rolled up like a burrito in her squishy duvet, her face beaming out of the middle: 'Do you think we can take these home?' she asked, grinning. (In the UK in the early eighties, most of us still had blankets on our beds.)

In 1984, 'Last Christmas' reached Number 2 – held off the Number 1 spot by Band Aid's 'Do They Know It's Christmas?', which George (and Martin) also sang on.

Back to the set in the Alpine mountains ... I'm so proud of that song and the video, and the fact that so many people still feel that Christmas starts when they hear it for the first time. Some of the rumours and stories about the video make me laugh, too. There are lots of fan theories. Some people are convinced that Martin appears in the video with me, playing my boyfriend. I'm not sure if it's true but I wouldn't be surprised to hear that they had thought it funny to find a Martin lookalike to appear with me because the first thing I saw when I saw him was how much he looked like Martin.

However, after Christmas Day 2016, when George's sister Melanie telephoned with the awful news, everything went dark. Constant rotations of 'Last Christmas' brought me pain, not pride. George's face was everywhere – and it felt as though I was being haunted by my own young ghost, every time I turned on the TV and saw a clip from the video. That girl was so carefree and full of joy – I didn't think I'd ever feel joy again.

The press were desperate to speak to Martin and me. There was one low point when a breakfast television programme asked if I'd present a segment live, from George's funeral. George would have found this darkly hilarious. In one way, this was comforting, and in another, it made it much harder to bear.

There was constant, cruel speculation about the hows and whys of the tragedy. Grief is so very private and personal. It was strange, in a way. I knew how much George meant to his fans and that millions of people felt that they knew him. He was their friend and he had helped them through some of the hardest parts of their life. But the man the tabloids described wasn't the man I had loved. It should have been comforting, to know that the world was grieving too, but it felt utterly alienating.

Pepsi and I have talked about how one of the most painful parts of grief is the way that it doesn't get any easier as you get older and that experience doesn't help at all. Mourning one person doesn't mean that you know what to do the next time. Instead, grief makes old feelings fresh. In 2009, Martin's lovely mum and dad died within days of each other. I'd adored Frank and Eileen, who were so sweet, gentle and loving. I'd also lost my own parents. There is no way to prepare yourself for grief, but having Martin by my side helped me enormously with the loss of my parents. I felt a huge hole in my family, because my kids no longer had any grandparents and Christmas suddenly got a lot quieter.

Still, I never felt more appreciative of my amazing family than I did that Christmas. The outside world was becoming too much to bear, so we all drew closer together. And of course, I had Pepsi. I didn't have the strength to call her, Harley did it for us. I felt sorry for Pepsi because she wasn't with any of us. We could all be together and comfort each other, but Pepsi was too far away for that. But we managed to talk and it made us talk more often. I guess we both realised how short life is and that you should never pass up an opportunity to catch up with someone even if it's just a quick hello. But just knowing she shared so many of those memories was enough. She understood and shared the loss. We weren't grieving a celebrity, we were grieving our friend. And we didn't have to pretend to each other. I don't think there's anything more precious than a friend you're so comfortable with that you can answer 'How are you?' with 'Terrible.'

When we were asked to give a tribute to George at the BRITs, it felt more like an honour to do it. It was really nice to have three old friends standing up there rather than some random celebrities who didn't know him: we wanted to pay tribute and everything we said was from the heart. We wrote our speeches together. Pepsi flew in from St Lucia and it was the first time I had seen her since it happened. And as soon as I saw her, she fell into my arms. It must have been so raw for her to see us without him being there. During the day, Andrew, Pepsi and I rehearsed our speeches in the centre of the O2. We all read our speeches perfectly but when it came to the evening and seeing the whole arena fill up, you could literally hear a pin drop as soon as we started to speak.

You could feel the genuine love and respect for George from every artist, executive and fan in the room. I'd read the speech perfectly but when it came to it, my heart started pounding, my lips were trembling and my emotions took over. I looked over at Peps and saw tears falling from her eyes. It felt so surreal to actually be there, standing and talking about one of our best friends, who was no longer with us.

Being reunited with Pepsi and Andrew was strange, and special. The circumstances made the reunion unbearable at times. Every so often I'd remember why we were together, what we were doing and who was missing. However, it was strangely joyous too. We'd been given the opportunity to travel back in time and relive the feeling of being young, carefree and invulnerable. When Andrew became exasperated with me for not projecting in a rehearsal, we could have been back in a little theatre in Aberdeen – 'I *know*. I'll *do it on the night*,' I said, sounding like an over-grown teenager. It broke the tension and made me happy. As long as the three of us could be together, George would be with us in spirit, somewhere.

We will never stop missing George and wishing that we'd been allowed to have him with us for much, much longer. We were the luckiest girls to have spent so much time of our life and careers with him. The trick to life is that you have to appreciate the people around you.

Gratitude and fate are important parts of our lives. There isn't a single day that I don't think about what's happened, but I can't change the things that have happened. You have to look forward and learn to accept them and in time, your heart heals. Being friends with Pepsi taught me this and so much more. Now, whenever I feel low, without knowing how I'm feeling, she will call me. She is one of the rarest and most precious people I know. Our lives have been so rich in adventure but we have also seen our share of super highs and the deep lows. The one thing that has remained constant, the one thing that's always been written in black and white, is the way we have cared for each other.

20

Pepsi & Shirlie's rules for friendship

History beats geography. If someone has been a big part of your life, you can find a way to keep them in it, no matter how many oceans separate you.

Celebrate similarities – and differences. Good friends have plenty in common, opposites attract, and great friends know that it's all about balancing the two sides of the equation.

Comfort is key. A friend is someone you can totally relax with and be yourself with. Anyone can dazzle you at a fancy showbiz party, it's only a true friend who can make you laugh when she puts on your mum's slippers.

True friends become your family. You know a friend is for keeps when you want them to share every aspect of your life and all of the people in it.

Friendship needs space. You'll have periods of time when you live in each other's pockets and others when you don't necessarily speak every single day. If a friendship is going to go the distance and last for decades, you need to let it wax and wane. There will inevitably be times when your lives run in different directions, but you'll probably come back together.

Good friends know each other inside out. *Great* friends keep asking each other questions. Friendship becomes much more interesting when you're excited to see each other evolve and you want to know where you've both come from – and where you're both going to.

The foundation of nearly every great friendship is usually a shared passion for snacks.

Travelling creates a big bond. Pepsi and Shirlie kept each other company on countless long-haul flights, but for them, it all began on a car journey from Finsbury Park. If you want to know if someone is a true friend, go travelling with them – it doesn't matter whether you go to Bangkok or Brighton!

Another great place to forge a friendship is on the dancefloor – having the moves is good, but unbridled enthusiasm is better. You can really get to know some-one when you're both whirling around to ABC's 'Poison Arrow.'

Working together is the Waterloo of many a friendship. You need to express yourself clearly, listen carefully and remember that the most powerful tool you can have in your belt is a sense of humour. Laugh often – and laugh at yourself.

Sometimes we know our friends better than we know ourselves. It's our job to guide our friends, support them when they have to make difficult decisions and encourage them to do what makes them happy, even if it doesn't feel safe or straightforward. The best friend to have is a happy friend.

If you need to say 'I love you' to someone in other words, make them a perfect cup of tea.

Give people their flowers now – don't wait to tell your friends that you love them, and what you love about them. It's fun to tease them and make each other laugh, but you also need to tell them just how amazing they are, in case they need reminding.

Sometimes we need to be brave for our friends and talk them into *that* figure-hugging outfit. However, sometimes we need to listen to our friends if they're feeling self-conscious and shy about what they're wearing.

Friends come and support you and cheerlead for you – sometimes literally. They guide you through major highs and lows. A friend is there for you, no matter what. That means not only do they come through for you when life is really hard, but when things are going really well, they're in the front row, applauding as loudly as they can.

Good friends sometimes know you better than you know yourself – and it's really important to trust them and ask them for what you need. The only way to let your friend down is to let yourself down.

One of the hardest things you can go through is grief – but grief is the price we pay for love. Grieving our friends is devastating, but grieving *with* friends can be deeply healing.

The best thing about your best friend having kids is that you end up with brand new best friends in miniature.

Self-help books can be really useful – and when you share them with your friend, they become help-each-other books too! Even if you don't always completely agree on what you've read.

For some people, coming to the party in the same outfit as someone else is a disaster. For best friends, it's the beginning of a dance routine.

And finally: Your friends should always be your biggest fans.

Shirlie on Pepsi

Peps is 'sure-footed'. I'll never forget seeing her walking up the steps at Finsbury Park station. Perhaps it's a strange comparison to make, but the way she moved reminded me of my favourite horses at the stables – just the right balance of confidence and caution. She's one of the most grounded people I've ever met.

I love Pepsi's enormous appetite. Not just seeing the joy she gets from a stack of room service pancakes, but her appetite for life. She's handled so many challenges with such grace and enthusiasm. She's done so many exciting things because she's hungry for adventure.

When I was young, skinny and insecure, I would have done *anything* for Pepsi's fabulous boobs! I was sure she was the one all the boys fancied. In fact, I think I sometimes bossed her about and told her what to wear because I wanted to live vicariously through her. She looked fabulous in those form-fitting outfits!

Touring was really hard for me, and if it wasn't for Pepsi's kindness and patience, I don't think I could have kept going. Looking back, I can't believe how much I went on about missing Martin. Pepsi was always the one who would be beside me, waiting by the phone with me – and she'd be the first to hug me when I was crying and homesick.

Some of my favourite memories of the eighties are being holed up with Peps in the *Top of the Pops* canteen! Everyone else would be rushing to get to the infamous Television Centre bar, but we'd be holed up with our tea and a big pile of biscuits.

One of the proudest moments of my life was sitting on the front row of the Old Vic, seeing Pepsi on stage in *Hair*. She was brilliant!

In many ways, Pepsi is my opposite. We're both home-bodies, but I always want to be surrounded by people and she's so independent. I love our differences and I think they make our friendship even stronger, but I always thought she was so sophisticated, living in her own flat!

For me, a dance floor isn't really a proper dance floor if it doesn't have Pepsi on it!

Pepsi taught me so much about the world when she told me about her family and their life in St Lucia. When I was younger, I was quite naïve and no one had ever told me much about the world beyond the UK. She shared so much, so generously, and opened my mind and heart. I married Martin in St Lucia because she had conjured up such a beautiful picture when she described it.

I'm so glad that Harley and Roman are close to Pepsi. They've grown up with her and she is their family too. I think Harley and Pepsi have a special bond, because Harley was there when we were away in LA, recording the second album. Also, I constantly confided in Pepsi about how much I wanted to be a mum – I think she longed for Harley almost as much as I did!

Suffering from endometriosis and worrying about infertility was really difficult. At times, I felt ashamed and embarrassed. Pepsi was the one who helped me through the darkest days when I was really struggling.

Pepsi & Shirlie will never, ever end. We're starting to work on new music together – but I believe we'll always be in a creative partnership, one way or another.

It's rare that any friendship can span decades – let alone survive fame, grief and a move across oceans. But Pepsi's friendship has kept me going through the good times and bad. I simply wouldn't be me without her.

Pepsi on Shirlie

I will never, ever forget the moment when I put my tape on in Shirlie's car and she told me that I sounded like Shirley Bassey. Years later, we'd meet Shirley Bassey at the Royal Variety Performance, bringing our families along for the occasion. It's one of my most cherished memories and I'm so glad that Shirlie and I can share it.

Shirlie makes the best ever veggie lasagne and it's my favourite cure if I'm feeling low. It always soothes my soul and puts a smile on my face.

We share a similar sense of humour and Shirlie must be the funniest person I know. When we've been together, I ache from laughing. I'm not sure I can even explain why her jokes make me laugh so hard – and I don't think anyone else appreciates them quite as much as I do!

I've lost count of the number of times that we've turned up for interviews, both wearing identical outfits. This has always made us laugh, but deep down, I believe it's an embodiment of our deep connection at a spiritual or quantum level.

Shirlie and I have really bonded over our self-help books. She has such a wise, intelligent interpretation of what she's reading. Quite often, we'll read the same words in an entirely different way from each other, but we never argue – we've taught each other how to agree to disagree.

She's the ultimate cheerleader. Shirlie is the one who is always excited for me when I have good news and when life is going well. When I'm feeling down, or I've been disappointed, she always knows exactly what to say – the perfect combination of emotional and practical advice.

Her nickname is still true – she's always Shirlie Shopper! When we go to a boutique together, she's bossy in the best way, telling me to put down that awful dress I've picked up, and then finding one that looks like it was made for me.

Shirlie asks the best questions and she was the first person I've ever met who was genuinely curious about me and my life. She's a really brilliant listener – although if you're chatting when it's late at night, there's a chance that she'll fall asleep!

I think Shirlie might be the kindest person I have ever met. She's adorable, and vulnerable, and has a truly enormous heart – even now, I always want to protect her and make sure no one ever takes advantage of her.

She has so much creative, playful energy. When Shirlie has her camera and she's truly in the flow, nothing and no one can stop her. She's so talented, visually, and I'm so proud of the work she creates.

Getting to know her gorgeous family – Martin, Harley and Roman – has brought me so much joy. Her kids are wonderful and so much like their parents. It's spooky how similar Harley and Shirlie are, and I can't wait to work with Harley on some future songwriting.

Speaking of spooky, Shirlie is very attuned to the rhythms of the Universe. Her ability to work out just what she needs and then manifest it is downright magical. She can be full of contradictions – sometimes nervous and lacking in confidence, and sometimes quietly but absolutely sure – and that's what I really love about her.

Shirlie has taught me to really listen to myself. There have been times when being away from her family brought her so much pain and as her friend, I knew it was vital for her to follow her heart and find her bliss – not to keep singing and dancing with a fake smile on her face. When I've seen Shirlie really shine, I've known she was following her heart. And everything I've done, from acting on stage to moving to St Lucia, has been inspired by her. She gives me the courage to follow my heart, too.

I have some really good girlfriends who are precious to me – but Shirlie is like a sister. We've travelled for thousands of miles together, literally and metaphorically, and we have a bond that can never be severed.

Acknowledgements

I owe my life to my parents Agatha and Roger. Our lives may not have been easy but there was Love. To my siblings Tecia, Charleston, David, Max and Robbie: we may be in different parts of the world, but you are always in my heart. To James, my husband, you've changed my life in so many wonderful, adventurous ways. You are my rock and the love of my life. To my pals George and Andrew: thank you for having me in your Wham! gang. Most of my journey would not have happened without you. Thank you to the Porter and Crockett families for welcoming me into the fold. To my extended family and friends of which there are too many to mention, you know who you are and I love you very much.

A big thank you to Ajda Vucicevic for encouraging us to tell our story. Thank you Daisy Buchanan for all your help. Thank you Issy for your patience and all at Insanity Management. A big thank you to all at Welbeck Publishing for making this book real.

And last, but definitely not least, to the girl who chose me to sing and dance around the world with her, my bestie Shirlie. Love ya girl, now and always. X

Pepsi

I would like to thank all the friends who have been a part of my journey... you have shaped me more than you will ever know.

My family, my parents, my brothers & sisters... I love you all so much.

A very big thank you to Ajda Vucicevic, this was all your idea! I hope we have written the book that you wanted to read.

A special thank you to Daisy Buchanan.

Thank you to Issy and Laura at Insanity Management – you're the best!

George and Andrew: how lucky I was to have shared the whole Wham! experience with you both.

Pepsi... you are like a sister to me. You have always been so caring and kind, qualities that drew me to you all those years ago and keep our friendship strong even now.

We hope you have enjoyed the extraordinary stories of two very ordinary girls.

Shirlie

Pepsi and Shirlie would like to give a special thanks to Suzanne Rose for her fashion inspiration, and to Cheryl Robson for keeping us singing and dancing when times were tough. Thank you to Shona Abhyankar from ED Public Relations. A further thank you to the whole Welbeck Team, with special thanks to Millie Acers, Alexandra Allden, Lyndsey Mayhew, Nico Poilblanc, Maddie Dunne-Kirby, Annabel Robinson and Rachel Burgess. We have loved working with you.